To Reach the Nation's Ear

# THE AMERICAN WAYS SERIES

General Editor: John David Smith
Charles H. Stone Distinguished Professor of American History
University of North Carolina at Charlotte

From the long arcs of America's history, to the short time frames that convey larger stories, American Ways provides concise, accessible topical histories informed by the latest scholarship and written by scholars who are both leading experts in their fields and polished writers.

Books in the series provide general readers and students with compelling introductions to America's social, cultural, political, and economic history, underscoring questions of class, gender, racial, and sectional diversity and inclusivity. The titles suggest the multiple ways that the past informs the present and shapes the future in often unforeseen ways.

## CURRENT TITLES IN THE SERIES

*How America Eats: A Social History of U.S. Food and Culture*, by Jennifer Jensen Wallach
*Popular Justice: A History of Lynching in America*, by Manfred Berg
*Bounds of their Habitation: Race and Religion in American History*, by Paul Harvey
*National Pastime: U.S. History through Baseball*, by Martin C. Babicz and Thomas W. Zeiler
*Wartime America: The World War II Home Front, Second Edition*, by John W. Jeffries
*Enemies of the State: The Radical Right in America from FDR to Trump*, by D. J. Mulloy
*Hard Times: Economic Depressions in America*, by Richard Striner
*Litigation Nation: How Lawsuits Represent Changing Ideas of Self, Business Practices, and Right and Wrong in American History*, by Peter Charles Hoffer
*We the People: The 500-Year Battle Over Who Is American*, by Ben Railton
*Of Thee I Sing: The Contested History of American Patriotism*, by Ben Railton

*American Agriculture: From Farm Families to Agribusiness*, by Mark V. Wetherington
*Hoops: A Cultural History of Basketball in America*, by Thomas Aiello
*Years of Rage: White Supremacy in the United States from the 1920s to Today*, by D. J. Mulloy
*Germans in America: A Concise History*, by Walter D. Kamphoefner
*American Exceptionalism*, by Volker Depkat
*Making America's Public Lands: The Contested History of Conservation on Federal Lands*, by Adam Sowards
*To Reach the Nation's Ear: A History of African American Public Speaking*, by Richard W. Leeman

# ORATION,

DELIVERED IN CORINTHIAN HALL, ROCHESTER,

BY FREDERICK DOUGLASS,

**JULY 5TH, 1852.**

Published by Request.

---

ROCHESTER:
PRINTED BY LEE, MANN & CO., AMERICAN BUILDING.
1852.

# TO REACH THE NATION'S EAR

*A History of African American Public Speaking*

Richard W. Leeman

ROWMAN & LITTLEFIELD
*Lanham • Boulder • New York • London*

Published by Rowman & Littlefield
An imprint of The Rowman & Littlefield Publishing Group, Inc.
4501 Forbes Boulevard, Suite 200, Lanham, Maryland 20706
www.rowman.com

86-90 Paul Street, London EC2A 4NE

Copyright © 2023 by The Rowman & Littlefield Publishing Group, Inc.

*All rights reserved.* No part of this book may be reproduced in any form or by any electronic or mechanical means, including information storage and retrieval systems, without written permission from the publisher, except by a reviewer who may quote passages in a review.

British Library Cataloguing in Publication Information Available

**Library of Congress Cataloging-in-Publication Data**
Names: Leeman, Richard W., author.
Title: To reach the nation's ear : a history of African American public speaking / Richard W. Leeman.
Description: Lanham : Rowman & Littlefield, [2022] | Series: American ways | Includes bibliographical references and index.
Identifiers: LCCN 2022021950 (print) | LCCN 2022021949 (ebook) | ISBN 9781538112311 (cloth) | ISBN 9781538112328 (ebook)
Subjects: LCSH: African Americans—History—Source. | Speeches, addresses, etc., American—African American authors. | Political oratory—United States—History.
Classification: LCC E185 .L435 2022 (ebook) | LCC E185 (print) | DDC 973/.0496073 23/eng/20220—dc22
LC record available at https://lccn.loc.gov/2022021950

# Contents

*Acknowledgments*  ix

*Introduction*  1

Chapter 1  Liberty, Equality, and Salvation: African Americans at the Start of the Nation  15

Chapter 2  All Manner of Reforms  37

Chapter 3  Emancipation, Segregation, and Migration  65

Chapter 4  Lifting as We Climb: Advancing the Cause  95

Chapter 5  Waves of Reform and Revolution: The Modern Civil Rights Movement  121

Chapter 6  "I Am Somebody": Public Speaking in the Age of Integration  159

Chapter 7  Barack Obama and the "Post-Racial" Society  189

*A Note on Sources*  221

*Index*  231

*About the Author*  243

# Acknowledgments

THIS BOOK HAS BEEN MANY YEARS in the making. My abiding interest in African American public speaking was sparked in the fall of 1979, when I was fortunate enough to take Dr. Lyndrey Niles's Rhetoric of Black America class at the University of Maryland. Dr. Niles was then chair of the Department of Communication Studies at Howard University and kind enough to come to our campus one evening a week to lead a class that no one else had the background to teach. I knew very little about so many of the leaders we discussed, and even less about their actual speeches. I was frustrated that there were so few accounts of these speakers, nor a single source to consult as a starting place. Speeches and analyses of those speeches were dispersed in many different, often hard-to-find locations. A decade later, when I returned studying African American public speaking, I quickly discovered that I hoped to eventually write an introductory text that would provide readers with a helpful starting place. This book is the culmination of that aim.

In a larger sense, however, the making of this book began in colonial times, when African Americans first began speaking to audiences large and small. In the introduction, I outline how important public speaking has been to African Americans and their community as well as to Americans of all races. These speakers have contributed mightily to what the nation has thought and what it has done. Theirs is a long, rich, and complex story that continues today in forums large and small, poor and wealthy, religious and secular.

Of course, this volume is also the product of contributions made by many colleagues and collaborators. I want to thank series editor John David Smith for bringing to me this opportunity to fulfill a (scholarly) lifetime ambition and for his many helpful comments. He made this a far better book. I also appreciate Cynthia King and Andre Johnson for reading and commenting on the manuscript. Jordan Whitley and Heather Stegner were helpful in identifying potential photographs and for tracking down hard-to-find speech texts. My colleagues at UNC Charlotte have continued to nurture a supportive environment within which to conduct scholarship, and I particularly thank my chair, Jason Black, and my dean, Nancy Gutierrez, for their work as groundskeepers of that space. From the Rowman & Littlefield team, I want to thank Jon Sisk for his editorial support, guidance, and patience and Sarah Sichina and Katherine Berlatsky, assistant acquisition editors, for their conscientious and efficient work to help complete this project. I also benefited from the work of Crystal Branson, production editor, and photographic help early on from Dina Guilak and Bejamin Knepp. Any errors in the book are of course of my own making.

For my part, I found this to be the most difficult book I have written. I wanted the volume to be comprehensive but detailed enough to provide readers with an appreciation for the speakers and their speeches. Without the love, support, and encouragement of my wife, Carol, this book would not have been completed. As always, she has been my helpmate on this journey.

Finally, the largest debt of gratitude belongs to the speakers and the audiences to whom they spoke. Without the rich and courageous tapestry of their words and the ears of those who listened, this book would not exist. As always when I have worked with this subject, my hope is that I have done justice in describing and interpreting these speakers, their work, and the communities to whom and for whom they spoke.

# Introduction

On March 21, 2022, the Senate Judiciary Committee began consideration hearings of Judge Ketanji Brown Jackson's nomination to the Supreme Court. In her opening statement, Judge Jackson spoke to her place in American history, but not simply as the first African American woman to be nominated for a seat on the highest court in the nation. After some brief introductory remarks, she turned to her own history, which she began by simultaneously referencing the racial discrimination her parents had faced and the evolution of American law. Judge Jackson had been born, she said, shortly after the civil rights legislation passed in the 1960s, and her parents had moved from Miami, Florida, to Washington, D.C., "to experience new freedom." Her parents gave her an African name—Ketanji Onyika—which means "lovely one," signifying her parents' "pride in their heritage and hope for the future." As African American speakers have traditionally done, Judge Jackson combined what W. E. B. Du Bois called the "twoness" of African Americans: their lives as Americans and as Blacks. As Black speakers often do, Judge Jackson made Black history personal as well. "I stand on the shoulders of so many who have come before me," she said, "including Judge Constance Baker Motley, who was the first African American woman to be appointed to the federal bench."

Drawing upon their duality, African American speakers like Judge Jackson articulate America's core principles powerfully. While a child, her parents said that "her path was clearer" than theirs had been, so that if she "worked hard and believed in myself, in America I could do anything or be anything I wanted to be." Later in her statement, she again affirmed these principles, vowing that "if I am confirmed, I commit to you that I will work productively to support and defend the Constitution and the grand experiment of American democracy that has endured over these past 246 years." As she concluded her remarks, she once more referenced the central governing principle of America: "Like Justice Motley, I have dedicated my career to ensuring that the words engraved on the front of the Supreme Court building—'Equal Justice Under Law'—are a reality and not just an ideal. Thank you for this historic chance to join the highest Court, to work with brilliant colleagues, to inspire future generations, and to ensure liberty and justice for all."

Public speaking has always occupied a central place in American democracy. Revivalists catalyzed the Great Awakenings; patriots and Tories debated separation from Great Britain; Chautauqua speakers disseminated the latest ideas about life, politics, and the arts. Many of the nation's most famous and resilient messages were first set out in a public speech. Jonathan Edwards told his audience that they were sinners in the hands of an angry God. Washington warned the nation about the perils of becoming involved in foreign alliances, although it was Jefferson who later used the adjective "entangling." Lincoln hoped that "government of the people, by the people and for the people" would not "perish from this earth." Bryan rejected a "Cross of Gold" while Roosevelt reassured the public that "the only thing we have to fear, is fear itself."

Beyond such famous utterances, speeches have performed much of the everyday work of reforming the nation and its citizens, or encouraging resistance to reform. A system of free public education, the abolition of slavery, woman suffrage, legal protection of labor unions, the ratification of civil rights, and the legalization of gay marriage were all changes made possible by innumerable speeches. Wars have been fought and wars have been avoided through Americans speaking in public. Although newspapers, books, television, YouTube, Twitter, and many other communication technologies have emerged alongside public speaking, nothing has fully replaced it as a method for disseminating and defending ideas. Alexis de Tocqueville observed that Americans were a noisy and boisterous people, inclined to argue every political idea, whether local or national. Many of those arguments still take place through the modality of public speaking.

But if public speaking has occupied a central place force in American life generally, it has been a critical force for those Americans descended from Africans. During colonial times and the early years of the nation, clergy like Richard Allen and Absalom Jones built community among Blacks through their churches, while others like Prince Hall did the same through fraternal organizations like the Masons. Still other speakers integrated Blacks into the larger community, with evangelists like Flora addressing audiences of mixed race. African Americans also entered the political arena, speaking especially in support of the abolition of slavery and about the immorality of race discrimination.

Throughout the antebellum era, religion, abolition, and racial equality continued to be major themes of African American oratory. Some clergy, like Theodore Wright and Henry Highland Garnet, were college-trained and sometimes appointed to minister to integrated congregations. These preachers were leaders in the abolition movement as well. Other sermonizers were folk preachers, usually emerging organically through their ability to speak, often surreptitiously, and thus minister to congregants who were anxious to hear a word of spiritual comfort. Before he ever spoke at an abolitionist meeting, Frederick Douglass led a covert Sunday school on the plantation where he was held in slavery.

African American speakers were leaders in the abolition movement, no matter whether they had been born free like Charles Lenox Remond and Frances Harper or had fled slavery like Garnet, Douglass, and William Wells Brown. But these speakers did not confine their remarks to the abolition of slavery. All of them spoke about human rights and dignity, and as slavery was abolished or gradually dismantled in the Northern states, these speakers challenged the legal and de facto discrimination against Blacks that they experienced throughout the "free" states. In the antebellum period, African American speakers participated actively in the reform movements of the day. They preached temperance and supported woman suffrage. During the Civil War, they were strong and vocal supporters of the Union cause generally, but they especially agitated for the immediate emancipation of those enslaved and for the full and equal participation of Black soldiers in the Union Army.

The latter half of the nineteenth century posed a series of unique challenges for African American speakers. In the immediate aftermath of the Civil War, political opportunities previously denied to African Americans were now open, and these presented new forums for speaking. Many able and articulate legislators emerged who spoke eloquently in Congress as well as in state houses across the U.S. Through their speaking, they demonstrated themselves to be the equal of anyone, and they helped pass progressive legislation.

The end of Reconstruction, however, brought with it a wave of even more pronounced hostility and racial discrimination, and the hard-won gains of the decade following the Civil War slipped away. Segregation became the law of the land in the South, and de facto discrimination took hold across the rest of the country. Lynching, riots, and discriminatory criminal statutes enforced those changes. African Americans resisted these changes in a wide variety of ways. Many spoke in condemnatory terms, usually appealing to the principles of freedom and equality that America professed. Some, though, warned that resistance should or would become violent. Still other speakers turned inward and focused on using education and self-improvement to build the community from the ground up. The women's club movement was a major force of this era, and its leaders like Mary Church Terrell and Frances Harper advocated strongly for legal equality while also emphasizing self-improvement and moral reforms such as woman suffrage and temperance. Still other speakers were important catalysts of emigration. Some favored emigration westward, while others were back-to-Africa advocates. Ultimately, it would be those arguing for migration northward to the cities who had the largest impact.

With the dawn of the new century, many of the post-Reconstruction challenges remained. As it became clear that the problems of de jure and de facto segregation were firmly entrenched, however, a movement emerged that advocated challenging the legality of racial discrimination at every turn. Coalescing in the National Association for the Advancement of Colored People (NAACP), this integrated organization led by speakers and writers like W. E. B. Du Bois fueled the rise of lawyers, lobbyists, and community organizers who pushed for legal equality at every turn. Educators and clergy, too, remained prominent speakers. Mary McCleod Bethune, Mary Church Terrell, Mordecai Johnson, Francis Grimké, and Archibald Grimké all addressed the issues of legal equality as well as how the African American community could better itself without the help of white America.

Meanwhile, several waves of the Great Migration had moved large numbers of African Americans from the rural South to the cities of the North. Here were large, concentrated populations who found that they still faced racial discrimination and economic exploitation in the North. Race riots, where whites entered Black neighborhoods to burn, murder, and terrorize, were as common up North as they had been down South.

While mainstream churches, the women's club movement, and politically oriented organizations like the NAACP continued to be important community forces, this was an era that also saw the emergence of mass movements among African Americans, often led by a fiery and charismatic speaker. Many of these speakers were ministers who came from the Pentecostal folk-preaching tradition, such as Father Divine and "Big Daddy" Grace. Others combined politics with community building and, like Marcus Garvey, often supported the idea of Black nationalism. The continuing influence of these speakers has been profound. Echoes of the ministerial voices can be heard in the voice of later reformers, such as Adam Clayton Powell, Jesse Jackson, and Al Sharpton. The famed labor organizer A. Phillip Randolph employed many of the speaking techniques used by Marcus Garvey. Garveyites like Malcolm X's father, Earl Little, continued to promote separatism long after Garvey had been deported from the United States.

Beginning in the mid-1950s, the modern civil rights movement was sustained by grassroots public speaking. Typically dated to the *Brown v. Board of Education* decision, the murder of Emmett Till, and the Montgomery bus boycott, the movement and the speeches that fueled it had deep roots in earlier public speaking by African Americans. Television, however, now brought those speeches out of the segregated spaces to which they had often been confined. White Americans now heard Martin Luther King, Malcolm X, Fannie Lou Hamer, and Stokely Carmichael. African American oratory helped pass the 1964 Civil Rights Act, the 1965 Voting Rights Act, and the 1966 Open Housing Act. The antiwar movement and the women's liberation movement of the 1960s were also shaped by the Black civil rights speakers who came before them and who also spoke in support of these human rights reforms.

In this era, African American speakers also reached a larger, more extended audience among Blacks. Black power and Black pride were two important themes that had always been present historically but now caught fire. Many Black youth heard the calls of Malcolm X, Stokely Carmichael, Huey Newton, and Angela Davis and became more militant in their outlook. Afrocentrism and Black studies emerged more prominently as intellectual and scholarly endeavors. These speakers and those who continued their legacy would call greater attention to systemic racism and social injustice.

As civil rights reforms took hold African American speakers emerged even more prominently as central voices addressing a variety of societal issues. Martin Luther King and Shirley Chisholm spoke out forcefully against the Vietnam War, and one of the most famous denunciations of Richard Nixon's offenses was Barbara Jordan's speech to the House Judiciary Committee. Marian Wright Edelman founded the Children's Defense Fund, and Faye Wattleton was the activist president of Planned Parenthood. Audre Lorde, bell hooks, Henry Louis Gates, and Cornel West were among the Black intellectuals who popularized their ideas through lectures and debates and whose influence permeated throughout the academy. African American speakers successfully made South African apartheid a touchstone in the American political landscape.

African Americans also spoke from positions of political power. Cities across the country elected African Americans to the positions of mayor and members of city councils, and the number and power of Black legislators grew at the state and national levels. Douglas Wilder was elected governor of Virginia, and Shirley Chisholm and Jesse Jackson mounted credible campaigns for the presidency. Colin Powell was named director of the National Security Council and then chairman of the Joint Chiefs of Staff. All these positions provided African Americans with platforms from which to speak and influence audiences of all backgrounds.

Some African Americans continued to speak from "outside" the "establishment." Louis Farrakhan revived the Nation of Islam and drew upon the legacy of Malcolm X. Benjamin Chavis organized the First National People of Color Environmental Summit and along with many other speakers brought attention to the issue of environmental racism. Lenora Fulani ran for president as the nominee of the New Alliance Party. Angela Davis continued to be a much sought after lecturer and advocate for the American Communist Party. Public speaking thus remained a vibrant element of the African American experience but was now reaching a wider audience on a more regular basis.

No speaker captured both the promise and the problems that this change represented better than Barack Obama. Highly regarded for his powerful speaking style, Obama appealed to audiences from all racial backgrounds and was twice elected president. Early in his presidency, his eloquence secured the passage of a health care reform bill and helped catalyze the Arab Spring. So enthusiastic were observers that many declared that America had become "post-racial."

However, it became quickly apparent that Martin Luther King's dream of complete racial equality had not arrived. The "birther movement" questioned Obama's legitimacy in a way no white president had been questioned since the whisper campaigns of a century earlier that had suggested that Jackson and Lincoln were of mixed race. After Trayvon Martin was killed and his white assailant freed, and videos were posted online of Black men being shot and killed at the hands of police, the Black Lives Matter movement took hold. It began as a social media movement gone viral, but many speakers, and especially the mothers and wives of victims, gave voice and form to the cause. At the start, these speakers addressed systemic racial discrimination in the criminal justice system, but the discussion widened to include all matters of systemic social injustice, including economic discrimination. "Post-racial" America had not yet arrived, and these speakers made audiences aware of that fact. More importantly, they helped illuminate the many aspects of racial discrimination that continue to challenge the nation.

Public speaking has played such a prominent role in African American history for several reasons. Broadly, public speaking is "free," and that feature was a boon to people who were disadvantaged economically. Newspapers were financially difficult to sustain, and licenses for radio and television stations were hard for African Americans to come by. Public speaking, however, was readily available.

Over time, magazines and organizational news magazines like *The Crisis* would provide a viable alternative to speaking, and in the 1980s, the rise of cable television created outlets that had not previously been affordable. Inexpensive and free Internet platforms, ranging from formal websites to the wide variety of social media, have provided additional avenues through which African American advocates can reach an audience. Still, the "free" nature of public speaking means that advocates continue to talk at demonstrations, catalyze audiences by speaking at meetings, and create community through inspirational speeches delivered in a wide variety of settings and occasions.

The other side of the financial ledger is that public speaking has often provided income for African Americans by which they could pursue their advocacy. Abolitionist speakers like Douglass, Harper, and Brown supported themselves by charging admission to their lectures or by passing the collection plate. For Douglass, it was his lectures and the sales of his autobiographies that financially sustained his newspapers. When Frances Harper wrote to William Still that she wished to abandon the lecture circuit and work directly with the Underground Railroad, Still pleaded with her to continue her speaking because the money she was sending back was vital to sustaining the Railroad. Even today, the money raised through lectures by speakers like Bryan Stevenson provides financial support to their organizations like the Equal Justice Initiative.

Finally, Afrocentric scholars like Molefi K. Asante and Audre Lorde observe that African Americans brought with them a culture that emphasized orality. Indeed, these authors believe that oral communication is inherently integral to the understanding of community for those of African descent. They argue that the division between speaker and audience is an artificial, Eurocentric idea, and that the act of public speaking is a communal performance of unity. In this way, public speaking is not a tool by which to accomplish an end, but is itself an inherent part of the community's identity.

So vital has public speaking been for African American experience that many of those perceived as leaders of that community achieved their reputation through their public speaking. Frederick Douglass stood up to speak at an abolition meeting, and his emotional testimony as a fugitive slave captured the imagination of the movement. Sojourner Truth could not read or write, but she was highly regarded for her profoundly eloquent speeches. Booker T. Washington built Tuskegee Institute, but it was his public speaking that made Tuskegee possible and gave Washington his standing at the turn of the nineteenth century. Marcus Garvey frightened his critics with his power to attract and energize huge crowds in Harlem.

Adam Clayton Powell, Malcolm X, Stokely Carmichael, Jesse Jackson, Shirley Chisholm, Barbara Jordan, Louis Farrakhan, and Al Sharpton are just a few figures whose efforts focused heavily on public speaking.

The modern archetype for this manner considering African American speakers is Martin Luther King Jr. He first attracted attention through the nightly speeches he gave during the Montgomery bus boycott. His ability to keep the boycotters energized and organized over the course of the year was the springboard he used to organize the Southern Christian Leadership Conference. Through his oratory, King articulated the nation's moral obligation to treat its citizens of color with dignity and equality. He called America to account for its racial transgressions and espoused the principle of nonviolent civil disobedience. He gave voice to the economic legacy of slavery, segregation, and racial discrimination, insisting that the United States redress the institutional poverty that racial inequality had left in its wake. In the last year of his life, he was a powerful speaker against the U.S. war in Vietnam. Although he would also pen eloquent essays, such as "Letter from a Birmingham Jail," it was his public speaking that commanded public attention.

Many scholars and lay observers have worried about the importance that has been attached to these speakers. In part, they are concerned that the attention is reductionist; that the African American community has never had one "leader" and that the range of ideas, values, and opinions held by African Americans cannot be conveyed through a single speaker. Some have also worried that by focusing on a single leader—the "Moses" who will lead the community to the Promised Land—Americans white and Black absolve themselves of their individual responsibility to address the nation's issue of race.

Similarly, the singular attention devoted to speakers like King means that, for many Americans, Black public speaking takes a single form. In general, King spoke in the folk style of the Black Baptist preacher. Such speaking is often extemporized, with biblical quotations woven throughout. Many invitations for the audience to interact with the speaker will be included, using the call-and-response technique. It is heavily stylized, using many metaphors, parallelisms, and other figures of speech. Humor and irony are often employed, both to make a point with a bit of a bite and also to bind the speaker and audience through implied, but mutually understood, messages. There will often be singing or quasi-singing, and the speech inevitably leads to an emotional climax. Many speakers who have followed King and gained national attention, like Jesse Jackson, Al Sharpton, and William Barber, draw upon the same tradition.

Black folk preaching is indeed a powerful form of public address, but it is unfortunate that it is so often regarded as the only method of Black public speaking. Just as African Americans have spoken about a wide range of subjects and have often taken conflicting positions, so too there are many styles of public speaking that they have employed. Reducing the African American public speaking style to a single archetype obscures the many different types of oratorical eloquence that African Americans have displayed.

As the speakers analyzed in this volume demonstrate, Black folk preaching is just one of many styles of speaking that African Americans have employed. Sojourner Truth used piercing logic to cut to the heart of her opponents' illogic and then yoked that logic to lessons from the Bible. Frances Harper was a poetically eloquent orator, as was Frederick Douglass, while Ida B. Wells-Barnett reported the stories of lynching with a journalistic eye for detail that reflected her training. Garvey's speaking was enthusiastic; Du Bois's was learned. Many preachers—like Theodore Wright, Alexander Crummell, the Grimké brothers, and Vernon Johns—were more theological than energetic, while Shirley Chisholm, Barbara Jordan, and Marian Wright Edelman were debaters at heart. Variety performed at a high level of excellence has long been the true hallmark of African American public speaking.

Barack Obama provides a case in point. Obama emerged nationally in 2004 due to his eloquent keynote address to the Democratic National Convention. As he conducted his unlikely campaign for president in 2007 and 2008, his eloquence became legendary, and his style was often analogized to that of King. With rare exceptions, however, such as when he broke into song during his eulogy at Mother Emmanuel Church, Obama's public speaking bore little stylistic resemblance to that of King. He rarely engaged in runs—extemporaneous speaking that weaves patterns out of repeated language—and wove few biblical passages into his speaking. Although he employed many parallelisms, his other figures of speech were more muted. Indeed, Obama's reputed "coolness" stood in stark contrast to the heat generated by a minister preaching in the folk tradition. To identify Obama's speaking too closely with King's is to miss how artfully Obama blended an inspirational call to America's values with the pragmatic necessities of government administration.

Public speaking has thus been integral to and often identified with the life of the African American community, but it has also been an integral part of the American community as a whole. African American speakers have addressed every major issue, reform, and philosophical development that has arisen throughout the history of the United States. Moreover, the special influence of African American public speaking on movements such as woman suffrage, the Vietnam War protests, women's liberation, and the LGBTQ movement is undeniable. Cause and effect are always difficult to prove when discussing the evolution of a community or a culture. It is clear, however, that African American oratory has been an indispensable feature of American history.

This volume surveys that history, and in doing so has three aims. First, the volume seeks to convey how integral African American public speaking has been to U.S. history. Black speakers have addressed every important issue that has arisen since the nation's founding, and as this history demonstrates, they have proven themselves influential contributors to American thought. Second, this survey of their work should illumine the richness of the speaking. As noted above, public speaking has been one of the few resources of influence consistently available to Blacks, and their rhetorical virtuosity is on full display in this volume. The third aim of this book is to describe themes and motifs that have been present throughout African American public speech. Public speaking practices continually evolve over time, but changes are invariably influenced by what has gone before. Malcolm X, for example, is not a Garveyite, yet his speaking included some important commonalities to that of Marcus Garvey, such as arguing for Black economic self-sufficiency and the importance of self-discipline. In turn, Black Power speakers explicitly acknowledged the influence Malcolm X had on their own development as speakers, and the emancipatory rhetoric honed by those speakers continues to be evidenced by those in the twenty-first century who advocate for social justice. There is a danger of oversimplification when describing such influences and motifs, but public speaking never emerges in a vacuum. There has always been some public conversation going on in the community before the speaker ever stands up to address an audience, and some of that conversation is what the speaker will often echo, in content or in style, and in that way motifs emerge and evolve.

In order to examine these continuities and changes, this volume tells the stories of some of the most influential African American public speakers as well as some of those who are less well remembered. To tell these stories requires some attention to individual speeches and passages that illustrate the content and style of those speakers. No speech or speaker can be fully covered in the space of such a survey, but some close analysis of situation, audience, and speech can provide a deeper appreciation for how these speakers worked to bring about change and to build community.

The volume is composed of seven chapters, divided broadly into eras in which speakers faced similar issues and situations and responded in ways that were echoed by other speakers during that time. It is always artificial to suggest that one era of speaking abruptly ends and another suddenly appears, but within some general time frames common themes do emerge.

Chapter 1 examines the colonial and early national period. Speakers of this era worked to build a community among those of African descent who had come from many different places and represented many different ethnic groups. All faced racial discrimination, however, and speeches helped create a common vocabulary of community. As with the population generally, religious speaking played an especially important role, as lay and clerical speakers developed two different paths—one that integrated African Americans into the religious movements that arose and one that created separate churches in which Blacks could worship free of discrimination. During this era, Black speakers were also thought leaders in creating an abolitionist community that agitated against the system of slavery.

Chapter 2 looks at the antebellum era, when cotton became king and slavery expanded widely and became even more entrenched. Abolitionist speaking took center stage, and Black abolitionists became increasingly militant in their agitation against slavery. Fugitive slaves, like Henry Highland Garnet, Frederick Douglass, and William Wells Brown, became prominent speakers who could speak personally to the evils of slavery and also, through their eloquence, demonstrate that African Americans were entitled to full citizenship. Religion, temperance, and woman suffrage were also subjects addressed by Black speakers who, like Frances Harper and Sojourner Truth, spoke widely in support of many different reforms. This was an era, too, when Black separatist speakers rose to national prominence, primarily arguing that African Americans should leave the United States and that Blacks would never be treated as equals in the United States.

With the onset of the Civil War and subsequent passage of the Reconstruction amendments, African Americans gained a new legal status, at least nationally. Chapter 3 examines the Civil War, Reconstruction, and post-Reconstruction periods. The ability to be elected to political office opened up new vistas for African American public speakers, as did their work in education. Religion, too, could now be practiced publicly, whereas during the antebellum period, the more indigenous practices of Black religion had often been suppressed. Women's clubs proliferated during this era, and those also afforded new speaking opportunities for many. The brief window of Reconstruction, however, was followed by the rise of segregation and lynching in the South and racial discrimination in the North. The challenges raised in the post-Reconstruction era posed a dilemma for

African American speakers, with some arguing for accommodation, others for agitation and integration, and still others for emigration.

Chapter 4 discusses public speaking from post–World War I until 1954, which traditionally marks the rise of the modern civil rights era. Scholars often treat these three decades as a fallow period, but they were actually a time of great activity. Formed in 1909, the National Association for the Advancement of Colored People spearheaded the move to challenge segregation and discrimination through court cases and legislative lobbying. The 1954 *Brown v. Board of Education* decision, which legally overturned segregation, was the culmination of a great many speeches—in the courts, in the community, and at fundraising meetings. Meanwhile the Great Migration saw many African Americans flee the rural South and move to the urban North. The rise of concentrated populations and the advent of microphones, loudspeakers, and then radio allowed charismatic speakers like Marcus Garvey to gain national and international attention. Some, like Garvey and A. Philip Randolph, built political and labor organizations through their speaking. Others, like Charles "Big Daddy" Grace, used their speaking talents to evangelize. Still others, like Adam Clayton Powell Jr., bridged both of those worlds by using the pulpit to organize boycotts and effect political change. Educators like Mary McLeod Bethune also continued to be highly regarded speakers who addressed a wide range of moral and practical issues.

Chapter 5 explores the vibrant period of the modern civil rights movement. This was an era rich in public speaking that often overshadows the speaking of earlier and later times. It was a period marked by the nonviolent protests led by Black preachers like Martin Luther King Jr. as well as civil rights organizers like John Lewis and Fannie Lou Hamer. In reaction to the slow pace of change, a young, militant group of speakers came forward. Malcolm X was the widely acknowledged progenitor of this brand of speaking, and he was followed by the "Black Power" style of speakers, such as Stokely Carmichael, H. Rap Brown, Eldridge Cleaver, and Angela Davis. Between the hammer of militancy and the anvil of nonviolent protests, civil rights policy changed in America. Into this mix came the Vietnam War, which disproportionately sent the poor and African Americans into combat. Initially a point of contention between the "mainstream" movement and the militants, by 1968 most leaders in both camps were speaking in opposition to the war.

Chapter 6 looks at the four decades of speaking following the assassination of Martin Luther King Jr. in 1968. With the passage of 1960s civil rights legislation, many activist speakers transitioned into political positions. Other speakers reached national audiences as leaders of organizations, some with traditional civil rights organizations like the NAACP, others with new civil rights groups like Operation PUSH, and still others at the head of organizations that were not focused on civil rights, such as the Children's Defense Fund and Planned Parenthood. African Americans also found larger opportunities and audiences in the intellectual community, while religion continued to be an important locus of public speaking. As a result, African American speakers were able to address a wider range of social and political issues to more and larger audiences than they had typically been able to reach in the past. In all these endeavors, African American speakers continued to draw on the traditions of public speaking that had characterized earlier eras.

Chapter 7 examines African American public speaking in the era many hoped would be "post-racial" but was not. In 2008, the United States elected Barack Obama to the presidency, the first African American to earn this national office. Many in the U.S. and around the world who had never heard a speech by an African American now did so, and like many who had preceded him, Obama drew on the speaking traditions of African Americans. The election of an African American to the presidency signaled to many that the U.S. was finally "post-racial." However, racial resentment to his presidency was evident, while issues of social injustice persisted. The Black Lives Matter movement emerged, and with it came speakers who addressed issues of systemic discrimination and unequal treatment by the police and the criminal justice system. In 2020, that movement grew more powerful and even more integrated as protests erupted over the death of George Floyd. In an era marked by many radically new communication technologies, public speaking has remained a vital tool for African American advocacy and for the development of community. Even in the twenty-first century, the echoes of the African American speaking traditions first forged four hundred years earlier can still be heard.

# 1

## Liberty, Equality, and Salvation

*African Americans at the Start of the Nation*

FROM THE EARLIEST MOMENTS of Blacks' arrival on the North American continent, public speaking played a vital role in the life of the African American community. Like Americans from all backgrounds, Blacks preached, spoke in community groups, and discussed politics. Although their access to meeting venues was often limited, African Americans from many walks of life still spoke. Like those of most American speakers of that era, few texts of speeches delivered by African Americans have been preserved, but we do have historical accounts of their speaking as well as some texts that were saved in personal journals or printed in newspapers or as pamphlets.

Unsurprisingly, the themes these speakers addressed have largely persisted to the present day. In colonial times and the early years of the United States, African American speakers discussed their political place in American society, the hypocrisy of slavery and racial discrimination in a society that preached Christian love and political freedom, their identity as a community, and the nature of their religious beliefs. Although the earliest recorded speakers talked about religion, antislavery speakers also emerged during colonial times as did those who sought to build a community among those Blacks who had immigrated—voluntarily as well as forcibly—to the shores of what would become the United States. The distinction between these three kinds of speaking should not be too sharply drawn, however. Religious speakers addressed political issues and often sought to build a stronger community among Blacks, and political and community activists usually made religious appeals a part of their speeches.

## SPREADING THE GOSPEL

Preaching—the speaking of religious matters—occurred among Blacks from the earliest days of the British colonies. Many scholars argue that the roots of Black preaching may be found in the African culture from which Blacks had been taken. Africans who were enslaved or who came as indentured servants spoke among themselves, often in secret meetings, about the religious beliefs they brought from Africa, and this practice continued throughout the period of slavery. Most religious practices and beliefs in sub-Saharan Africa were tolerant, and so Blacks were often open to adapting Christianity to their existing theology.

### *Folk Preaching and the Great Awakening*

One of the earliest forms of speaking recorded is typically characterized as "folk preaching," and it often incorporated singing, shouting, and an emphasis on stories and the application of religious beliefs to the difficulties of life enslaved. In his study of *The Slave Community*, historian John Blassingame wrote that music, or spirituals, was integral to plantation worship and that slave accounts are consistent in writing that music was closely intertwined with preaching at Blacks' religious meetings. Black congregations wove together shouting, singing, and praying to create a holistic religious experience that eased the spiritual and physical burdens of slavery. The practice of whooping—a form of preaching in which the words are delivered in an a cappella "chant"—was a speaking form that emerged from this practice. The call-and-response pattern, when the preacher implicitly or explicitly invited a response from the congregation who then answered that call, was another style of speaking that emerged from the earliest practices of folk preaching.

Because these religious meetings were held in secret, and because Blacks were excluded from the pulpit of established churches, the "Black church" was what historians like Martha Simmons and Frank Thomas have called "the invisible institution." There were meetings, preaching, forms of worship, and theologies, but those forms were not "visible" to the dominant white culture and therefore rarely recorded. Still, these were important public speaking occasions for speaker and audience alike. Before escaping slavery, for example, Frederick Douglass's first public speaking experience occurred when he surreptitiously taught "Sunday school" on the plantation.

Black preaching became somewhat more visible when the Methodist preacher George Whitefield toured the colonies and sparked the Second

Great Awakening in 1740. Whitefield stimulated change in two regards. First, he practiced "emotionalism," a style of preaching that emphasized one's personal experience with God, and he applied that experience to one's everyday encounter with God. In contrast to the stiff, doctrine-oriented preaching prevalent at the time among white colonists, Whitefield's style of speaking was far more closely aligned with the Black style of folk preaching. Second, Whitefield emphasized the importance of reaching every individual with the Gospel—young and old, poor and rich, male and female. While many whites had previously proselytized among Blacks, Whitefield's message energized that impulse, encouraging Black membership in churches and asking Blacks to testify regarding their faith and salvation.

A common kind of preaching during the Great Awakening was performed by "exhorters," individuals who felt the urge to take up the religious spirit of the revival and speak. Establishment ministers often looked down upon these lay preachers. Anglican missionary Charles Brockwell and Charles Chauncy, minister of Boston's First Congregational Church, both condemned the rise of exhorters, writing disparagingly about the children, women, and "Negroes" who had the audacity to preach the Gospel at revivals. Revivalist ministers, though, were more complimentary. In 1742, itinerant preacher Daniel Rogers provided one of the earliest known descriptions of African American public speaking: "A Negroe man servant of Colonel Pepperell's broke out and spoke in a wonderful manner of the sweet love of Jesus which he said he felt in his heart to great degree that he could die for Christ. He exhorted all to come and talke of the love of Christ. Another negroe man servant of Colonel Pepperell cryed out in distress."

One such exhorter was Flora, an enslaved woman in the town of Ipswich, Massachusetts. Although none of her speeches survive, Flora's *Confession* was published in 1746, and it probably reflected the substance of her talks. Flora's faithfulness had lapsed during the six years since she had first participated in revivals, and she confessed to committing the sins of ingratitude, spiritual pride, unwatchfulness, and levity. She marveled at the gift of God's grace, which had filled her heart, nurtured in her a prayerful attitude, and brought her heart "home" to "some Texts of holy Scripture." As historian Christopher Cameron writes, Flora's religious expressions were consonant with the Calvinist beliefs prevalent throughout New England.

Of note, too, was Flora's mention of "scripture." As Simmons and Gardner observe, scriptures, or the Bible, have been central to Black preaching, with particular attention paid to making the Bible relevant to African Americans' experience. Reporting about a young African American woman exhorter he heard in 1743, Daniel Rogers wrote that she

Mrs. Juliann Jane Tillman, preaching in the A.M.E. Church, circa 1790. Library of Congress.

spoke about a vision of the coming kingdom of God and the entrance of African Americans into that kingdom. She found the biblical support for her vision in Psalm 68, in which the psalmist celebrated God's release of captives and prisoners, his care for widows and orphans, and the triumph of God's people over their enemies. Psalm 68 foretold that "Ethiopia shall stretch forth her hand to the Lord." Blacks' inclusion in Christian religious practice was thus both justified—God foretells it—and necessary. Until the descendants of African—that is, Ethiopia—were counted among the faithful, God's triumph could not occur. Psalm 68 thus functioned as both a comfort to African Americans because it prophesied a better day coming and an argument that whites who denied Blacks equal treatment in the church or under the law were sinning against God's will.

*Ministers*

Not all Black preachers during the colonial and early national periods were "folk" preachers, however. By the 1770s and 1780s, Black preachers and the Black church had become more visible. In 1758, an African Baptist church was founded in Mecklenburg County, Virginia, and a Silver Bluff Baptist church in Silver Bluff, South Carolina, was established in 1773. Frustrated with the discriminatory practices found in the white-controlled churches of the Episcopalian faith, in 1791 Absalom Jones and Richard Allen founded the St. Thomas African Episcopal Church in Philadelphia, and Peter Williams Sr. and others soon followed suit in New York City. These churches became the foundation of the African Methodist Episcopal (A.M.E.) Church. Other preachers of the era, such as John Chavis (Presbyterian), Lemuel Haynes (Congregationalist) and Peter Williams Jr. (Episcopalian), were ordained by and preached to predominantly white congregations. According to Simmons and Thomas, African American preaching served three major roles for Black congregations: it provided hope, taught church doctrine, and agitated for political and social change.

Hope came in part because Christianity promised individual salvation. Those who had faith in Jesus Christ would be the beneficiaries of his grace and thus gain heaven. George White's 1809 "A Sermon Preached on the Funeral Occasion of Mary Henery" is representative. Freed by his dying master, White became an itinerant Methodist preacher and deacon. In 1809, he preached at the funeral of Mary Henery, a twenty-year-old enslaved woman on Long Island, New York, whom White had earlier converted. Black preachers were usually well versed in both the Old and New Testaments of the Bible and paid close attention to the text. White was no exception, taking as his text the Gospel of Luke: "Strive to enter in at the strait gate, for many I say unto you shall seek to enter in, and shall not be able." His sermon was well organized, as he drew three lessons from his text: that Jesus Christ was the "strait gate" who required repentance, faith, and atonement in order to gain entry to heaven; that the gate is called "strait" because Christ's demands ran contrary to human nature and thus required that we have God's grace; and that his hearers must heed Christ's call now and without delay, lest their faith come "too late." White's sermon was simultaneously a call to Christian faith and a message of comfort to the congregants: "But hush the heaving sigh, and dry the briny tear, for your deceased relative, and our much-loved Christian sister, has, no doubt, found a safe passage through the strait and narrow gate to the blissful regions of eternal day; where she now joins the Church triumphant, around the dazzling throne of God, in songs of praise and shouts of victory."

Church doctrine, as supported by scripture, was important to Black preachers in part because it provided instruction in daily, faithful living, but also because religion made the case that those of African descent were equally human to those of European descent. In his 1787 speech "I Speak to Those in Slavery," Cyril Bustil referenced no fewer than twenty-one passages from the Bible, ranging from the Psalms and Proverbs through the Gospels, Letters of Paul, and the Book of Revelation. Although a baker by trade, Bustil's speech was a sermon to those in slavery, and he used the occasion to counsel them to live faithful, biblical lives. Bustil was an abolitionist and emancipated slave who had been manumitted by his Quaker owner, but he urged his audience to trust that the Lord would deliver them from their condition. The message woven throughout Bustil's sermon was that, because Blacks were the equal of whites, their religious path to salvation was identical to whites. There was no special "path" for African Americans because all people are equal in the eyes of God. Bustil made this point in part by noting that "God is no respecter of persons," a quotation from Acts 10 that is echoed in Paul's second letter to the Romans. That God is no respecter of persons and does not discriminate between "nations" was a Scriptural phrase repeated by many African American speakers, whether religious or secular, and in many different settings.

African American preaching was not solely concerned with how religion helped define issues of race or race relations, however. African Americans were also interested in the theological matters of faith, hope, grace, and salvation, and African American preachers reflected on all of these. Lemuel Haynes's 1805 sermon "Universal Salvation" was an extemporaneous rebuttal of the Universalist minister Hosea Ballou's lecture that all people could be saved by adhering to the Gospel. Haynes was an ordained Congregationalist minister and, from the earliest days of the American Revolution, an outspoken abolitionist. From a pragmatic standpoint, Haynes could have served his own political agenda by preaching a message of universal salvation and by supporting a political ally. Instead, Haynes remained true to his spiritual convictions and forcefully advanced the Calvinist doctrine, comparing Ballou's sermon to the flattering appeals Satan used on Adam and Eve in the Garden of Eden.

Although African American religious sermons and lectures in this era touched on many different messages, what emerged broadly were principles and speaker roles that have recurred since colonial times. In *Preaching with Sacred Fire*, Martha Simmons and Frank Thomas outline several principles of African American sermonizing. First, they argue that for African American preachers, the Bible has been central though not necessarily literal. Specifically, the role of the preacher has been to "bring alive" the stories and meanings of the Bible. That desire to bring the Bible "alive" to the audience has been manifest in many speeches, from the exhortations recorded by Daniel Rogers to George White's funeral sermon on the "strait gate." Simmons and Thomas note that a related principle is the emphasis on relevance. African Americans of all backgrounds faced lives of hardship caused by discrimination. For Black preachers, the Bible has been a source of comfort, resolve, and pride. Typically, their preaching has reflected a deep study of the Bible, but with particular attention to understanding the Bible's relevance to the listener's everyday life and to using the Bible to understand the world in a very different way. Finally, Simmons and Thomas note the emphasis on God's transcendent power, a power that was not of the preacher's making nor one that could be controlled by any human, no matter how rich or politically powerful or of whatever race.

## BUILDING COMMUNITY

Although religious meetings and church services provided one of the primary opportunities for African Americans to speak in public, those were not the only settings in which African Americans formally addressed audiences. Within the Black community, social organizations arose where African Americans gathered, provided aid and support, and exchanged ideas. Through these community associations, Blacks also organized, agitated, and lobbied for political change. In 1775, Prince Hall provisionally founded the Masonic African Lodge No. 1 in Boston and gained a permanent charter for the lodge in 1787. The Wilberforce Association was an example of the literary/debating societies where African Americans met and discussed the political and philosophical ideas of the day. The New York African Society for Mutual Relief, the Brooklyn African Woolman Benevolent Society, and the Wilberforce Philanthropic Association were a few of the groups organized by African Americans to aid the widowed, sick, and poor.

Portrait of Prince Hall. Grand Lodge of British Columbia and Yukon[1] Portrait: http://freemasonry.bcy.ca/prince_hall/PrnceHll.jpg.

Like Lemuel Haynes's sermon on universal salvation, many of the speeches and talks given at community meetings did not directly address matters of race. Temperance, education, philosophy, and history were just some of the subjects that were addressed at these meetings. However, most of the speeches published in pamphlets or recorded on broadsides discussed the issue of race.

*Building Pride*

One important function of all of these organizations was to build community among African Americans. Most African Americans of the era were themselves or were descended from persons who had been forcibly taken from their homes in Africa. Through slavery, most had been deprived of the benefits of permanent social relationships. All Black Americans lived amid a culture that consistently denigrated them. African Americans thus faced many challenges that coming together as a community could help address. In community meetings, African Americans could find dignity and support, and an important component of building community was to find honor in one's origins, what in later times would be called "race pride" or "Black pride." John Marrant's message, captured in the title of his speech "You Stand on the Level with the Greatest Kings," was representative. Delivered at the African Lodge No. 1 in 1789, Marrant painstakingly constructed a logic drawn from history and biblical stories that established that the Egyptians were "expert Masons" as they built the pyramids and that the Egyptians of that time drew from sub-Saharan Africa as well. While Americans of European descent thought of Africa as a primitive, savage, and uncivilized place, Marrant argued that history revealed many "Africans who were truly good, wise, and learned men, and as eloquent as any other nation whatever."

In 1792, Prince Hall developed a similar message for his fellow Masons in "A Charge Delivered to the Brethren of the African Lodge," saying explicitly that his speech was building upon the foundation laid by Marrant's 1789 address. Although Hall's charge to his listeners was to live their lives justly and according to the precepts of Masonry, the primary point of his lecture was to instill in his audience pride in their African ancestry. While Marrant had focused on the architectural and engineering evidence that supported the claim that Masonry extended back through history to Africa, Hall emphasized Africans' place in the Bible and early Christian church.

Hall noted, for example, how the "compassion of a Black man"— Ebedmelech the Ethiopian—was extended to the prophet Jeremiah when no one else would support him. Hall also pointed to important early church leaders who had been African, including Tertullian, Cyprian, and Augustine. He developed the Gospel story of the Good Samaritan as an example of a member of a race looked upon as "unworthy" who acted in the most spiritual and benevolent way. He urged his audience to imitate all these good and noble Africans, reassuring them that God's fortune was with them because, like the exhorter Flora, he observed that the "great Architect of the universal world" has told the faithful in Psalm 68 that "Aethiopia shall stretch forth her hands unto me."

Hall also used contemporary evidence to support his point. Referring to the American Revolution, Hall asked his audience to consider "our conduct in the late war" when we marched "shoulder to shoulder, brother soldier and brother soldier, to the field of battle." Given these biblical and historical instances, Hall could conclude theologically that whoever "despises a Black man for the sake of his colour, reproacheth his Maker."

*Rebutting Prejudice*

African Americans also used speeches to reject whites' prejudice. These speeches performed two important functions. Ostensibly, the audience for these remarks were African Americans, and the purpose of the arguments was to help Blacks reject the popular prejudices that surrounded them. Two religiously based themes were that Africans were descended from Adam's son Cain, who had killed his own brother, Abel, or that they came from Ham, Noah's disgraced son. Both of these biblical ancestors were persons of bad repute, and thus, according to the prejudicial logic, Blacks were not entitled to the same religious favor in God's eyes as were those of European descent. Hall's arguments contradicted those claims, reassuring Blacks that they did indeed stand firmly in God's good graces.

However, arguments like Hall's functioned to build community in a second way as well, by supplying his audience with evidence and reasons that could be used to rebut whites and their cultural prejudices. It was useful to remind white Americans that Blacks had fought alongside whites in the Revolution, that God was no "respecter of persons," and that African civilizations had flourished while Europeans were still living in houses made of mud. Although African Americans constituted the immediate audience seated in the hall, published reprints of speeches like Marrant's and Hall's were distributed to Americans of all races.

The 1791 Haitian slave revolt and 1804 establishment of a government there run by former slaves provided a contemporary example of what Blacks were capable of and aspired to. Haiti was frequently cited by speakers as proof that Blacks did want freedom, that they were willing to fight for it, and that they were capable of self-government. In his 1826 commencement address at Bowdoin College, delivered as a graduating student, John Brown Russwurm took Haiti as his case study. A year later, Russwurm became one of the cofounders of *Freedom's Journal*, the first African American–owned newspaper.

In his graduation speech, Russwurm argued that liberty ran in every person's "breast," and so the Haitians—paraphrasing the motto of the French Revolution—intended to "live free or die gloriously." In the process of fighting for their liberty and establishing their nation, Haitians had "stepped forth as men." They had adopted a representative form of government, and nowhere were the rights and privileges of all people "more respected, and crimes less frequent" than in Haiti. The public proceedings and state papers written by Haitian officials were, he said, "distinguished from those of many European courts only by their superior energy and nonexalted sentiments." Russwurm pragmatically acknowledged the ongoing Haitian civil war but characterized it as a monarchic leader fighting against a democratic one. That Haitians were prone to the same divisions as other nations simply proved their membership in the human race.

## Abraham Johnstone's "Address" on Community

One of the most unique speeches of this era that has survived to the present is Abraham Johnstone's "Address to the People of Color." Johnstone had been born into slavery in Delaware and then gained his freedom. In 1790, Johnstone was convicted of murdering another free Black man and sentenced to death. On the surface, his statement to the court was directed toward African Americans, but he clearly understood that white Americans were also listening. Indeed, his first point was that his conviction should not be used to make prejudicial generalizations about African Americans. Such stereotypes, Johnstone says, will only be made "by the low-minded illiberal and sordid persons who are the enemies of our color." Referencing his own situation, Johnstone held that if an impartial count was made, one would find that the "vast majority" of those who had died on the gallows had been white. He thus concluded ironically that this was "a plain proof that there are some whites (with all due deference to them) capable of being equally as depraved and more generally so, than Blacks or people of color."

Johnstone then turned to describe the cruelty of slavery. "From the first," he said, those of "our color" were forced "to drudge incessantly yet without the smallest hopes of a reward, denied a sufficient portion of food . . . or raiment sufficient to hide their nakedness." "The most unheard of cruelties and punishments were daily inflicted upon us," he said, and he testified that he had "personal knowledge" of these facts because "I speak from experience."

After thus denouncing slavery, he considered the religious case. He believed it was a "foolishly chimerical notion" that African Americans could not enter the kingdom of heaven. "Some other speaking idiots," he said mockingly, "would have us as the seed of Cain." He dismissed such fools out of hand. It was "enough to make any unconcerned or disinterested person merry to hear such foolishly frivolous arguments adduced with such solemnity against us." It was nonsensical, he argued, because "God is neither a respecter of persons, nor color," and because "Scripture tells us expressly, 'That all that believe shall be saved.'"

Having established the intellectual, physical, and spiritual personhood of Blacks, Johnstone described again the vicious nature of slavery and its "affecting tortures" inflicted by the "merciless callous-hearted monster of a master." He recited a list of slavery's brutal practices—the pangs of hunger, the distempered bodies, and the cutting stripes and scourges that are caused by the lash. "And why [is this]?" he asked. "Because our color happens to be Black?" He condemned the wanton cruelty of slavery and the absurdity of those who justified the cruelty because of their supposed superiority. On the precipice of his own execution, Johnstone remarked instead on the injustice of prejudice and slavery and, instead of commenting on his own fate, attempted to better the condition of those of his race whom he left behind.

Building community also meant working together for the common good. African Americans must "teach our children," said Rev. Absalom Jones in his 1808 Sermon of Thanksgiving marking the legal end of the external slave trade. The children must "acquire a knowledge of useful trades" so they may "advance themselves." Speaking to the New York African Mutual Relief Association on the first anniversary of that ban, William Hamilton congratulated his audience on their work. "Deep poverty and distress is the bane of improvement," he told them. Working together as an association, those better off could help relieve their brethren's poverty and thereby improve the outlook for the African American community as a whole.

## OPPOSING SLAVERY

The African American community could never fully thrive, however, as long as the institution of racialized slavery continued. For one thing, the American practice of slavery depended upon and thus nurtured racial prejudice. Also, those enslaved who either bought their freedom or fled to freedom left behind family and friends. Communal bonds between free and enslaved Blacks were either discouraged or illegal. Thus, slavery was an institution the African American community felt the need to oppose loudly and often. Johnstone's speech at his sentencing, which alternately defended Blacks' personhood and attacked the cruelty of slavery, was representative. Many speeches were devoted to the abolition of the institution, and few speeches by African Americans did not comment upon its evil presence.

African American petitions for the abolition of slavery suggest the scope of public speaking that was devoted to the topic, for speeches were the tool by which people organized to write and sign petitions, and speeches typically accompanied the delivery of such petitions to the targeted legislature. In 1773, a committee of enslaved persons formed in Massachusetts for the purpose of opposing slavery and submitted a petition to the state legislature urging it to abolish slavery. In 1777, Prince Hall led another drive among African Americans to petition the Massachusetts legislature, and similar antislavery petitions were signed in New Hampshire and Connecticut. Historian Christopher Cameron notes that these petition drives predated and rhetorically influenced later abolition efforts by white-led organizations. In 1799, Absalom Jones and seventy-two other signees submitted a petition to the president of the United States and both houses of Congress urging the immediate abolition of slavery. In their petitions and speeches, African Americans consistently and clearly voiced their case against slavery.

*The Cruelty of Slavery*

In no small measure, that case began and ended with the cruelty of the institution, in a manner similar to Johnstone's description. Rev. Absalom Jones's 1808 Thanksgiving Sermon, marking the start of the prohibition against the slave trade, illustrated the graphic description that speakers often provided. He observed that Africans arriving in the New World were treated like "horses and cattle" or "bales of goods." God, he said, had seen their "pangs of separation" as family members were sold to different plantations, compelled to work under the burning sun "with scarcely as much clothing upon them as modesty required," returning in the evening to "smoky huts," with "nothing to satisfy their hunger but a scanty allowance of roots." God had "seen all the different modes of torture" used to keep those enslaved in check: "the whip, the screw, the pincers, and the red-hot iron." Jones concluded, denouncing the "masters and mistresses educated in fashionable life" as "Inhuman wretches!"

Speaking in 1809 at the one year anniversary of the prohibition, William Hamilton, a carpenter and cofounder of the New York Society for Mutual Relief, wondered aloud about who would not be horrified by the acts of cruelty committed against an "unoffending part of the human family." Whites were flattered by the name "master," he said, when they should be smart enough to shun the "odium" that the name implied. Yet in their ignorance they congratulated themselves on being "demigods." Hamilton likened white slaveholders to Shakespeare's character of Shylock, who demanded of his debtor the promised "pound of flesh." "If these [cruelties of slavery] are some of the marks of superiority," Hamilton concluded, "may heaven in mercy always keep us inferior: go, proud white men, go, boast of your superior cunning."

On the Fourth of July of 1827, Austin Steward, an escaped slave from Virginia who established a meat market and grocery in Rochester, New

York, reminded his audience there about the cruelties of slavery even as he spoke in celebration of the partial abolition of slavery in New York that was taking effect on that day. He spoke about the "deceit, the forcible fraud and treachery" that had "been so long practiced," as slavery had caused fathers to be torn from their families, wives taken from the "embrace of their husbands," and children stripped of their parents. With notable irony, Steward asked his audience on this day of celebration, "Why should we remember, in joy and exultation, the thousands of our countrymen who are to-day, in this land of gospel light, this boasted land of civil and religious liberty, writhing under the lash and groaning beneath the grinding weight of Slavery's chain. I ask, Almighty God, are they who do such things thy chosen and favorite people?" Like most Black speakers, Steward could not ignore those African Americans still in slavery even when gathering to celebrate a tangible gain the community had made.

## The Hypocrisy of Slavery

In addition to condemning the cruel nature of slavery, Black speakers charged that white Americans who supported or tacitly allowed the institution were hypocrites. White Americans were political hypocrites because they boasted that the American Revolution had been fought and the United States founded to secure people's liberty. Liberty, said Russwurm in his 1826 commencement speech, runs through every man, not just whites. In his 1815 address "O, Africa!" the carpenter and community organizer William Hamilton contrasted the American Revolution with the institution of slavery: "While the siren song of liberty and equality was sung though the land, . . . the groans of the oppressed made the music very discordant." How, speakers asked, could white Americans unashamedly claim moral superiority over other nations, saying that the United States was devoted to the ideals of democracy, while that same nation protected and nurtured the institution of slavery?

Black speakers also condemned white Americans as religious hypocrites. While professing Christian love for their neighbor, whites were enslaving many of those self-same neighbors. In his Thanksgiving sermon, Absalom Jones described the Old Testament Egyptian enslavement of the Hebrews with details that made it clear he was seeing parallels with contemporary American slavery. Egypt was the "hottest climate" where those enslaved worked "laboriously" at difficult manual labor such as making bricks for the pyramids, and despite these oppressive working conditions, the Hebrew slaves were criticized for their "laziness" and punished severely for the least offense. White Christian Americans could conveniently condemn the pharaoh for enslaving the Hebrews yet hypocritically support their own nation's enslavement of Blacks.

The New Testament, too, was a resource for making the point that white Christian Americans were being hypocritical. The Gospel message of the golden rule—to treat others as you would have them treat you—was an effective yardstick by which to measure slavery and find it deficient. William Hamilton made a similar point, although using a bit more condemnatory stance, citing the Gospel of Mark, "I shall content myself with observing that the [slave] trade was begun by white men, and by Europeans, by men who boast of the proud trust they put in the book that tells us, 'with what measure you mete to others, shall be meted to you again.'"

The religious argument was often made with a more positive spin as well. Those slaveowners who emancipated their slaves during the owner's lifetime, or those who, like George Washington, manumitted their slaves in their wills, were living according to their creed said these speakers. Antislavery allies such as the Quakers John Woolman and Anthony Benezet were, said the Episcopalian rector Peter Williams Jr., "conscious that slavery was unfavorable to the benign influences of Christianity." African American speakers were quick to congratulate white advocates like Woolman, Benezet, William Wilberforce, and others for *not* being hypocritical, although they could not help but note that these exceptional individuals were few in number.

## Power and the "Benevolence" of Whites

The good works by white Christian allies who thus avoided being hypocrites also exposed a rhetorical problem that African American speakers faced. Power, such as that represented by the slaveowners' control over those whom they enslaved, could only be redistributed by two means: either voluntarily or by force. Although slave rebellions large and small occurred with regularity, most African Americans of this era sought to achieve abolition through persuasion. They argued for voluntary abolition through manumission, and they argued for forceful abolition through the mechanism of government. In both cases, they had to convince a white audience to cede power.

In support of such cession of power, a number of African American speakers focused on the idea of "benevolence," that is, to act out of charity and without concern for self-interest. Peter Williams Jr.'s speech in 1808, marking the effective start date of the Act to Prohibit the Importation of

Slaves, made just such a case. Williams's speech was an epideictic speech, that is, a speech that marks a particular occasion like a eulogy, the Fourth of July, or the beginning of a ban on the slave trade. These are speeches that, when done well, promote a value, condemn a vice, or do both in concert with one another. By rehearsing such ethical concerns in a public forum, speakers reinforce communal norms and reinvigorate those values a community holds important.

For his speech, Williams used the vice/virtue set of avarice and benevolence. Avarice, the insatiable appetite of greed, was what had sent Europeans to Africa for slaves, had made the Middle Passage a cruel shipment of "goods" rather than people, and had fostered the American form of slavery that sought to wring the last penny out of the slaves' labor. The opposite of avarice was benevolence. Benevolence was what spurred antislavery advocates to speak out and agitate for change, and benevolence was what Congress displayed when it passed the law banning the slave trade. There was no interest of property when it took this profitable trade away from New England merchants and removed this cheap source of labor from Southern planters.

However, Williams did not just praise the benevolence of white antislavery allies or the U.S. government. He also urged his predominantly Black audience to act in a way that reflected well upon their allies and that would thus demonstrate the wisdom of the ban and support their call for more legislation, such as the abolition of slavery itself. The benevolence of these "friends of humanity," Williams said, had made the "the pledges of our integrity." Those who opposed African American rights, either from prejudice or monetary interest, were bound to assail white allies. In his conclusion, Williams urged his audience to return benevolence with gratitude: "Let us, therefore, by a steady and upright deportment, by a strict obedience and respect to the laws of the land, form an invulnerable bulwark against the shafts of malice."

Peter Williams Jr. was hardly alone in making this persuasive appeal to the Black community. On the same day that Williams was speaking in New York City, Absalom Jones was marking the occasion with his Thanksgiving sermon in Philadelphia. Jones, a vocal antislavery advocate, was so disgruntled by prejudice in the white church that he cofounded what became the A.M.E. Church. In his speech, Jones emphasized the hand of God in the passage of the ban, but he, too, urged his congregation to "let us be grateful to our benefactors, who, by enlightening the minds of the rulers of the earth, by means of their publications and remonstrances against the trade in our countrymen, have produced the great events we are this day celebrating."

Like Williams, Jones also told his audience to behave in a way that would not invite reproach: "Let us conduct ourselves in such a manner as to furnish no cause of regret to the deliverers of our nation, for their kindness to us."

This particular time was, though, a moment of hopefulness. These speeches we still have copies of suggest that the community believed that the ban on the importation of slaves marked the beginning of the end and that the total abolition of slavery was not far off. With the invention of the cotton gin and the rise of cotton as a cash crop, however, it soon became apparent that slavery was becoming even more deeply entrenched in American culture. Two speeches by William Hamilton, each of them marking the anniversary of the ban, reveal an evolving attitude. In 1809, one year after the ban's enactment, Hamilton was still upbeat. He "congratulated" the audience on this first anniversary, rejoiced in the progress they had made, praised the "spirit of Liberty" that was alive in the land, and supported the philanthropy and beneficence of whites and Blacks who had moved the community forward.

By 1815, Hamilton had turned pessimistic. His speech was almost entirely devoted to condemning the cruelty of the slave trade and slavery. Who should be surprised, he asked, that in some nations the image of the devil is painted "in the complexion of a white man"? After describing in some detail the torture, starvation, and cruel deaths experienced during the Middle Passage by captives, Hamilton wondered, "Now tell me my brethren, is there in God's domain other and worse fiends than these [slave traders]?" The antislavery advocates Benezet and Wilberforce were still mentioned but only briefly in passing. The community should thank these friends, Hamilton said, but only by singing their praises and not through any conduct that was somehow owed to them. Whatever progress had been made was the Lord's doing, and Hamilton expressed some comfort in the notion that God was just. Hamilton referenced Thomas Jefferson's often quoted line from his *Notes on the State of Virginia*, written in 1781. As he reflected on the institution of slavery, Jefferson confessed that "indeed I tremble for my country when I reflect that God is just: that his justice cannot sleep forever." In his 1815 speech, Hamilton was hoping that God's justice would be soon awakened.

## HOSEA EASTON'S THANKSGIVING ADDRESS OF 1828

The Reverend Hosea Easton was born free in 1798, the son of a Native American father and mixed-race mother. He would later work with the noted abolitionist William Lloyd Garrison and would serve as the minister to the Black Talcott Congregational Church in Hartford, Connecticut. He opened a trade school to train African Americans and in 1836 watched as his church was burned. Black churches were often burned because they were sites for speaking and community organizing. In 1828, eight years prior to the church burning, Easton delivered a Thanksgiving Day address to an African American audience in Providence, Rhode Island. His speech was exemplary in regard to how public speaking among African Americans had evolved during the colonial and early national periods.

The Reverend Easton began his sermon by touching on those themes that would serve just as well on Thanksgiving Day in twenty-first century America. There should be rejoicing, he said, that Providence had bestowed so many blessings upon the nation. Americans enjoyed a land of "plenty and happiness." The "rapid growth of this Nation" was a testament to its prosperity and energy. Thanks be to God, he said, for "rearing us from nothing, to a great and mighty nation."

Prosperity and happiness were not the nation's only blessings, however. America was also a land of liberty. "Who can say," Easton asked rhetorically, "that our Constitution is not founded on the principles of liberty and equality!" Liberty made possible Americans' material, intellectual, and spiritual prosperity. In response to the country's many blessings, the minister invoked Psalm 92: "It is a good thing to give thanks unto the Lord."

After thus establishing his credentials as a patriotic American, appreciative of the blessings bestowed upon and offered by the nation, Easton paraphrased Jefferson to highlight the nation's hypocrisy: "But while I have endeavored to inspire your hearts with thankfulness to God, there has reflections forced themselves into my mind which has caused me to tremble for the fate of this country." Although his immediate audience was comprised of African Americans, in his sermon Easton pleaded on their behalf to white America: "O, America! Listen to your subjects. Allied to you by birth and blood. Shut out from [them] all slavery which you have riveted on their necks."

The cruelty of slavery, said Easton, demanded that slavery be "shut out." He described the "merciless stripes [whippings]" and "forced marches" taking husbands from wives and children from parents, just to "gratify the avarice of proud America." Here Easton turned America's pride on its head. What he had commended at the beginning of the speech simply heightened the hypocrisy. His descriptions of slavery and the slave trade were graphic, putting into words the outrage and frustration of his audience:

Brethren, what was the sensation of your minds, when you beheld many of the female sex, pregnant with their young, tied to a tree or stake, and whipt by their masters, until nature gave way, and both mother and infant yielded up the ghost while bearing the hellish scourge of these candidates for hell? . . . When you saw your brethren shot or beat with clubs? Saw their master vent his rage, by murdering them by degrees, either, by roasting them alive, dissecting them limb by limb, or starving them to death for not complying with their unjust requirements?

For Easton, the hellish nature of slavery illustrated with stark clarity the hypocrisy of white Christians, who by their laws and customs also prohibited Blacks from congregating for worship and from learning to read the Bible. The barbarous practice of slavery pointed up the hypocrisy of white, democratic Americans who preached liberty but enslaved their fellow human beings. "Did not the spirit of Liberty cry within you, for vengeance to fall upon this country?" Easton inquired, for this country "has so falsified the principles of Liberty, and trampled justice under foot."

While the free Blacks in his congregation suffered in kinship with those who were enslaved, Easton went on to describe the injustices inflicted upon even those who were technically free. Throughout his recitation of the unjust treatment inflicted upon him, he interwove the hypocrisy of the nation because it deprived all African Americans of the blessings of democracy and religion that he had celebrated at the beginning of his sermon.

As his audience was already fully aware, free Blacks could not truly count themselves as citizens in this land of liberty. "It becomes our duty," Easton declared, "to consider how far our liberty extends." His answer: not very far indeed. Free Blacks were not eligible for office, were not considered citizens, could not attend the free public schools, could not get the better salaried jobs, or, if they tried to be their own entrepreneur, could not count on the patronage of any white American unless the Black's occupation was cutting wood or hauling water. Sensitive to John Locke's political theory of the social compact and its relationship to the principles of the American Revolution and U.S. Constitution, Easton asked, "Are we taken into social compact with Society at large? No."

Expanding upon this initial recitation of injustices, Easton turned to "religious improvement" and the hypocrisy of white Christians as it extended to their treatment of free Blacks as well. Highly educated Black ministers would not be hired to preach in white churches, could not earn a living preaching to small Black congregations, and, if they chose itinerancy as a means to evangelize the Gospel, could not even be assured of safe travel.

Easton then turned to the foundation of democracy: education. In those cases where free Blacks did gain access to public education at the primary school, they were assigned the worst seats, given the worst materials, ignored in the classroom, and disparagingly dismissed as being "Negroes." If they did not get discouraged by such treatment and managed to persevere in acquiring an education, Black youth "know enough only to feel sensible of their misery." They apply for positions as clerks, and "they are rejected." They apply to attorneys for legal apprenticeship, and "they are rejected." They turn to the merchants who trade on the sea, and the only jobs offered them are as deck hands, cooks, or stewards. At every turn, Easton reminded his audience, "custom" takes away what "liberty" has supposedly offered. For those few able to secure some measure of economic success, they face Jim Crow laws and customs that give them the worst mode of travel, the worst food to eat, and the worst place at the inn. Money is loaned to the Black businessman at 75 percent interest. Yet after all this, Easton said, "the question is asked by whites: Why is it that Negroes cannot do business like other people?"

Easton then returned to the matter of religion. Free Blacks are told to sit in the back of the church if they are allowed to sit at all, he said. They take the Sacraments last, if they are allowed to take them. And when, at the last, the white minister invites the free Blacks to "partake of the sacred elements [communion]," he will say without the least sense of shame, "Come coloured brethren, now come and partake of the broken body of Christ. It is free for all without any distinction." Easton was not content to leave the matter of hypocrisy there. He went on to comment that almost inevitably the white minister will, at some point in the service, single out the free Blacks, identifying them as "Africans or Ethiopians," while, Easton declared, "in fact they are Americans, and perhaps distantly related to some of the white members, by reason of the brutal conduct of their fathers." Easton thus blended his charge of religious hypocrisy with a reminder of the sexual violence that had been and was still being perpetrated by white slave owners. His sermon had traveled quite far from his opening paean to the blessings of liberty.

Easton then turned his religious wrath upon the colonization movement, the attempt by whites to "return" free Blacks back to Africa. It is, Easton pronounced, "a diabolical pursuit, which a great part of our Christian community are engaged in." The hypocrisy and prejudice of the movement was clear—to remove from the country free Blacks while retaining those African Americans who were still enslaved. If white Americans were genuinely interested in helping African Americans and restoring what they had taken from Blacks by force, "they can do it to better advantage in the bosom of our country, than at several thousand miles off." But the colonization effort is a hoax, he said. It is like a thief stealing another's goods and then trying to smuggle them out of the country before being detected. "The deception is not so well practiced," Easton said referencing the Book of Revelation, "but that we can discover [in it] the mark of the beast."

Easton concluded: "My heart is filled with sorrow for this nation." The "blessings of Liberty" he had praised in his opening are barely remembered in his conclusion, except as hollow promises that might, however, yet be realized. Still, Easton argued, "the time has come, when our necessities call aloud for our exertions, to prepare ourselves for the great events which are about heaving in view." Easton perceived that change was afoot, and African Americans needed to prepare for that day of change. His conclusion urged them to seek "moral improvement," in other words, to educate themselves, to be hardworking and industrious, and to study religion. He did not urge them to do so in gratitude to benevolent whites who had helped them, as Peter Williams Jr. had. He did hope that showing themselves to be "pious, industrious, and intelligent men and women" would "demand respect from those who exalt themselves above you," but that purpose was to show that white prejudice was wrong, and not to show that African Americans had somehow now earned the rights and liberties that were in fact owed to them as part of the social compact.

Even then, Easton's charge to his congregation that they engage in moral improvement was less about disproving white prejudice and more about preparing themselves for the change that God was bringing. Easton expressed faith that God's will was at work for the future, that the day Jefferson had "trembled" about was indeed on the horizon. Easton's sermon was not a message of peace; it was a message about radical change and upending the social order. As he told his congregation in his concluding lines: "I assure you my heart mourns daily, while beholding the clouds of evil thickening over this Republic. The awful consequences are plain to be seen, by the aid of both ancient and modern history. Let him that readeth understand. But, O, for a Gideon, with his three hundred men, chosen of God, to go up against the towering walls of evil, and cause them to fall, forever fall, to rise no more."

Easton was correct. In 1828, the winds of change were on the American horizon, and African American public speakers would play a vital role in making that change, as they expanded and built upon the rhetorical foundation that had been laid during the colonial and early national periods.

# 2

# All Manner of Reforms

AFRICAN AMERICAN SPEAKERS in the antebellum period built rapidly upon the oratorical foundation laid by speakers during the colonial and early national periods. Ministers, practiced in the art of speaking, continued to occupy a central role, but they were joined by an ever-growing number of business leaders, schoolteachers, literary figures, lay preachers, and fugitive slaves. The antebellum period also saw women take to the platform in increasing numbers, addressing men as well as women. The abolition of slavery and elimination of discrimination in law and practice still occupied a central place for these speakers, and sermons were still preached in order to spread the Christian Gospel. This was an era of reform, however. Mental improvement, temperance, and women's rights became central subjects of the speeches by African Americans. Emigration back to Africa also emerged as an important theme.

## ALL MANNER OF SPEAKERS

The range of subjects addressed by African American speakers in this era was matched only by the variety of speakers and speaking situations. Conventions called by antislavery societies were widespread, as were conventions organized by the "free colored citizens" of the North. Literary societies for the purpose of self-improvement sprung up across the U.S., and they often sponsored political debates and evolved into political organizations. Antislavery societies sponsored African Americans to travel and spread the message of abolition. Black women attended and spoke at women's rights conventions as well. Church services and days of celebration were yet other occasions that required someone to say a few words. In all, it was a robust era of public speaking by African Americans.

*Preachers*

Some African American ministers had been born free and received an education from an early age. Nathaniel Paul, pastor of the First African Baptist Church in Albany, New York, was born in New Hampshire. He toured with William Lloyd Garrison raising funds to combat the American Colonization Society until, frustrated with racial discrimination across the North, he immigrated to Canada. There he continued to speak against slavery and prejudice. The Reverend Daniel Payne was born a free black in Charleston, South Carolina, where he opened a school for Blacks, but then left when the Black Codes made it illegal to teach African Americans to read and write regardless of whether they were enslaved or free. One of his better known speeches was the sermon he gave upon being ordained by the Franckean Synod of the Lutheran Church in 1839. In "Slavery Brutalizes Man," Payne argued that no American could truly be free while the American government and its social compact upheld the enslavement of others.

One famous minister of the era was Theodore S. Wright, who was born in 1797 in New Jersey and attended the African Free School in New York City. After graduating from Princeton Seminary, he became pastor of the First Colored Presbyterian Church in New York. In 1832, Wright was one of the founders of the American Anti-Slavery Society, and throughout his life he mentored many young African Americans. At a time when it was still unusual to have Black Americans speak in front of mixed-race antislavery societies, in 1836 Wright delivered "The Slave Has a Friend in Heaven, Though He May Have None Here" to the New England Anti-Slavery Society's convention with about five hundred delegates in attendance. A year later, Wright gave two speeches to the New York State Anti-Slavery Society. One of those, "Prejudice Against the Colored Man," addressed the discrimination that free blacks encountered across the Northern states. The other speech confronted the racism that permeated the various antislavery societies. White Americans joined these societies because they believed slavery to be immoral, but many who did so still believed that Blacks were inferior to whites and these white members carried that prejudice with them, even into their antislavery work.

Other African American ministers had been born into slavery and became free later through manumission, through purchase of their freedom, or, most commonly, by fleeing North. Henry Highland Garnet, for example, escaped slavery in 1824 at the age of nine when his family ran away from a Maryland plantation. While away working as a deckhand, fugitive slave hunters recaptured his sister and his parents fled. On a second, subsequent voyage, Garnet injured his leg, which was eventually amputated. With the encouragement of Theodore Wright, Garnet pursued an education and became a Presbyterian minister. In 1843, Garnet delivered "An Address to the Slaves of the United States of America" to the National Convention of Negro Citizens in Buffalo, New York. His speech was a radical call for those enslaved to rebel and demand their freedom, and he implied that free African Americans should agitate for abolition more aggressively. Garnet later promoted repatriation of Blacks to Liberia as a means of escaping racial discrimination in America. On February 12, 1865, Garnet became the first African American so speak in the U.S. Capitol, when he delivered a sermon in the House of Representatives celebrating the passage of the Thirteenth Amendment outlawing slavery.

At the age of twenty-one, Jermain Wesley Loguen fled slavery in Tennessee in 1834 and escaped to Syracuse, New York. There he became a schoolteacher, a bishop in the A.M.E. Zion Church, and an agent for the Underground Railroad. Following the 1850 passage of the Fugitive Slave Law, his speech "I Won't Obey the Fugitive Slave Law" helped rally the city in protest. At that city meeting, the attendees voted 395 to 96 in favor of declaring Syracuse an "open city" for fugitive slaves. The Reverend Loguen later served as an officer of the Liberty Party and helped recruit African Americans to fight with the militant abolitionist John Brown.

James W. C. Pennington was another fugitive slave who became a minister and an outspoken activist. Trained as a blacksmith on the Eastern Shore of Maryland, Pennington ran away from slavery in 1830 at the age of twenty-one. He received some tutoring and attended evening schools, including auditing classes at Yale College despite being prohibited from officially enrolling. He served as pastor of several African Congregational churches, in Connecticut, Long Island, and New York City, and was politically active on local and international stages. In the 1850s, he attended world antislavery conventions as a delegate and also participated in a world peace convention. In New York City, he worked with James McCune Smith and Henry Highland Garnet to abolish segregated streetcars. When draft riots against conscription into the Union army broke out in July 1863, and African Americans were attacked and killed by white rioters, Pennington gave a widely circulated speech arguing that Blacks needed to arm and defend themselves against their attackers.

Not all African American preaching was conducted by educated, formally appointed ministers. Folk preaching did not end at the close of the Great Awakening. On plantations, preaching and teaching were both conducted by self-taught speakers. According to his *Narrative*, Frederick Douglass's first public speaking experience was gained through "Sunday school" talks he gave to his fellow slaves after he had been returned from Baltimore to his owner's plantation on Maryland's Eastern Shore. Free Blacks also continued to preach in the "folk" style. One such minister was Rebecca Cox Jackson, a preacher and Shaker "eldress," who biographer Jean Humez says generated enthusiastic responses from whites as well as Blacks at revival meetings in the 1830s. Humez writes that a recurring theme of Jackson's sermons was that her audience should practice self-control as a means to power.

The most famous folk preacher of the era was Sojourner Truth. Born into slavery as "Isabella" on an Upstate New York farm around 1797, Truth was finally freed by law in 1827. She continued to work on the farm until the early 1840s, when she changed her name to Sojourner Truth and left New York to search for her children who had been sold South. She managed to rescue one son, Peter, from slavery in Alabama. A native speaker of Dutch and illiterate, for a time Truth joined the Millerites, a group who believed the Second Coming of Christ was imminent. After leaving that group, she became an itinerant preacher as well as an abolitionist and woman's rights advocate.

Like the folk preachers of colonial times, Sojourner Truth used biblical stories with great facility. In her most famous speech, "Ar'n't I a Woman?" at the 1851 Woman's Rights Convention, the *Anti-Slavery Bugle* version reports that, in response to the cliché that Jesus was a man and therefore men should be the dominant gender, Truth pointed to the origin of Jesus. "And how came Jesus into the world?" she asked. From God and woman—man had nothing to do with it. Sojourner Truth's easy merging of religion, abolition, and woman's rights was typical of the reform-oriented speaking of the era.

## *Lay Speakers*

Not all African American public speakers were ministers and preachers. Business leaders were also politically and socially active throughout the community. William Whipper, born around 1804 to a white businessman and a Black servant woman, was a model of the range of interests and the intellectual energy that African Americans brought to the platform.

Often regarded as the first Black millionaire in the United States, Whipper owned and operated a lumberyard in Columbia, Pennsylvania, along the Susquehanna River. Located just thirty miles north of the Mason-Dixon Line, Whipper's lumberyard was a major stop on the Underground Railroad. There, fugitive slaves could blend in with Whipper's employees while plans were made for the next leg of their journey.

Whipper was active in literary societies and attended state and national conventions of African Americans. He was a founder of the Colored Reading Society in Philadelphia and the American Moral Reform Society and was the first editor of the *National Reformer*. In 1833, he, James Forten, and Robert Purvis presented a petition to the Pennsylvania state legislature arguing against a bill that would ban the immigration of Blacks into the state. That bill was defeated, although in 1837 the state amended its constitution to ban Blacks from voting. In addition to his political activism, Whipper encouraged African Americans to acquire a liberal education, supported temperance, and spoke against prejudice and discrimination.

One of his most famous speeches, "Non-Resistance to Offensive Aggression," set forth a rationale for nonviolent protest that Martin Luther King Jr.'s philosophy echoed a little more than a century later. In his speeches, Whipper was committed to the enlightened development of the individual and a Christian philosophy of love that treated all persons without respect to race. After the 1850 Fugitive Slave Law, Whipper's activism became sharper, however, and reportedly he helped physically repel fugitive slave hunters from the premises of his lumberyard. He remained committed to integration, however, and in the 1850s vocally opposed those who were advocating black separatism and a return to Africa.

James Forten Jr. worked his way up from cabin boy on a merchant vessel to owner of a sail-making business that employed more than twenty workers. He frequently spoke before antislavery societies and in 1836 delivered a speech that staunchly supported the entry of women into the public sphere, arguing that women abolitionists energized the movement. Robert Purvis was born a free Black in Charleston, South Carolina, the son of an English merchant and a mother of Jewish and Moorish descent. He, too, was active in the antislavery movement, giving speeches, petitioning legislatures, helping finance William Lloyd Garrison's *Liberator*, and working with the Underground Railroad.

The Langston brothers, John Mercer and Charles C., exemplified the emergence of highly educated African Americans who moved easily between the worlds of education, public affairs, and political activism. The brothers were free-born Blacks from Virginia who graduated from Oberlin

College in Ohio. John Mercer went on to earn a master's degree, pass the Ohio bar in 1854, be elected as a town clerk and later as a representative of Virginia, and be appointed U.S. ambassador to Haiti. He also served as dean of the Howard School of Law and during the Civil War helped recruit African Americans for the famed "Glory Brigade," the Fifty-fourth Regiment. His brother Charles moved to Kansas during the Civil War, where he worked as a teacher, a school administrator, and in state government. Both men spoke frequently on behalf of the abolition of slavery and the repeal of discriminatory Jim Crow laws.

*Lecturers*

For many African Americans, public speaking was an extension of their roles as ministers, educators, business persons, and community leaders. For others, however, public speaking became their profession. During this era, antislavery organizations at the state level, such as in Massachusetts, and the national level, such as the American Anti-Slavery Society, sponsored agents to go on public speaking tours promoting the cause of abolition. While some of these speakers were white, many were African American. Typically, the society would purchase a train ticket or two and provide the speaker with introductions to members who lived in the various towns on the tour. Most of the speaker's subsistence, however, would come from selling tickets for admission or from taking up collections at the lecture.

Early African American agents were usually free Blacks, such as Charles Lenox Remond. Born in Salem, Massachusetts, in 1810, Remond became a devotee of William Lloyd Garrison and began speaking professionally at age twenty-one. He was a founding member as well as agent for the New England Anti-Slavery Society and the American Anti-Slavery Society. With Garrison, Remond argued that the Constitution was a slavery document that abolitionists should not legitimize through involvement in politics. "Moral suasion"—reaching the hearts of the individual through public speaking—was the means they advocated for ending slavery. However, Remond actively lobbied and agitated for the end to Jim Crow laws in Massachusetts. He was also one of a series of African Americans who toured Britain and Ireland, raising consciousness about the American form of slavery and raising funds in support of the American antislavery societies. Remond was a very popular speaker at home and abroad during the 1830s and 1840s. As a highly literate African American, Remond and other free Blacks provided evidence that Blacks were the intellectual and moral equals of whites.

One of the most notable female lecturers was Frances Ellen Watkins (later Harper). Born free in 1825, Watkins was orphaned at the age of three and then raised and educated by her uncle, William Watkins, who ran the William Watkins Academy for Negro Youth in Baltimore. William Watkins also organized the East Baltimore Mental Improvement Society, a group whose meetings were attended by Frederick Douglass, a slave in town who worked as a ship caulker. Frances Watkins gained fame as a poet, and in 1854 she left her teaching position to travel the lecture circuit as an agent of the Maine Anti-Slavery Society. Although abolition was her primary focus during the antebellum period, her speaking and poetry also argued in support of women's rights, temperance, and self-improvement. At times lyrical and other times forceful in her logic, Watkins was a very popular speaker. In the 1850s, she wrote to William Still, an organizer for the Underground Railroad, to ask his permission to work directly with the escape of fugitive slaves. In his reply, Still implored Watkins to continue with her lecturing, writing that the financial contributions she was able to make from speaking fees were vital to the success of the Railroad.

While free Blacks formed the initial vanguard of antislavery agents, fugitive slaves who could provide firsthand testimony about the cruelties of Southern slavery gained prominence in the 1840s. Some, like Lewis Richardson, H. Ford Douglas, and Stephen Pembroke were primarily asked

Frederick Douglass, 1840. Albert Cook Myers Collection, Chester County Historical Society.

to describe their experiences. Richardson, for example, had been enslaved on the Kentucky plantation of Henry Clay, the senator and presidential candidate known as the "Great Compromiser" and an advocate of gradualism and the recolonization of free blacks back to Africa. Speaking in 1846 in Amherstburgh, Canada, to which he had escaped, observers recorded that Richardson's account of Southern slavery was filled with emotion and humor and "elicited sympathy, tears and increased interest in abolition."

Other fugitive slaves were sponsored as agents by antislavery societies. Like Richardson, William Wells Brown was born into slavery in Kentucky, but as a child he was moved to the St. Louis area where, enslaved, he labored in a variety of capacities. His most emotionally wrenching work was for a slave trader, when he had to tend to other slaves as they were transported down the Mississippi for auction. Brown escaped slavery in 1834. In 1836, he began speaking at antislavery conventions, and in 1843 he was hired to speak full-time as an agent of the Western New York Anti-Slavery Society. In 1847, he published his autobiographical *Narrative*, and in 1853 he became the first African American novelist on record. Like Remond, Brown toured the British isles for several years, delivering many lectures there. Also like Remond, Brown initially argued that moral suasion was the right path to abolition, but with the passage of the Fugitive Slave Law in 1850, he became more militant in his politics.

Easily the best known fugitive slave and antislavery speaking agent of the era was Frederick Douglass. The son of an enslaved woman and an unnamed white man, probably related to the plantation owner, Douglass was hired out in his teen years to learn the ship-caulking trade in Baltimore. There he taught himself to read and sought out educational opportunities such as the meetings of the East Baltimore Mental Improvement Society organized by William Watkins. Returned to his plantation "home" on Maryland's Eastern Shore, Douglass continued his independent and rebellious ways, finally escaping North in 1838, at about the age of twenty, by posing as a free Black seaman.

Settling in New Bedford, Massachusetts, Douglass worked in the shipbuilding industry and attended antislavery meetings. After hearing Douglass speak at a meeting in 1841, William Lloyd Garrison hired him to speak as an agent of the Massachusetts Anti-Slavery Society. An intelligent and powerful speaker, Douglass's lectures brought to life the experiences of slavery. One of his set pieces was the "Slavemaster's Sermon," which was a parody of the talks given by plantation owners as they used selected portions of the Bible to justify to their enslaved workers the "moral rightness" of slavery. A white abolitionist, James Madison, recorded this account of Douglass's version of the "Sermon":

[The Sermon was] a brilliant example of irony, parody, caricature, and *reductio ad absurdum*, all combined. It abounded in phrases which, though innocent in the original preacher, when delivered by Mr. Douglass with suggestive tone and emphasis . . . became irresistibly ludicrous. . . . To do him justice . . . you must imagine his marvelous power of imitation and characterization —the holy tone of the preacher—the pious snuffle—the upturned eye—the funny affectation of profound wisdom.

When audiences began doubting that the educated-sounding Douglass could ever have been enslaved, he published his autobiography, *Narrative of the Life of Frederick Douglass, an American Slave*, in 1845. His freedom in jeopardy, Douglass sailed to Britain where, like Remond, Brown, and others, he was popular as a lecturer. When he returned to the United States in 1847, his freedom purchased by British supporters over his objections, he established himself as a newspaper editor, activist, and widely traveled lecturer. Like Brown, Whipper, and others, Douglass initially subscribed to the moral suasion point of view regarding abolition but became increasingly militant in his activism, particularly with the passage of the Fugitive Slave Law.

Frances Ellen Watkins Harper, 1872. Library of Congress.

## Women Speakers

The antebellum period was also the era in which African American women speakers became increasingly prominent. One of the most famous of the early women to speak on a public platform was Maria Miller Stewart. Born in 1803, Stewart gained fame as an essayist, first writing in Garrison's *Liberator* and then publishing a collection of essays in 1831. When her second collection was published the next year, Stewart was invited to speak to the Afric-American Female Intelligence Society in Boston. That speech was well-received though controversial because until that time women rarely took the stage, even to address a female-only audience.

The controversy increased exponentially, however, when the following fall Stewart addressed a mixed audience of men and women, which she did one more time the following February. In these speeches, Stewart challenged slavery, prejudice, and discrimination. She also challenged the African American men in the audience to engage in "self-improvement," and she challenged African Americans of both genders to be more militant in their abolitionism. At one of these speeches, Stewart was reportedly pelted with rotten tomatoes, as some were offended by her moral condemnation. Stewart's last public speech, her "Farewell Address to Her Friends in the City of Boston," defended women's right to speak and called for unity within the Black community, something she herself had not experienced in her public speaking. As many later African Americans would do, Stewart linked Black rights with women's rights. "Let us no longer talk of prejudice" in the South, she admonished her audience, "till prejudice becomes extinct at home." Stewart then moved to New York City, taking employment as a teacher, and there is no record of her taking to the stage again.

Other African American women followed, however. Although Sojourner Truth and Frances Ellen Watkins were two of the most widely known female speakers of this era, many other African American women spoke in public as well. Sarah Douglass, a free Black born to an affluent family in Philadelphia, was a teacher who started her own school for Blacks. In her 1832 speech to the Female Literary Society of Philadelphia, Douglass pleaded with her audience on behalf of "our brethren and sisters, who are in this land of Christian light and liberty held in bondage the most cruel and degrading—to make their cause our own!" Elizabeth Jennings, too, was a schoolteacher who attended the first Anti-Slavery Convention of American Women, held in 1837, and in 1854 she sued the New York City Third Avenue Railroad Company when she would not move to a Jim Crow car. In 1837, Jennings spoke to the Ladies' Literary Society of New

York on an occasion that included men in the audience. There she argued that African American women needed to pursue every opportunity to educate themselves, in no small part as a rebuttal to those who claimed that the intellect of Blacks was inferior to that of whites. There is no record of Jennings receiving the harsh reception that had greeted Stewart just five years earlier.

Sarah Parker Remond, sister of Charles Lenox Remond, was a popular lecturer of the era, and her public speaking tours included stops in Great Britain. Mary Ann Shadd (Cary) initially taught school, emigrating to Canada after the passage of the Fugitive Slave Law. In 1853, she became the first Black woman to edit and publish a newspaper in North America, the *Provincial Freeman*. She lectured widely in the 1850s, connecting equal rights for Blacks with those for women. In her 1858 speech "Break Every Yoke, Let the Oppressed Go Free," for example, Shadd spoke of the double discrimination that African American women confronted. "Those with whom I am identified," she said, "namely the colored people of this country and the women of the land [have been cast out into] the pit." For Shadd, the sin of "enslaving [Black] men" had a common origin with that of the "political proscription[s]" against women. Both kinds of oppression were contrary to God's Second Commandment to love one another, and both ran counter to the example of Jesus in the New Testament.

African American women addressed a range of reforms in their speeches. Lucy Stanton, the first female graduate of Oberlin College's four-year program and president of the Oberlin Ladies Literary Society, provided another example of their interest in reform. In her 1850 "A Plea for the Oppressed," delivered as a commencement speech at Oberlin College, Stanton argued, "Ye that advocate the great principles of Temperance, Peace, and Moral Reform" have an obligation to "raise your voice" against slavery, for "Slavery is the combination of all crime. It is War." Slavery, she said, is itself intemperate, for it "intoxicates the master with power and leads to a madness of passion and cruelty. It opposes peace, for it makes war upon the enslaved. And it opposes Moral Reform, because only ignorance can keep those enslaved in chains. One cannot hope to reform society, unless the reformer embraces and agitates for 'universal freedom.'"

## SPEAKING FOR ABOLITION

African Americans spoke publicly on a wide range of reforms, from temperance and self-improvement to civil rights and women's rights. It was abolition, however, that occupied the chief place during the thirty years preceding the Civil War. African Americans spoke out against slavery during the colonial and early national periods, but with the explosive growth of the institution in the nineteenth century, public speaking called forth organizations devoted solely to the antislavery cause and those organizations presented new and greater opportunities for speakers to reach an audience.

*The Immorality of Slavery*

As noted earlier, many African American speakers of the 1830s and 1840s focused their efforts on "moral suasion," the belief that the hearts and minds of white Americans needed to be reformed in order for slavery to be abolished. Certain arguments emerged that were central to this appeal to whites' morals. The first was that slavery was a cruel institution. Slaveholders often claimed that, as valuable property, those they enslaved were well cared for. They also claimed that Blacks were lesser intellectual beings than whites and therefore "happy" in their status. In order to awaken their listeners' moral feelings, African American speakers needed to challenge these assertions. Daniel Payne's 1839 sermon at his ordination, "Slavery Brutalizes Man," was illustrative. To enslave and treat someone as a piece of property, said Payne, is to treat them as one would an animal. Just as a farmer would sell a calf to the butcher, "so slavery tears the child from the arms of the reluctant mother." Just as the bird catcher will take a nesting mother from its nest, "so slavery separates the groaning husband from the embraces of his distracted and weeping wife!" And just as the hunter tracks and kills prey for food in the forest, "so are the slaves hunted, tortured and slain by the cruel monster of slavery!" As Payne sharply pointed out, "To treat a man like a brute is to brutalize him."

Payne's formula assumed that his listeners believed that African Americans were persons equal to all other races; however, the pernicious argument Blacks faced was the prejudice that they were not. This was an old argument, confronted earlier by speakers like Prince Hall and John Marrant, but it remained a persistent prejudice. Such prejudice supported discrimination in the Northern states, even as they gradually abolished slavery. In "Prejudice Against the Colored Man," delivered to an antislavery meeting in 1837, Theodore Wright aptly summarized the problem. Unfortunately, he noted, even many whites who supported abolition were in favor of discriminatory laws and the "re-colonization" of free Blacks back to Africa. "Unless men come out and take their stand on the principle of recognizing man as man," said Wright, "I fear our society will become like the expatriation society. . . . It is an easy thing to ask about the vileness of slavery at the South, but to call a dark man brother, . . . to treat the man of color in all circumstances as a man and brother—that is the test."

Speakers commonly observed that discrimination on the basis of skin complexion effectively made all Blacks guilty of the "crime of color." Speaking on the fifth of July in 1832—because most African Americans refused to celebrate the Fourth of July as "Independence Day"—Peter Osborne urged his audience, "Let us make it known to America that we are not barbarians; that we are not inhuman beings." Thomas Paul, addressing the Massachusetts Anti-Slavery Society, reflected on the difficult rhetorical situation that Blacks faced in this matter: "Here we meet, time after time, to prove—what? Why, that a man is a man, and that he is the only human possessor of himself. But these propositions are self-evident propositions," which are, he noted ironically, "the most difficult to prove."

Many strategies for supporting this claim were devised, however. Speakers reminded their audiences that African Americans had fought and died in the War for Independence and during the War of 1812 had been commended by Andrew Jackson for their valor at the Battle of New Orleans. Audiences were reminded that African Americans like Phyllis Wheatley had published poetry and others like Theodore Wright had graduated from college and seminary. Charles Lenox Remond remarked that he asked one white man what he would think if his red-haired brother were made to sit in a separate railroad car due to the color of his hair, saying that segregation based on skin color was no different. Even the Boston Baptist minister Thomas Paul, after referencing the Declaration of Independence by noting that it is difficult to prove the "self-evident," advanced his own argument. If a person started believing their dog was a human, no matter how smartly the canine behaved, we would think the person "a fit subject for an insane hospital," he said. We should consider the slaveholder in the same manner, for "if you cannot metamorphose a brute into a man, can you make a man a brute?"

*The Hypocrisy of Slavery*

Once the humanity of African Americans was established, speakers could argue that slaveholding was contrary to white Americans' avowed beliefs in democracy and Christianity. On both counts, the United States was hypocritical when it legalized and supported slavery. "No people in the world profess so high a respect for liberty and equality as the people of the United States," Peter Williams Jr. observed in 1830, "and yet no people hold so many slaves, or make such great distinctions between man and man." Speaking in 1841, Thomas Paul similarly pointed out that Americans "present the rare spectacle of a nation boasting of equal rights, while a large part of the population are the most oppressed and degraded beings that crawl on the face of the earth."

At its core, Daniel Payne's sermon of 1839 was an argumentative brief that established the hypocrisy of those who profess to be Christian yet own slaves or support the institution of slavery. God commanded his followers to obey his laws, Payne remarked, and yet slaveholders destroyed the bonds of matrimony, prevented parents from raising their children, and even forced adultery upon them. Jesus instructed his disciples to evangelize the Gospel, but those enslaved were prohibited from learning how to read the Bible, meeting together to worship, and traveling to spread the Word. Those enslaved understand, Payne said, that "oppression and slavery are inconsistent with the Christian religion," and so they "sneer and laugh" at the pious mouthings of their masters and "scoff at religion itself."

Speakers also addressed the other side of the equation, looking not only at what values white Americans had abandoned through their support of slavery but also at what values their actions embodied; to wit, avarice, and greed. Robbery, stealing, marketing, selling, auctioning: references to money permeated these speeches. Nor were slaveholders the only Americans guilty of sacrificing their principles for money, these speakers said. The Northern merchants who shipped the slaves and the goods that the slaves produced were just as guilty, as was the federal treasury, which received a tariff of ten dollars a head for every imported slave.

For nineteenth-century speakers, evil was often treated as an animate, malignant spirit with a will of its own, and abolitionists spoke of it in a similar manner. Slavery was a form of "intemperance," said William Whipper, and Lucy Stanton, a noted abolitionist and in 1850 the first recorded African American woman to graduate from college, took up a similar theme in "A Plea for the Oppressed," delivered that same year. "Such passions" of intemperance and madness "does Slavery foster," she said, "yea—they are a part of herself [i.e., Slavery]. It is full of pollution." In his 1843 "Address to the Slaves of the United States," Garnet, too, treated slavery as an active form of evil. Despite the best efforts of those who had opposed slavery early in the nation's history, "all was vain." Paraphrasing the Book of Jeremiah, Garnet declared that "slavery had stretched its dark wings of death over the land, the Church stood silently by, the priests prophesied falsely, and the people loved to have it so. Its throne is established, and now it reigns triumphantly." Evil knew no political boundaries, and so speakers like William

Wells Brown argued that slavery was a *"national institution*, and that the guilt of maintaining it is *national guilt."*

Many speakers in the antislavery movement, Black and white, held that American hypocrisy ran so deep that the structure of government needed to be torn down and rebuilt anew. In May of 1844, the American Anti-Slavery Union adopted the motto "No Union with Slaveholders." Later that month, Charles Lenox Remond spoke to the New England Anti-Slavery Society in support of that position. In "For the Dissolution of the Union," Remond began by dividing his audience into those nine-tenths who benefited from the U.S. Constitution and the 10 percent who did not, and he told them that he spoke on behalf of the "few who identify themselves with the outcast," that is, African Americans, who were the Americans who did not benefit from the Constitution. "What does it matter," he asked, if the Constitution speaks of "peace—tranquility—domestic enjoyments—civil rights," when the Union meant no such thing to them? "Look at them," Remond commanded his audience, "as they are falling, generation after generation, beneath the sway of the Union, sinking into their ignominious graves unwept, uncared for, unprayed for, enslaved, and say what has the Union been to them."

Remond took issue with the argument that the words "slave" and "slavery" did not appear in the Constitution but instead referred to those enslaved as "all Other Persons" after enumerating free persons, servants who are indentured for a set period of time, and "Indians." "What if the word 'slave' is not in it?" Remond asked, highlighting the practical implication of the document: "It does not matter to me nor mine. Slavery was in the understanding that framed it—Slavery is in the will that administers it." "If the Union had been formed upon the supposition that the colored man was a *man*," he said, "a man he would have been considered." But, he concluded, "under the Union as it was, and as it is, he is kicked, stoned, insulted, [and] enslaved." And so Remond called for the "dissolution of the union between Freedom and Slavery," and therefore the dissolution of the United States.

*Moving to Militancy*

Other speakers argued that moral suasion was not enough. Abolitionists must become politically involved, they said, and they supported the rise of the Liberty Party. Still others argued that slavery was a violent institution and must therefore be resisted by force. David Walker's 1829 pamphlet "Appeal to the Coloured Persons of the World" is generally credited as the first widely circulated radical call for resistance by force. Walker passed away one year later, but his arguments were echoed by many others, most famously captured in Henry Highland Garnet's 1843 "An Address to the Slaves of the United States." A staunch supporter of the Liberty Party and an opponent of the moral suasion advocates, Garnet had already debated Frederick Douglass on this point at a meeting earlier that year. In August, a group of free Blacks called for a National Convention of Colored Citizens to be held in Buffalo, New York. Twenty-five African American delegates attended, as well as some white observers.

On its face, Garnet's speech addressed those who were currently enslaved, and it was part of a resolution that his speech be printed as a pamphlet and distributed throughout the South. Just below the surface, however, it was an exhortative call for free Blacks to become more radical in their abolitionism. He first defined slavery as evil, describing its inherently inhuman character. He then focused on urging those enslaved to action. Garnet, himself a fugitive slave, was assertive, telling slaves that "you had better all die—*die immediately*, than entail your wretchedness on your posterity." Twice he repeated the motto *"Rather die freemen, than live to be slaves."* Go up to your "lordly enslavers," Garnet commanded, and "tell them plainly, that *you are determined to be free."*

Garnet's speech was a passionate appeal, stirring up the emotions so as to move his audience to action. He reminded his audience not only of the cruelty and brutality of slavery but of the "lust" of the slaveholders. In doing so, he challenged the masculinity of his presumably all-male audience: "You act as though you were made for the special use of these devils. You act as though your daughters were born to pamper the lusts of your masters and overseers. And worse than all, you tamely submit while your lords tear your wives from your embraces and defile them before your eyes. In the name of God, we ask, are you men? Where is the blood of your fathers?" Now is the time, Garnet told them, to "strike for your lives and liberty."

Garnet analogized the slaves' condition to that of the American Revolution—as did many other speakers—and reminded his audience of Patrick Henry's call to "give me liberty or give me death." To the enslaved as well as the free Blacks who were "overhearing" this speech, Garnet said, "Let it no longer be a debatable question whether it is better to choose *Liberty or death."* Garnet was not being poetic here. He cited the examples of four leaders of slave revolts: Denmark Vesey, Nathaniel Turner, Joseph Cinque, and Madison Washington—two of whom died leading their revolts. For Garnet, a Presbyterian minister, these were the political leaders whom free Blacks as well as those enslaved should emulate.

The outcome of Garnet's speech at this 1843 conference was representative of the times. In 1843, African Americans were still deeply divided between militancy and moral suasion, and the resolution failed by a vote of thirteen to twelve. After the conference, however, the twelve delegates on the losing end of the resolution met in a church across the street and decided to take up a collection and publish the pamphlet anyway. For the most part, this internal disagreement on how to proceed with abolishing slavery melted away in 1850 with the passage of the Fugitive Slave Law. In stark terms, the Fugitive Slave Law convinced audiences that slavery was a national institution in ways that allusions to avarice and greed had not been able. The law helped slave hunters pursue and capture fugitive slaves throughout the North and made it easier for bounty hunters to enslave African Americans who had been born free. In courts, the law created the presumption that *all* Blacks must be either slaves or fugitive slaves. The burden was on African Americans to prove that they were free citizens.

*Frederick Douglass's "Fourth of July" Oration*

Frederick Douglass's 1852 Fourth of July speech, commonly titled "What to the American Slave Is the Fourth of July?" eloquently summarized the abolitionists' arguments during the antebellum period and also marked the movement's coalescence around a radically resistant political platform. Douglass spoke at the invitation of the Rochester Ladies' Anti-Slavery Society, delivering the speech at Corinthian Hall, an auditorium built in support of the antislavery cause. Douglass had been living in Rochester, New York, since 1848, when he began publishing his weekly newspaper, *The North Star*.

Unlike many African American speakers who condemned the slaveholding patriots as hypocrites, in this speech Douglass praised the Founding Fathers as radical defenders of freedom and liberty in order to later heighten his condemnation of white Americans living in 1852. As he praised these "men of action," he foreshadowed his arguments that they were also hypocrites, both secular and religious. In 1776, he said, these American patriots were considered "plotters of mischief, agitators and rebels, dangerous men." He would later note that it was the abolitionists whom opponents now called "agitators." "But, your fathers," he told the audience, "had not adopted the fashionable idea of this day, of the infallibility of government."

Into this opening section, Douglass also wove religious analogies. He noted that "to you" white Americans, Independence Day was "what the Passover was to the emancipated people of God." He thus reminded the audience that God freed the Hebrew slaves from the Egyptian pharaoh, implying that white Americans should do the same for their slaves of African descent. Douglass returned to this analogy shortly after. He reminded his audience that in the Gospels Jesus criticized the Jews for taking refuge in their heredity—"we have Abraham to our father"—rather than acting in a way faithful to the principles of Abraham. On the Fourth of July, Douglass noted, white Americans were quick to say, "We have Washington to *our father*," even as they held people in slavery and condemned those who spoke on behalf of the enslaved.

Douglass scathingly summarized this hypocrisy in the passage which gave the speech its title:

> What, to the American slave, is your 4th of July? I answer: a day that reveals to him, more than all other days in the year, the gross injustice and cruelty to which he is the constant victim. To him, your celebration is a sham; your boasted liberty, an unholy license; your national greatness, swelling vanity; your sounds of rejoicing are empty and heartless; your denunciations of tyrants, brass fronted impudence; your shouts of liberty and equality, hollow mockery; your prayers and hymns, your sermons and thanksgivings, with all your religious parade, and solemnity, are, to him, mere bombast, fraud, deception, impiety, and hypocrisy—a thin veil to cover up crimes which would disgrace a nation of savages.

In this passage and throughout the speech, Douglass used the second person pronoun "you" to refer to his white audience and thus separate the African American perspective from that of white Americans. For example, in one use of "you" and "I," Douglass employed a model of antithesis, the placing of opposite terms in parallel structure in order to heighten the contrast. Regarding the Fourth of July, Douglass said, "*You* may rejoice, *I* must mourn." Each element paired an opposite. He divided his white audience from himself—You versus I. He contrasted their ability to celebrate their Independence with his need to mourn those who were still enslaved. Most importantly, his antithesis contrasted white Americans' choice—they *may*—with his necessity—he *must*—and extended to the audience an implicit invitation for them to mourn with him.

Regarding his preference for action over endless discussion, Douglass asked his audience rhetorically, "What would you have me argue?" He then took up the standard arguments about abolition. Must I argue that slaves are persons? he asked. He noted that Virginia had seventy-two crimes for which an African American could be executed but only two such crimes for white men. When cattle can be executed for committing such crimes, said

Douglass, then I may take up our time arguing about whether a slave is a human being. He continued: Are men entitled to liberty and citizenship? How can he be bothered to argue *that* point on the Fourth of July, which *celebrates* the Declaration of *Independence*?

Douglass then turned to describing the internal slave trade. Since 1808, border states such as Virginia and Maryland had become slave breeding states, where slave owners forced their slaves to reproduce so that the offspring could be sold down South in the cotton-producing states. On its face, Douglass's discussion highlighted the white Americans' hypocrisy, as they congratulated themselves for passing the 1808 law that banned the importation of slaves even as their internal slave trade was booming. However, Douglass's discussion also allowed him to remind his audience about the cruel nature of American slavery. Douglass vividly described the horror of the auction block, the slave drive, the sugar mills, cotton fields, and chain gangs. His had strong epithets for those who bought, sold, or oversaw those who were enslaved. They were flesh-mongers, flesh-jobbers, savage, blood-chilling, and murderous.

The Fugitive Slave Law, Douglass noted, had made the slave power "co-extensive with the Star-Spangled Banner and American Christianity." Where the flag and the cross went, he said, may also go the "merciless slave-hunter." Because the law enforced the institution of slavery everywhere, New York was a slave power no different from Virginia. Meanwhile, the Christian Church in America had "made itself the bulwark of American slavery, and the shield of American slavery." The church's sins were omission as well as commission. Some helped preach that slavery was legitimate; others forgot to remind their followers that Christ's Second Commandment—to do unto others as you would have them do unto you—constituted a bold declaration against slavery. Organized religion in England, he observed, had rallied against the practice of slavery. In America, organized religion had pledged to "support and perpetuate" it.

About the Constitution, Douglass had broken with his mentor, William Lloyd Garrison, who continued to advocate moral suasion and nonparticipation in politics. Douglass argued instead that the Constitution was a "GLORIOUS LIBERTY DOCUMENT." The "principles and purposes" of the Constitution were to preserve the people's liberty, and if the audience was to be true to the legacy of the patriots whom Douglass celebrated at the beginning of the speech, his audience must be abolitionists.

Even as Douglass logically developed his case against slavery, he told the audience that no such case was necessary. "At a time like this," he said, "scorching irony, not convincing argument, is needed." He continued: "O!

had I the ability, and could I reach the nation's ear, I would, to-day, pour out a fiery stream of biting ridicule, blasting reproach, withering sarcasm and stern rebuke. For it is not light that is needed, but fire; it is not the gentle shower, but thunder. We need the storm, the whirlwind, and the earthquake." Within a decade, the storm would arrive, aided by the increasingly militant tone of Black abolitionist speakers who were indeed pouring out fiery streams of stern rebuke.

## THE WIDE CIRCLE OF REFORM

During the antebellum period, African American speakers addressed a wide range of reforms besides abolition. They especially advocated on behalf of temperance, moral reform, women's rights, and equal treatment for free Blacks. They also spoke avidly against gradualism and the American Colonization Society.

### *Temperance*

Temperance was an important reform movement during the antebellum decades. Many reformers of all races and genders, such as Susan B. Anthony and Elizabeth Cady Stanton, spoke first on behalf of temperance and expanded their work from there. Frederick Douglass, William Wells Brown, Theodore Wright, and William Whipper were just a few of the prominent African Americans who advocated temperance. Benjamin Quarles, a historian of Black abolitionists, wrote that "a supporter of abolition was likely to be a supporter of temperance." Frances Watkins spoke for temperance in the antebellum period and later served as an officer of the Woman's Christian Temperance Union. At the 1833 "Third Annual Convention for the Improvement of the Free People of Colour" held in Philadelphia, one of the major reports delivered to the members was on temperance reform, and the delegates approved the resolution that they form the Coloured American Conventional Temperance Society.

In his 1834 presidential address to the Colored Temperance Society of Philadelphia, William Whipper argued that intemperance was a form of slavery. Whipper referred his audience to other speakers regarding the religious and medical arguments against the use of alcohol. His argument, he said, rested on the similarities between the "two greatest evils that ever scourged the human family, viz., Intemperance and Slavery." Like slavery, intemperance was an animate evil. It was a "blighting monster" with a "ghastly countenance and destructive mien" that had "slain mankind." Both slavery and intemperance were "poisons" that attacked the human soul. Slavery cultivated cruelty and sloth in the slave owner and conditioned those enslaved to live in a brutish environment. From the very start, Whipper said, alcohol fueled the slave trade and it continued to hold back the advancement of free Blacks. Whipper walked a careful line here because of the double-bind that all African American temperance speakers faced: to encourage reform in the Black community without legitimizing white criticism. "I wish not to be understood to insinuate, that we [African Americans] are more intemperate than the whites, for I do not believe it," Whipper said, "but that we must be more pure than they, before we can be duly respected, [is] self-evident."

*Moral Reform*

As a movement, "moral reform" often included temperance and abolition, but it extended its interests more broadly to include education and the improvement of human behavior generally. The rise of literary societies in this era was a manifestation of the moral reform movement. Speaking to the Ladies' Literary Society of New York in 1837, Elizabeth Jennings summarized the movement's purpose. Jennings was the New York City schoolteacher who had later sued the Third Avenue Streetcar Company over its Jim Crow policies. "Now [is] a momentous time," she told her 1837 audience, "a time that calls us to exert all our powers, [of which] the mind is the greatest, and great care should be taken to improve it with diligence."

America was still an agrarian society, and agricultural metaphors often marked the approach these reformers took to encouraging improvement and diligence. Too often there had been a "neglect of cultivation" of the mind, as Jennings admonished her audience. Two decades later, the Boston journalist William Nell instructed the young men in his audience to tend to their education in the same terms: "Do not waste your spring of youth in idle dalliance, but plant rich seeds to blossom in your manhood and bear fruit when you are old."

But this was a militant age as well, and while the mind must be nurtured, African Americans also argued that they needed to attack with vigor both the work of reform and the prejudicial attitudes that opposed them. "Put on your armor, ye daughters of America, and start forth in the field of improvement," Jennings commanded. "The mind is powerful, and by its efforts your influence may be as near perfection, as that of those which have extended over kingdoms, and is applauded by thousands."

According to these speakers, this fight was being waged with a threefold purpose. The first was that they believed moral improvement would disprove white Americans' prejudice. If we do not pursue mental and moral improvement, Jennings said, "our enemies will rejoice" and they will say that their claims that whites are superior are true. Second, mental and moral improvement was, as Nell said, "useful," for it opened to the educated "future prospects" of employment and wealth. Third, however, education produced honor and pride. Learning and good behavior served the "cause of humanity" and provided the individual with appropriate pride of place. Speaking in 1855 to celebrate the desegregation of the Boston city schools, Nell told the youth in his audience that "your parents have labored to achieve this good for you, and to them you must ever render due honor." That honor would be rendered by becoming educated and learning good moral comportment.

*Women's Rights*

As women became reform activists and took to the public speaking stage, the movement for women's rights, and especially woman suffrage, quickly emerged. Beginning with Maria Miller Stewart's assertion of her right to take the stage and address audiences of mixed races and genders, African American women spoke forcefully in defense of women's rights. Elizabeth Jennings, Lucy Stanton, Sara Stanley, Frances Watkins, Mary Ann Shadd, and other women argued that women must insist on their right to an education, the right to vote, and the right to control their own destinies. In his speech on the desegregation of Boston's public schools, William Nell observed that it was the mothers who had served as the major agents of change. It was the mothers, he said, who accompanied him to city hall to protest segregation, and it was the mothers who accompanied their children in force on the first day of desegregation. While "some men would become lukewarm and indifferent, despairing of victory," it was African American women who kept the "flame alive."

From the start, many African American men perceived the connection between rights for Blacks and rights for women, and they embraced both causes. In 1844, Charles Lenox Remond remarked to his audience that "I belong to that class of persons called women's rights men" and noted that he looked upon the entire issue of slavery from that point of view. That is, he said that among its many sins the institution of slavery violated the rights and personhood of women. At the Seneca Falls convention of 1848, Frederick Douglass was one of the men who signed in support of the

Declaration of Sentiments, the woman's rights manifesto patterned after the Declaration of Independence.

The most famous women's rights speech of the era is Sojourner Truth's "Ar'n't I a Woman?" delivered to the 1851 Women's Rights Convention. It is doubtful that Truth ever asked the title question specifically but, rather, that both the question and the extensive use of dialect were inventions of Frances Gage, who "recorded" the speech twelve years later in *The History of Woman Suffrage*. Still, the contemporaneous account of Truth's speech that appeared in the *Anti-Slavery Bugle* captured what that reporter called "one of the most unique and interesting speeches of the convention." Truth's speech was apparently an extemporaneous rebuttal of speakers who had taken to the floor to argue against women's rights. Throughout the speech, Truth countered with innovative replies.

To the belief that men and women were not equal, Truth described her work on the farm: plowing, reaping, husking, chopping, mowing—and eating, she pointed out—as much as any man. In the midst of an upper middle-class, "citified" audience, standing around six feet tall, muscular, and speaking in an uneducated fashion, Truth reminded her audience visually and verbally that most American women, and almost all African American women, were engaged in dirty and difficult manual labor on the farm. There they worked alongside the men, having equal responsibility for tending the farm even while they did not have equal rights.

As for a man's claim that women were not the intellectual equals of men, Truth did not respond with the usual rebuttal, which would be to give examples of women who were leaders, educators, doctors, and lawyers. Rather, Truth shifted the discussion to one of selfishness. If man's intellect was a "quart" and woman's was a "pint," she said, then at least let women have their "pint" full. It was selfish to take a quart and not let women use their pint. She also advanced the argument that, if men quit "taking" women's rights from them and simply returned them "to her," that men would feel much better. Men would find it much simpler if they stuck to tending to their own rights and let women take care of their own.

Finally, Truth took up the religious argument that the story of Eve in Genesis, where Eve brought the apple to Adam, illustrated the immoral nature of women and the lesson that men must therefore control politics and business. This was an illogical but pervasive rationalization against women's rights. Many women speakers pointed out the contradiction that while nineteenth-century American men would not allow women's "immoral" nature to play a role in the "public sphere," those same men argued that it was woman's sphere to be the parent responsible for the moral upbringing of her children. Women speakers usually argued that the expulsion from Eden was as much Adam's fault as it was Eve's. As usual with her speeches, Sojourner Truth took a different tack. If "Eve caused man to sin," said Truth, essentially *allowing* the blame to be placed on Eve, then why not give woman the chance to turn the world "right side up again"? Truth embraced Eve, focusing on her power and, by extension, the power of all women—if only they would be given a chance.

Although most of Sojourner Truth's arguments were innovative and original, the conclusion of her speech, as reported in the *Bugle*, was consistent with other speakers, as she connected the two reforms of abolition and women's rights. "Man is in a tight place," Truth reportedly observed; "the poor slave is on him, woman is coming on him, and he is surely between a hawk and a buzzard."

*Discrimination*

Although not formally enslaved, free African Americans continued to face many of the same obstacles they had confronted during the colonial and early national periods. Employers with good jobs would not hire them; if public schooling was available to them, it was usually segregated; and public accommodations such as inns, steamships, and streetcars were segregated as well. Most states did not extend the right to vote to Blacks, and in some of the states that did, the right could only be exercised with the payment of a poll tax. African American reformers spoke out against all these social ills.

Speakers began with the fundamentals: that these discriminatory practices were unjust. Like David Walker in his 1828 speech, "The Necessity of a General Union Among Us," speakers pointed to and described the "miseries and degradations" that free Blacks were forced to endure. Look at our Ohio penitentiaries, said John Mercer Langston in 1855. We pay taxes, but cannot vote or send our children to public school. If convicted of even the least felony, however, we are mixed equally with the "worst white criminals"—until mealtime. Then, segregation is reinstituted and you may "see the prisoners marching [to their meal]—horse-thieves in front—colored people behind."

Many speakers remarked that America, reputedly the land of the free and equal, was also the land of castes: whites, slaves, and free Blacks. Only in the United States were Blacks guilty of the "crime of color." Reformers asked for employment. In her 1832 speech "Why Sit Ye Here and Die?" Maria Miller Stewart implored the white women in her audience to hire Black women as seamstresses. That, as least, was a better paying job than cleaning floors and taking in laundry. On behalf of Black men, Stewart made a similar emotional appeal to the white members of her audience: "Look at our young men, smart, active and energetic, [but] if they look forward, alas! What are their prospects? They can be nothing but the humblest laborers, on account of their dark complexions."

Other appeals to whites' consciences were made as well. Some tried shaming. "We are NATIVES of this country," said Peter Williams Jr. in 1830, "we ask only to be treated as well as FOREIGNERS." As James Forten and many other speakers pointed out, "Our ancestors—not from choice—were the first successful cultivators of the wilds of America," and so "we, their descendants, feel ourselves entitled to participate in the blessings of her luxuriant soil, which their blood and sweat enriched."

Inevitably, those who traveled abroad contrasted the color-blind treatment they experienced outside of the United States with the discrimination they encountered at "home." In 1842, Charles Lenox Remond testified before the Massachusetts legislature against its Jim Crow laws regarding public transportation. "In the course of nineteenth months' traveling in England, Ireland and Scotland," Remond said, "I was received, treated and recognized in public and private society, without any regard to my complexion." He made a point of mentioning that "from the moment" he departed the *American* ship in Liverpool until the time he stepped back aboard an *American* vessel, "in no instance was I insulted or treated in any way distinct or dissimilar from other passengers or travelers, either in coaches, railroads, steam packets or hotels."

Most speakers understood, as Lucy Stanton said in 1850, that "the freedom of the slave and the gaining of our rights, social and political, are inseparably connected." As long as slavery existed, it was easy for white Americans to perpetuate their prejudice. Conversely, if free Blacks were treated as equal citizens, it would imply that the enslavement of Blacks was immoral. Thus, David Walker argued on behalf of a united effort on both fronts by free Blacks because "it is indispensably our duty to try every scheme that we think will have a tendency to facilitate our salvation."

At the 1843 National Convention of Colored Citizens at which Henry Highland Garnet gave his "Address to the Slaves," the chairman of the convention, Samuel Davis, aptly summarized the frustration free Blacks felt as he delivered his keynote speech, "We Must Assert Our Rightful Claims and Plead Our Own Cause." "Our grievances are many and great," Davis noted, and ranged from the deprivation of voting rights to the denial of access to the public schools. Davis observed succinctly that the heart of the problem was that "the color of skin is made the criterion of the law." Shall we petition the legislatures for our rights? he asked. He answered, "We have petitioned again and again, and what has been the result? Our humblest prayers have not been permitted a hearing."

He continued: Should we appeal to the "Christian community" and its conscience? The American church supported slavery, so there was not much hope there. Neither political party would stand with the African American, and so the matter of reform was left to free Blacks themselves. For Davis, African Americans needed to form their own Liberty Party and thereby exert political control over their own destinies: "We ourselves must be willing to contend for the rich boon of freedom and equal rights, or we shall never enjoy that boon."

*Colonization vs. Emigration*

The one "reform" that African American speakers universally opposed was the "encouraged" emigration of blacks back to Africa, as promoted by the American Colonization Society (ACS). Founded in 1816 by an amalgamation of Quakers, clergy, and slave owners, most African Americans saw the organization as a thinly veiled attempt to control the free Black population by sending them to the West Coast of Africa and thus relieve the abolitionist pressure to end slavery.

In 1833, the Reverend Nathaniel Paul—brother of the Reverend Thomas Paul—and William Lloyd Garrison toured England, speaking in support of abolition. At the time, the ACS was conducting a fundraising tour to help finance the "benevolent" repatriation of free African Americans back to Africa. In "Let Us Alone," Paul set out the African American case against the society. "I brand it a cruel institution," Paul told his audience, because it sought to expel a man from the country of his birth due solely to the complexion of his skin. The society not only robbed him of the political, civil, and religious rights to which his birth entitled him but also robbed him of employment so that he would feel compelled to go back to Africa.

"In the next place, I condemn the Society on account of its hypocrisy," Paul continued. The society operated on the pretense of being opposed to slavery but wished to expel free Blacks, actively persecuted those who sought to educate African Americans, and counted slaveholders such as Henry Clay among its officers. "Instead of the American Colonization Society seeking the welfare of the free people of color," said Paul, "it is their most bitter enemy."

Speaking at the Fourth Convention of Colored Citizens in 1834, William Hamilton similarly articulated the society's deviousness whereby it claimed to be "helping" Blacks while the effect of its "reform" was to reinforce discrimination and support slavery. "The society says one thing up North and another down South," Hamilton argued. African Americans were "ignorant, idle, a nuisance and a drawback" to the country while in the United States, but if shipped back to Africa, "we shall civilize and Christianize" that continent. The society had "resorted to every artifice to effect their purposes," Hamilton said. It had stoked fears of Black insurrections and of race-mixing, petitioned legislatures to send free Blacks to Africa, and worked to deny Blacks access to public education. And yet, Hamilton lamented, "such are the men of that society that the [national] community are blind to their absurdities, contradictions and paradoxes." "I do not know of a solitary colored individual who entertains the least favorable view of the American Colonization Society," concluded Nathaniel Paul. To a person, he said, the message of free blacks to the Society was "*Let us alone.*"

In 1858, disheartened by the slow progress of equal rights, an increasing number of African Americans did begin speaking about a return to Africa. Henry Highland Garnet helped found the African Civilization Society, and others such as Martin Delany also promoted Black migration to Africa. Unlike the colonizationists, however, these speakers never argued that African Americans were unsuited for life in the United States, that they should not be entitled to full citizenship in the U.S., or that free African Americans were a "problem" that needed to be solved. They simply held that, taken as a whole, white Americans would never accept Black Americans as equals and that Africa, not the U.S., was their true "land of opportunity."

## CONCLUSION

For African American public speakers, the antebellum period was a time of attention to reform. In their view, there was much to be done. Temperance, women's rights, civil rights, education, and moral reforms all caught their attention, and African Americans from many walks of life stepped forward to address the need to shape the still young nation. Central to all these reforms was abolition. At first, African American speakers were divided by how militantly they should become involved in politics in order to abolish slavery, but by the 1850s and the passage of the Fugitive Slave Law, their militancy was almost universal, accompanied by a rising chorus of those who urged immigration to Canada, Haiti, or Africa.

After the British Empire had declared slavery illegal beginning August 1, 1837, African Americans gathered together each first of August to celebrate it as the true day of independence and freedom, and they continued to shun Fourth of July celebrations as shameless hypocrisy. August 1 was typically marked by speeches celebrating true freedom and condemning the continued institution of slavery in the United States. In his 1857 August 1 speech, Frederick Douglass aptly summarized most African American reformers' attitude toward their work. "Let me give you a word of the philosophy of reform," Douglass said. "The whole history of the progress of human liberty shows that all concessions yet made to her august claims have been born of earnest struggle." He continued with what has become one of his most often quoted passages: "If there is no struggle there is no progress. Those who profess to favor freedom and yet deprecate agitation are men who want crops without plowing up the ground; they want rain without thunder or lightning. . . . This struggle may be a moral one, or it may be a physical one, and it may be both moral and physical, but it must be a struggle. Power concedes nothing without a demand. It never did and it never will."

Although his observations applied to all types of reforms, Douglass was, like most African Americans in 1857, already seeing signs of the "thunder and lightning" that attended the reform movement of abolition and the storm that would break in 1861.

# 3

# Emancipation, Segregation, and Migration

IN ITS SIMPLEST TERMS, the last four decades of the nineteenth century for African Americans centered on fighting a hard-fought battle for legal freedoms and equal rights—and then watching those rights be taken away through the force of prejudice. During the Civil War, African American speakers agitated to make it a war of emancipation and to ensure that African Americans were provided the opportunity to be equal partners in their liberation. Reconstruction was a time of hope and political power, when Blacks lobbied for and passed the emancipation amendments, voting rights bills, and the Civil Rights Acts of 1868 and 1875. But through Supreme Court decisions, state laws, and federal neglect, those rights were eroded to the point that even the right to life was at risk with the rise of lynching. Increasingly, immigration—to the West, the North, and to Africa—became a topic that Black speakers addressed.

## FIGHTING THE CIVIL WAR

With the outbreak of the Civil War in April 1861, it seemed as if the United States might at long last forcibly eject slavery from the national culture. President Lincoln, however, quickly made it clear that while he was not a proponent of slavery, this was a war against secession but not for abolition. His first inaugural was conciliatory, staking out a conservative position of "preserving the Union." Over the first two years of the war, he often overturned decisions by his generals that threatened the institution of slavery, such as the confiscation of those enslaved or the enlistment of fugitive slaves into the Union Army. One important task African American public speakers set for themselves was to convince the president, the Congress, and the Northern population at large that the war was and should be a war for the abolition of slavery.

Although African American speakers never abandoned their position that slavery was immoral, early on they understood the attraction of the "necessity of war" argument, and they pointed out that it would be politically advantageous for the federal government to declare that the purpose of the Civil War was to abolish slavery. Abolition is a "military necessity," declared the noted dentist and lawyer John S. Rock in January 1862, and "the safety of the country is dependent upon emancipation." "It is true," acknowledged Rev. J. C. Pennington a month later, that "the government is but little more antislavery now that it was at the commencement of the war; but while fighting for its own existence, it has been obliged to take slavery by the throat, and sooner or later *must* choke her to death." In the fall of that year, Sarah Remond pressed the case that the war was an abolition war. Speaking in London to an international congress of philanthropic organizations, Remond urged her audience, "Let no diplomacy [by] statement, no intimidation [by] slaveholders, no scarcity of cotton, no fear of slave insurrections, prevent the people of Great Britain from maintaining their position as the friend of the oppressed negro."

One tack many African American speakers took in this cause was to advance a favorable interpretation of events whenever possible. Blacks understood, for example, that Lincoln's Emancipation Proclamation of January 1, 1863, only declared slavery void in the states that had rebelled. However, even radical speakers like the Philadelphia philanthropist and activist Robert Purvis celebrated the spirit of the Emancipation Proclamation, declaring that it converted the war to a "glorious contest," defining it finally as a "war between freedom and despotism the world over." "Our country is not yet free," Purvis concluded, "but thank God for those signs of the times that unmistakably indicate that it soon will be!"

Declaring that the war was an abolition war was strategic in two regards. First, it increased the chances that slavery actually would be abolished by the end of the war. The Thirteenth Amendment, which eliminated slavery, would be passed in February 1865, but in the early stages of the war, the abolition of slavery was uncertain. It was critically important for these speakers to elicit public commitments from the president and Congress that the war was in fact a struggle to abolish slavery. Second, defining the Civil War as an abolition war helped endorse the claim that African Americans were equal citizens of the nation and therefore entitled to all the rights of citizenship, including suffrage. "The slaveholders and their allies are biting the dust," declared Purvis, and "the Black man is a citizen."

There was a fine line these speakers walked, however. If the war was *not* an abolition war, then emancipation was not guaranteed. If, however, the war *was* an abolition war, then Blacks could be blamed as the "cause" of the war. Thus, speakers like Pennington, discussing the New York City draft riots of the summer of 1863, held that the war had not been *started* for the purpose of abolishing slavery, but that it had evolved—through necessity—into such a conflict. Isaiah C. Wears, a Philadelphia barber and Republican Party activist, argued that Blacks were the "cause" of the Civil War in the same way the Hebrews were the "cause" of the plagues on the pharaoh. White Americans were being selfish to suggest that Blacks should leave the United States now that the exploitation of their labor was coming to an end, he said, and African Americans were committed to fighting for their rights regardless of what discriminatory laws might come their way.

In "The Mission of the War," delivered in early 1864, Frederick Douglass argued that, although the North had begun the battle solely for the purpose of preserving the Union, the South had entered the conflict in order to preserve slavery. Regardless of Northern motivations, therefore, the "true character" of the war was the abolition of slavery. "I now hold that a sacred regard for truth, as well as sound policy," said Douglass, "makes it our duty to own and avow before heaven and earth that this war is, and of right ought to be, an Abolition war." Because the character of the war was defined as a battle in support of freedom and basic rights, Douglass urged the federal government to provide "immediate and unconditional emancipation in all states, invest the Black man everywhere with the right to vote and to be voted for, and remove all discriminations against his rights on account of his color, whether as a citizen or as a soldier."

"Rights" as a soldier were slow to come to African American troops during the Civil War. Although Blacks had fought in the Revolution and the War of 1812, initially they could not enlist in the Union Army. African American speakers understood that if Blacks were not part of the war effort, it would place them in the position where whites had "given" them emancipation. "Hardships and dangers are household words to us," John Rock observed, and so "we desire to take part in this contest. . . . We are not afraid to dig or to fight." Rock included digging here because initially Black soldiers were employed solely as manual laborers, digging trenches, cooking meals, and ferrying supplies. By 1863, however, Black combat soldiers constituted units such as the Fifty-fourth Massachusetts Regiment. There they had "a chance to prove their manhood," as J. Stanley said in a eulogy to one of the soldiers of the Fifty-fourth who was killed at the battle of Fort Wagner.

Discrimination continued, however, as Blacks were not allowed to serve as officers and were not paid equally to the white soldiers. In part, there was the issue of financial hardship. As New Orleans native Arnold Bertonneau related in a speech to Republican Party leaders in 1864, one regiment of Black troops was mustered for forty days and upon their discharge the soldiers were paid the "monthly" sum of $7.00, but then charged $13.97 for their uniform. Thus they owed the federal government $6.97 for the privilege of having served in defense of the city. The issue of unequal pay was also important symbolically. Equal pay would signify that Black soldiers were the equal of white soldiers and thus signal that Blacks were entitled to all rights of citizenship. Delivering a recruiting speech in Baltimore early in 1864, Reverend J. P. Campbell made the argument explicitly: "If we receive equal pay and bounty when we go into the war, we hope to receive equal rights and privileges when we come out of the war. If we go in equal in pay, we hope to come out equal in enfranchisement."

In June 1864, Congress passed legislation requiring that African American combat soldiers receive combat pay. As the end of the war came into view, emancipation, suffrage, and equal rights would become the central issues of the Reconstruction period.

## RECONSTRUCTION

In the waning days of the Civil War, the Reverend Henry Highland Garnet, who twenty-two years earlier had publicly called for slave insurrections, became the first African American to speak to Congress in the U.S. Capitol. On January 31, 1865, the House of Representatives had voted to send the Thirteenth Amendment abolishing slavery to the states for ratification. On February 12, the Reverend Garnet, now pastor of the Fifteenth Street Presbyterian Church in Washington, D.C., was invited to preach a sermon in celebration. Garnet's speech perfectly bridged the transformation of issues facing African Americans as the Civil War became the Reconstruction era.

As he rejoiced that Congress has passed the Thirteenth Amendment and he called on the states to ratify the amendment, Garnet rehearsed the arguments Blacks had arrayed against slavery since colonial times. Slavery was a monster, he said, a demonic institution that made brutes of all men— the slaveholder as well as those enslaved. He quoted the Bible, taking as his passage Jesus's condemnation of the scribes and Pharisees, who would quote the law of Moses but would not live by it. He reminded the audience that the chief force of slavery was to prevent those enslaved from following God's commands. Slavery was, he said, "the highly concentrated essence of all conceivable wickedness: theft, robbery, pollution, unbridled passion, incest, cruelty, cold-blooded murder, blasphemy and defiance of the laws of God." He recited antislavery quotations from the Founding Fathers, including Washington, Jefferson, Lafayette, and Patrick Henry. As many speakers would remark, the terrible human cost of the Civil War was God's punishment on America for its sin of slavery.

However, Garnet was already looking to the future as well. "If slavery has been destroyed merely from *necessity*," he said, "let every class be enfranchised at the dictation of *justice*." Garnet posed the question he imagined that America was asking: "When and where will the demands of the reformers of this and coming ages end?" He answered himself: "When emancipation shall be followed by enfranchisement, and all men holding allegiance to the government shall enjoy every right of American citizenship. ... When, in every respect, [the Black man] shall be equal before the law, and shall be left to make his own way in the social walks of life." Securing passage of the Thirteenth Amendment, the Fourteenth Amendment (equal citizenship rights) and the Fifteenth Amendment (voting rights) would occupy much of the attention of African American speakers in the first years following the Civil War.

*Emancipation and Universal Suffrage*

Although the new constitutional amendments were designed to lay these issues to rest, they remained unsettled. Speaking in 1867 at an organizational meeting of the Republican Party in Charleston, South Carolina, the Reverend Ennals J. Adams aptly identified three major issues that African American speakers would address throughout the Reconstruction years: the right to vote, access to an education, and equal economic opportunity. These, said the Rev. Adams, "will fit the colored man for any position, social or political."

Appropriately for a political meeting, Rev. Adams set out the case for providing universal suffrage. There were the benefits to democracy: "Justice, domestic tranquility, the common defense, the general welfare, and the blessing of liberty cannot be secured without universal suffrage." Universal suffrage was also needed so that the poor could protect their interests. The rich, he observed, will find ways to look out for themselves regardless of the political system. Only democracy could provide some relief for the poor. To this he added a religious justification. Just as God provided humans with volition—the ability to choose whether to follow God's will or not—so had he provided them with the will to select their political leaders. And finally, Adams noted, the right to vote was owed to African Americans for their many years of slavery and disfranchisement.

In his closing remarks, Rev. Adams also identified the pernicious argument advanced by white Americans who opposed giving African Americans voting rights, a sound education, or economic opportunities. "Social equality" was the code word used for "race mixing," in other words, sexual intercourse between the races. As a shibboleth, the specter raised by whites was that African American men would pursue white women. Many African American speakers of the era responded by reassuring white Americans that Blacks were not interested in such race mixing. Speaking in support of desegregating the District of Columbia schools, Senator Hiram Revels of Mississippi argued that "mixing" in schools would not bring about social equality. Some speakers, however, like Frederick Douglass, argued that it was nobody's business but that of the two individuals involved. Still others, like the Rev. Adams, turned the issue on its head. He pointed out that he did not "wish to be understood" as advocating social equality. As he concluded, "God forbid that. For some of my mean white drunken enemies may sneak into my house and marry my daughter."

In addition to the specter of social equality, Southern whites advanced the stereotypes that Blacks were uneducated, lazy, and undisciplined and therefore unfit to vote or hold office. African Americans were "children" they argued, and good policy was to have a paternalistic political and social system that would "do what was best" for them. This was a stereotype that Northern whites subscribed to as well and against which African Americans had consistently raised their voices. It was a stereotype repeated by Southern whites who found a receptive audience up North. Regarding the large numbers of newly emancipated African Americans in the South, this was often called "the Negro problem," and that, too, was an argument that African Americans would have to counter well past Reconstruction.

A common rebuttal to the stereotype was to relate the successes experienced by African Americans despite the obstacles they had to overcome. In "Coloured Women of America," a speech Frances Harper delivered to the Woman's Congress in 1877, she related story after story that illustrated how industrious and disciplined Blacks were. Just ten years after emancipation, she noted, Mrs. Montgomery manages a cotton farm of 130 acres; Mrs. Brown and Mrs. Halsey "formed a partnership . . . leased nine acres and a horse, . . . and are living independently." Mrs. Henry, an invalid, still managed to make "600 bushels of sweet potatoes, . . . has 100 hogs, thirty dozen chickens, a small lot of ducks and turkeys, and also a few sheep and goats." Harper used examples to refute the stereotype that Blacks were uneducated and unintelligent as well. "In higher walks of life, too," she said, "coloured women have made progress." The principal of the Coloured High School in Philadelphia was an ex-slave, and two African American women were studying law at Howard University while two others were studying medicine at the Woman's Medical College of Pennsylvania.

A second common response to the stereotype was to remind their Northern, Republican audiences that African Americans were being attacked—verbally and physically—by these ex-rebels, ex–slave masters, and the overwhelmingly *Democratic* white Southerners. In an 1867 Thanksgiving Day sermon in Fairfield, Ohio, the later principal of Clay Street School in Memphis B. K. Sampson reminded his audience that prejudice against African Americans had supported the institution of slavery and served as the cornerstone of the Democratic Party. Race prejudice was responsible for lighting up the "national sky" with the "fierce flames of war." At the present time, he said, "our coloured brethren are bowed down under the most depressing influences in the Southern states. They have been put to torture and death by the fiendish traitors who plotted treason against the government."

This appeal, known as waving the bloody shirt, conveyed three messages. It called up Northern resentment that Southern intransigence had led to so many deaths and injuries in the Civil War. It also reminded Northern white audiences that African Americans had fought loyally and bravely on the side of the North. Finally, it pointed up the fact that white Southerners were almost universally registered as Democrats while Blacks in all geographic regions were solidly Republican. This was an attractive appeal to make while speaking to Northern and western Republicans, who held power nationally throughout much of the last half of the nineteenth century.

Acquiring political rights seemed a never-ending and sometimes discouraging struggle, however. In 1868, the reconstructed Georgia state legislature voted against seating the African Americans who had been elected as representatives because, although the new state constitution said that Blacks could vote, it did not explicitly say that they could hold office. In 1865, following the Civil War, Bishop Henry McNeal Turner had organized the African Methodist Episcopal (A.M.E.) Church in Georgia and then used his same skills to organize the Republican Party in that state. He was a delegate to the state convention that drafted the new constitution, a convention largely boycotted by white Democrats who did not want to be "tainted" as having cooperated with the hated Yankee government.

As the unofficial leader of the Black representatives and speaking last to the legislature, the thirty-four-year-old Turner was suitably outraged that he was being turned out through the interpretation of a state constitution that he had helped write. His was a speech of fire, brimstone, and condemnation, the kind of jeremiad he would have preached to a wayward congregation. "I have come to hurl thunderbolts," he told the legislature, and he proceeded to do so. He called the Anglo-Saxon race cowards, sinners who were replacing God's judgment with theirs, and challenged them to a contest. If they would read the Bible in Latin, so would he. If they would read it in Greek, so would he. If they would read it in Hebrew, so would he. It was no hollow challenge. A brilliant scholar, largely self-taught, Turner could read all three.

"Go on with your oppressions," Turner dared his audience. He warned them: "Babylon fell. Where is Greece? Where is Nineveh? And where is Rome?" Like those great civilizations, the United States would fall into decay if it did not change its ways and stop persecuting African Americans for the color of their skin. Like a disciple shaking the dust from his sandal as he left a town that would not receive the Gospel, at the conclusion of his speech, Turner marched out of the hall and, at the top of the steps, turned to scrape the mud from his boots before leaving. Although Congress dissolved the Georgia legislature and forced them to write a new constitution that allowed Blacks to hold office, Turner did not return to politics. Instead, he became an advocate of emigration, preaching that those Blacks who were able to do so should return to Africa because, he said, they would never be treated equally in the United States.

*Woman Suffrage*

For African American women speakers, the role that race prejudice played in opposing the acquisition of suffrage confronted them with a dilemma. Should they seek suffrage for African Americans first, or universal suffrage for all regardless of gender as well as race? As they campaigned for the Fifteenth Amendment, African American men like Frederick Douglass, who had long supported woman suffrage, argued that if reformers attempted to pass a suffrage amendment for both Blacks and women, they would get neither. These speakers first wanted to secure universal suffrage for all men, regardless of color, and then return to the pursuit of woman suffrage. White women suffragists, such as Elizabeth Cady Stanton and Susan B. Anthony, were outraged, and they broke away to form the National Woman Suffrage Association.

For her part, Frances Harper elected to speak in support of race. Speaking at the eleventh Women's Rights Convention in 1866, for example, Harper chastised her white colleagues for their selfish attitudes about rights. Contrasting their privileged status with that of Blacks—male and female—Harper observed that "you white women speak here of rights. I speak of wrongs." She confronted two articles of faith for some woman suffragists—that giving women the right to vote would clean up politics and that white women held a superior place to Black women. "I do not believe that white women are dew drops just exhaled from the skies," she said, but rather "I think like men they may be divided into three classes, the good, the bad, and the indifferent." She repeated the common reform argument that the rights of each person were tied up together—"we are all one great bundle of humanity"—but she did so in order to support the claim that white women would ultimately benefit if equal rights were extended to include African American men. In her conclusion, Harper still avowed her support for woman suffrage but even here challenged the race prejudice of her fellow suffragists. "Talk of giving women the ballot box?" she asked rhetorically, and then answered, "Go on. It is a normal [teacher training] school, and the white women of the world need it. While there exists this brutal element in society which tramples upon the feeble and treads down the weak, I tell you that if there is any class of people who need to be lifted out of their airy nothings and selfishness, it is the white women of America."

In May of 1869, out of frustration that women had not been included in the Fifteenth Amendment, Elizabeth Cady Stanton, Susan B. Anthony, and other prominent white suffragists broke from the American Equal Rights Association to form the National Woman Suffrage Association. One of the few African American women who supported the new organization was Mary Ann Shadd Cary. Where Harper and other African American women focused on securing equal rights for African Americans, Shadd Cary believed it was critically important for Black women to gain the right to vote. Only suffrage for all women would bring that right to African American women as well. In her public arguments, Shadd Cary emphasized that Black women had also suffered the deprivations of slavery and were now facing the challenges of emancipation. The power of the ballot would be an important resource as they worked to improve their economic and social circumstances.

## *Civil Rights*

With the passage of the emancipation and suffrage amendments, African Americans had secured their freedom, the right to be treated as equal in the eyes of the law, and, for men, the right to vote and hold office. In everyday life, however, Blacks continued to experience widespread and pervasive discrimination, and so they turned their attention to civil rights. In contrast with voting rights, civil rights pertained to equal treatment in the public sphere, particularly in regard to schools, transportation, hotels, restaurants, and entertainment. A civil rights act had been passed in 1866, but it primarily addressed jobs and contracts and included very weak sanctions. As African Americans were elected to the Senate and the House of Representatives, they began advocating for stronger civil rights legislation, which was eventually passed as the Civil Rights Act of 1875.

In Congress, African Americans were represented by many impressive speakers, including Revels and Blanche K. Bruce (Mississippi) in the Senate and John R. Lynch (Mississippi), Richard H. Cain (South Carolina), John Mercer Langston (Virginia), and James T. Rapier (Alabama) in the House of Representatives. Between 1870 and 1901, twenty African Americans served in the House, and two served in the U.S. Senate.

James Rapier's 1874 speech in support of the civil rights bill was representative of these legislators' public speeches. Born a free Black in Alabama in 1837, Rapier had been educated in Canada and Scotland. His style of speaking was logical, precise, and highly polished. He began by noting the dilemma he faced. As a Black man, if he spoke in support of civil rights, he would be suspected of wanting "social equality." If he did not speak, however, then his silence was taken as assent to the current conditions. Referencing the Greek myth, Rapier observed that "in steering away from Scylla, I may run upon Charybdis." But, he concluded, the "anomalous" and "supremely ridiculous position" of African Americans—to be declared citizens but treated worse than the newly landed immigrant—compelled him to speak.

Repeatedly, Rapier noted that African Americans were punished for the "crime of color." Due solely to their skin color, they were deprived of an education and the basic amenities of food and lodging while traveling. Rapier used himself as an illustration: "Any white ex-convict . . . may start with me to-day in Montgomery, [and] all the way down he will be treated as a gentleman, while I will be treated as the convict. He will be allowed a berth in a sleeping-car with all its comforts, while I will be forced into a dirty, rough box with the drunkards, apple-sellers, railroad hands, and next to any dead that may be in transit, regardless of how far decomposition may have progressed."

Rapier also waved the bloody shirt. He prefaced this argument by noting first that "whatever liberty [the African American] enjoys has been paid for over and over again by more than two hundred years of forced toil," as well as by African Americans' participation in every war fought in defense of the nation. In the Civil War, however, African Americans played a pivotal role. "When the last ray of hope had nearly sunk below our political horizon," he said, "the Negro then came forward and offered himself as a sacrifice in the place of the nation, made bare his breast to the steel, and in it received the thrusts of the bayonet." Rapier sharply contrasted Black heroism with the role of Alexander Stephens, the former vice president of the Confederate States of America who was now serving as a representative from Georgia and had spoken against passage of the civil rights bill. Rapier noted ironically that African American soldiers had died from the "thrusts of the bayonet" that had been "aimed at the life of the nation by the soldiers of that government in which the gentleman from Georgia figured as second officer."

Throughout his speech, Rapier displayed a sharp sense of irony and pointed out the double standards that were evident in the behaviors of those who opposed civil rights. Opponents argued that the individual states could attend to the issue. Why then, Rapier asked, haven't they done anything? "I want someone to tell me," he said, "of any measure that was intended to benefit the Negro that [white Southerners] have approved of." Opponents held that Blacks newly emancipated were easily swayed in their votes. Rapier brought in the case of Joe Williams, a Black man in Alabama who campaigned in support of the Democratic Party. Williams was allowed to stay in the "best hotels" in Montgomery and extended every courtesy "because he was a Democrat, while at the same time they were hunting me down as the partridge on the mount, night and day, with their Ku Klux Klan, simply because I was a Republican and refused to bow at the foot of their Baal."

Rapier responded directly to the remarks of one congressional representative from Kentucky who had spoken against the bill. Said Rapier, Kentucky had an "army of fifty thousand ignorant white men, . . . many of whom I see every time I pass through that State, standing around the several depots continually harping on the stereotyped phrase, 'The damned Negro won't work.'" To heighten the irony, Rapier related the story of an African American who was dressed like "a gentleman" and was therefore threatened by a white mob at a railroad station in the South. He only escaped being the victim of violence by going into his luggage and bringing out his cards and dice in order to prove that he was a gambler. He was, Rapier noted, "forced to give satisfactory evidence that he was not a man who was working to elevate the moral and intellectual standards of the Negro before [the white mob] would respect him."

In his conclusion, Rapier returned to the issue of social equality that he had raised at the start. The bill "does not and cannot contemplate any such idea as social equality," nor did Rapier want any such legislation. In that one area, he said, he agreed with the "gentleman from North Carolina" who had once again raised that specter in regard to the civil rights bill. Indeed, concluded Rapier proudly, "I will tell him that I have seen many of his race to whose level I should object to being dragged."

An important persuasive device of these congressional speeches was the quality of the speech itself. The logic, vocabulary, and proud demeanor communicated through the speech served as a rebuttal to the stereotype that Blacks were not the intellectual equals of whites. Rapier argued that race prejudice was found most often in those whites who have "feeble minds and are conscious of it," thus clinging to an ill-founded sense of superiority. In contrast, he said, intellectually able white men are like the abolitionist preacher Henry Ward Beecher, who had said, "Turn the Negro loose; I am not afraid to run the race of life with him." As communication scholar Kirt Wilson observed, however, there was a danger in this appeal, for it implied that African Americans needed to "earn" the right to be equal citizens by "running the race" and attaining a similar level of education and accomplishments as their congressional representatives. Although all these congressional speakers consistently and explicitly asserted Blacks' natural rights to citizenship, too great a reliance on the *enactment* of equality through the quality of their speaking may have inadvertently distracted from the central point that, in the law, all persons were created equal.

This distraction was most clearly illustrated by the issue of literacy tests. Speakers like Representative Rapier, for example, were willing to accept the reading and writing requirements imposed by Massachusetts in order to contrast African American access to the ballot there with that of Southern states that used violence to discourage the Black vote. Before the Civil War, Massachusetts had simply required "that all male persons who could read and write should be entitled to suffrage" regardless of color, said Rapier, who asked rhetorically: "That was a case of equality before the law, and who had a right to complain?" The desire to have a literate, informed citizenry constitute the democracy was, these speakers held, a reasonable requirement, and it could even become a compelling reason for the government to make sound public education available to all children, Black and white. They did not foresee that literacy tests would be enshrined in revisions to Southern state constitutions in the last two decades of the century, and that those tests would be so unequally applied that African American access to the ballot box was reduced to virtually nothing.

*Migration*

Speeches about constitutional amendments, woman suffrage, and civil rights all focused on reforming the environment in which African Americans lived. There was, however, another option for improving one's life: leave for a better place. Liberia, Haiti, and Central America were commonly promoted as destinations for Black migration. Martin Delaney, Henry Highland Garnet, and Alexander Crummell all spoke in favor of immigration back to Africa. During Reconstruction, Kansas and other western destinations gave rise to the Exoduster movement. Estimates vary widely regarding the number of Blacks who moved west during Reconstruction. Historian Nell Painter reports that the Black population of Kansas increased by 26,000 people during the 1870s, with the movement reaching its height in 1878 to 1879, the years immediately following the official end of Reconstruction.

With limited resources and few models, the decision to migrate out of the South was a difficult one for many newly emancipated Blacks. Regardless of destination, those speakers who advocated migration faced two tasks: to remind the audience that the race prejudice in their lives was extreme and permanent and to convince them that the alternative was a viable option. Martin R. Delany, educated as a doctor and an officer in the Union Army, had advocated African emigration in the 1850s and continued to do so after the Civil War. Speaking in South Carolina in the summer of 1865 to an audience newly emancipated, Delany urged them to work hard on their own land and to protect their rights and the products of their labor. He pointed out that their former masters were scoundrels who had lived off their labor and would continue to do so at every chance because those masters were indolent. He warned his audience, too, that Northern whites—schoolteachers, emissaries, ministers, and agents—were not to be trusted either. He reminded his audience that many of their overseers had been Yankees from the North.

Those who advocated migration westward—the Exodusters—faced similar obstacles. One Exoduster leader, Benjamin "Pap" Singleton, was representative. Singleton was not highly educated but he was literate, escaping slavery by fleeing to Ontario, Canada, then moving to Detroit before coming back South to Nashville, Tennessee, to work as a carpenter making cabinets and coffins. In his speeches he cited his work making coffins for victims of white violence as the catalyst for his support of migration.

Singleton began his early work by organizing the Edgefield Real Estate and Homestead Association in Nashville as an association to help emancipated Blacks acquire their own farmland in Tennessee. Becoming convinced that Blacks would never be able to improve their situation in the South, however, he traveled to Kansas, doing the advance work necessary to create "colonies" to which African Americans could move. Singleton's speeches were not recorded, but as he and others reported them, he held "investigating meetings" to discuss the situation in Tennessee—where race prejudice had turned violent and conditions would never improve—and the promise of Kansas. In his talks, Singleton urged Blacks to stand together and "consolidate the race." It was, he said, their "duty to the race" to improve their situation, and only migration to Kansas would fulfill that purpose. Now was the time to leave for Kansas or, as Singleton reportedly phrased it, "Place and time have met and kissed each other."

Exodusters Fleeing the South. Homestead National Historical Park Trading Card, Flickr: TradingCardsNPS.

In 1880 Singleton was called to testify before Congress about his work with the Exoduster movement. There he reported his success in terms that were probably very much like the characterizations of Kansas he had given at his "investigating" meetings. Although he insisted that all migrants began their travels with sufficient means, by the time they got to Kansas, he said, many didn't have fifty cents left, [but] now they have got in my colony—Singleton colony—a house, nice cabins, their milk cows, and pigs, and sheep, perhaps a span of horses, and trees before their yards, and some three or four or ten acres broken up, and all of them has got little houses that I carried there. They didn't go under no relief assistance; they went on their own resources; and when they went in there first the country was not overrun with them; you see they could get good wages; the country was not overstocked with people; they went to work, and I never helped them as soon as I put them on the land.

Kansas, he said, was a place where hard work could pay off for Blacks.

There was another important element to Singleton's speeches, however: a sense of divine mission. Singleton himself said he had been called by God to do this work, and he referenced as his model the Book of Daniel, an apocalyptic book of the Old Testament that foretold God's judgment and the end of the Babylonian exile of the Jews. In his Senate testimony, Singleton reported that "I have held open air interviews with the living spirit of God for my people; and we are going to leave the South. We are going to leave it if there ain't an alteration and signs of change." From speech circulars and his testimony, it is clear that Singleton rejected African American politicians as "establishment" spokesmen who were exploiting the race for their own purposes.

For their part, many such "establishment" African Americans rejected the arguments of the emigrationists like "Pap" Singleton. Frederick Douglass, for example, argued that the emigration of African Americans away from the South would dilute their political power. He was also convinced that many of the proponents of Black migration were themselves opportunists. Historian Nell Painter, however, has argued that there was at this time a growing chasm between the "reputable conservative politicians" like Frederick Douglass or Blanche K. Bruce, who were no longer *of* the common people, and the community activists like Benjamin Singleton who spoke "their language." According to Painter, even some "establishment" proponents of African migration, such as Alexander Crummel and Henry McNeal Turner, tended to talk *at* the masses and not *with* them. The salvationist, community-organizing strains of Singleton's speaking resonated with audiences, and that style of speaking echoed across the sermons of many activist preachers.

*The Close of Reconstruction*

Reconstruction came to a legal end in 1877, when a deal in the House of Representatives gave the presidential election to the Republican Rutherford

B. Hayes in exchange for the removal of the last federal troops from the Southern states. In practice, the promise of Reconstruction had begun to fade long before it legally ended. In the same year that the Civil Rights Act of 1875 was finally adopted after five years of congressional debate, Tennessee passed a Jim Crow law that segregated public accommodations in the state. Even prior to 1875, Southern states had been codifying discrimination, for example, through legislation that prohibited interracial marriage or other laws that resegregated public schools.

Against this backdrop of hope and frustration, Frederick Douglass was asked to deliver the featured address at the unveiling of the Lincoln Monument in Washington, D.C. African Americans had collected money to erect the first national statue in honor of Abraham Lincoln, and at a ceremony on April 14, 1876, Douglass gave his "Oration in Memory of Abraham Lincoln." This was a challenging speech for Douglass to construct. During the war, he had been a sharp critic of Lincoln, chastising the president's slowness in declaring it a war for emancipation and his reluctance to bring African American soldiers into the Union Army. Further, in 1876, the initial gains made by African Americans during Reconstruction were visibly eroding. Even the statue itself could not be fully celebrated because it depicted the kneeling Black man in a subservient position to the apparently benevolent Lincoln.

In his speech, delivered on the eleventh anniversary of Lincoln's assassination to an audience that included President Grant, members of Congress, and the Supreme Court, Douglass frankly acknowledged Lincoln's shortcomings and pointed out the nation's racial divide. "It must be admitted," Douglass said, "even here in the presence of the monument we have erected to his memory, Abraham Lincoln was not, in the fullest sense of the word, either our man or our model. In his interests, in his associations, in his habits of thought, and in his prejudices, he was a white man. He was preeminently the white man's President, entirely devoted to the welfare of white men." Given Lincoln's iconic status as the heroic martyr who had ended slavery, Douglass was almost heretical as he reminded the audience that Lincoln had been quite willing to let slavery continue if doing so would bring the rebellious states back into the fold. Only when he was deep into the Civil War, and it was to the Union's international advantage to make it a war for emancipation, did Lincoln finally do so.

But, said Douglass, to Lincoln's credit he ultimately did make it an emancipation war and, once done, he was firm in his resolution to end the institution. Although African Americans were "at best only his step-children," Lincoln had ultimately served "at the head of a great movement" that abolished slavery. Douglass could thus extol the accomplishments of Lincoln, even if he could not completely laud the man himself. Using a series of antitheses, Douglass's appraisal of Lincoln was carefully balanced:

> Viewed from the genuine abolition ground, Mr. Lincoln seemed tardy, cold, dull, and indifferent, but measuring him by the sentiment of his country, a sentiment he was bound as a statesman to consult, he was swift, zealous, radical and determined. . . . He was assailed by Abolitionists; he was assailed by slaveholders; he was assailed by the men who were for peace at any price; he was assailed by those who were for a more vigorous prosecution of the war; he was assailed for not making the war an abolition war; and he was bitterly assailed for making the war an abolition war.

Although Douglass could have condemned Lincoln for selecting the middle path of compromise, he instead praised Lincoln for vigorously and steadfastly pursuing emancipation. Douglass thus celebrated what Lincoln *did* rather than making the president's character that of an idealized, heroic martyr.

Douglass confirmed that message in the close of his speech, as he praised not Lincoln but the African American people for having erected the monument. Tangible deeds were what mattered here, and this act of memorializing would, Douglass said, honor African Americans as much as it did Lincoln. When Blacks were assailed by prejudice—even as was happening in April of 1876 and would in the future—they could point to the monument as a testament to their character.

Despite Douglass's sharp criticism of Lincoln and his condemnation of race prejudice in the United States, his speech was widely praised. The *New York Times* reviewed the speech positively, even as it faithfully reported his condemnation of Lincoln as the white man's president and one who was often tardy, cold, and indifferent. A printing house quickly issued and sold his speech in pamphlet form. As Reconstruction evaporated, however, and the attention of the nation and the Republican Party turned away from equal rights for Blacks, so too did the positive reviews of such frank talk about race. Douglass would later be criticized in the white press for delivering similar messages that condemned the nation's double standard regarding race.

## POST-RECONSTRUCTION

For African Americans in the South, where the majority still resided, the post-Reconstruction era saw an increasing loss of legal rights and economic power. These changes were supported by a rise in lynching and other forms of white violence against the Black race. Some speakers argued that moral improvement, practical training, and education would produce economic wealth, which would then provide the basis for political power and the restitution of rights and protection. Others argued that the pursuit of political power—of which they still had some—was the best path to regaining their rights and protections. Some speakers held that violence against the race must be met by force, while still others believed that racial violence would never end and migration "back to Africa" was the only answer.

*Building the Race*

Speakers who promoted improvement of the race invariably focused on education. Women speakers most often focused on the education of African American females, while the men most typically advanced the idea of industrial education—the teaching of technical skills such as agriculture, mechanics, the trades, and small business practices.

The central forum for women speakers was the women's club movement. In the last part of the century, what had begun as female literary and moral improvement societies had now fully evolved into women's reform clubs. Usually excluded from or marginalized by the associations that were organized by white women, African American women formed their own organizations, such as the National Federation of African-American Women, the Colored Women's League, and the National Association of Colored Women, to promote women's reform. They advocated on behalf of temperance, woman suffrage, and moral reform. They sponsored "mother's meetings," which centered around these reforms as well as health education and promotion of "domestic" skills, particularly the economic management of a household.

In her 1886 speech given to the Alabama State Teacher's Association, Olivia Davidson divided the needed reforms into three categories. Davidson, the cofounder of Tuskegee Institute, said that women educators must promote physical health through temperance advocacy and education regarding malnutrition and disease, moral health through the teaching of modesty and Bible study, and intellectual health by establishing reading clubs. Journalist and short story writer Victoria Earle Matthews offered a similar list in 1897, as she spoke to the International Society of Christian Endeavor in San Francisco. In "The Awakening of the Afro-American Woman," Matthews celebrated the improvement that had been made "in the work of religion, of education, of temperance, of morality, of industrialism," while urging her audience to continue their efforts in these areas as well as to remove the barriers of popular prejudice and legal discrimination that still blocked the way for most African American women.

Many of those speaking in the "women's club" tradition in these decades addressed the progress that had been made by African American women since emancipation. Fannie Barrier Williams, one of only six African American women allowed to address the 1893 World's Congress of Representative Women held in Chicago concurrently with the Columbian Exposition, was representative. In her speech, she reminded the audience of where African American women had begun at the dawn of emancipation: impoverished, illiterate, often separated from husband and children, with no place to call their own and no capital to acquire something. From nothing, great "mental, social, and moral progress" had been made.

Speeches like Williams's address to the World's Congress had a threefold purpose. First, just as African American men were stereotyped as being sexually aggressive in order to justify the lynchings that were taking place, African American women were characterized as "Jezebels," sexual temptresses who were not interested in nurturing their children or building a home. Speakers like Williams refuted this image, sometimes implicitly but more often than not they did so explicitly. The "Jezebel" charge, said editor and activist Josephine St. Pierre Ruffin, often shocked African American women into "mortified silence," but Ruffin admonished them to be silent no more. Addressing the First National Conference of Colored Women in 1895, she said that the association's meeting served "to break this silence ... by a dignified showing of what we are and hope to become."

Second, speeches like Williams's sought to fully integrate African American women into national women's associations. Many U.S. women's organizations set up segregated chapters, and even when integrated, African American women were generally restricted in their ability to participate. Aside from the increased political power women might wield if Blacks and whites could join forces, it would be symbolically powerful if white women would fully embrace their Black sisters. African American women perceived an opening here. After all, white women, too, understood what it was to be discriminated against and to hold little political power. "Let woman's claim be as broad in the concrete as in the abstract," the writer and educator Anna Julia Cooper told the same 1893 Congress, for "we take our stand on the solidarity of humanity, the oneness of life, and the unnaturalness and injustice of all special favoritisms, whether of sex, race, country, or condition. If one link of the chain be broken, the chain is broken." Few white women were willing to fully admit Black women into their circle, however. For her part, Cooper would later travel to the Sorbonne in France to earn her doctorate of philosophy.

The third, and probably most important, purpose of speeches like Williams's was to cultivate unity among African American women. These speakers understood that while stereotypes and discriminatory practices needed to be refuted, in the immediate future only the pooling of their own resources, both financial and intellectual, could be counted on to improve their condition. The educator and activist Mary Church Terrell, the first president of the umbrella National Association of Colored Women (NACW), made unity the centerpiece of her first presidential address to the association. In her 1897 "In Union There is Strength," Terrell outlined the familiar arguments. "We take great pride," she noted, "in the unprecedented advancement" of the race since emancipation. "While rejoicing in our steady march, onward and upward," however, the organization realistically recognized that there was much that remained to be done. The home—the particular sphere of women—was the key to physical, intellectual, economic, and moral improvement. "It is only through the home," Terrell asserted to a receptive audience, "that a people can become good and truly great."

If home was the gateway, however, it was only through the united effort of African American women that the race would make progress. The NACW's motto, "Lifting as We Climb," summarized the organization's frame of mind. They could not rely on working closely with white women. "Our peculiar status," Terrell noted with understatement, "seems to demand that we stand by ourselves in our special work," and it was for this "special work" that "we have organized." "In Union there is strength," Terrell said at the opening of her speech, and she closed in similar fashion: "Let us not only preach, but practice race unity, race pride, reverence and respect for those capable of leading and advising us." "The greatest revolutions," Terrell said, "are wrought . . . by arduous persistence and effort" to work within the community to improve the community. It was there that "the heaviest blows are struck for virtue and right."

While women's voices like those of Williams and Terrell were important, the range of women's voices, like those of African American men, was wide. As historian Teresa Zackdonik wrote in *Press, Platform, Pulpit: Black Feminist Publics in the Era of Reform*, "Early Black feminisms were far from monolithic, and the politics Black feminists pursued were as varied as the publics who heard them. African American feminists pursued varied rhetorics, ranging from advocating a domestic and maternal feminism to arguing for ecstatic worship practices . . . and promoting the Black nationalist principles of communal unity and economic self-sufficiency."

Speakers of either gender who advocated for "industrial education" among Blacks thought of education broadly. For them it meant not only training in the trades but included lessons about moral conduct and economic management, education that would allow the race to acquire capital and build wealth. Addressing the National Education Association (NEA) in 1890, Joseph E. Price, the president and founder of Zion Wesley College in Salisbury, North Carolina, said, "We are told, directly and indirectly, that while there are rare and commendable exceptions, the race, as such, is ignorant, poverty-stricken, and degraded." It was, though, the environment that has caused this condition, and so the environment must be changed. "It is a generally recognized fact," Price asserted, "that the idea of morality in the general, as in the particular, becomes further and more strongly developed in proportion as culture, intelligence and knowledge of the necessary laws of the common weal increase." The "common weal," or wealth, could only be attained through education: "Labor, skilled or intelligent, coupled with the impetus arising from capital, will touch the South as with a magnetic hand, and that region with marvelous resources and immeasurable capabilities will blossom as the rose."

The most famous speech in support of industrial education was Booker T. Washington's "Atlanta Compromise" speech, delivered five years after Price's speech to the NEA. African Americans had been keenly disappointed when the 1893 Columbia World Exposition in Chicago had ignored them, as if they did not exist. In 1895, Atlanta held the Cotton States Exposition, where Southern promoters like Henry Grady, editor of the *Atlanta Constitution*, touted the "New South." With white, segregated power now firmly reestablished, white exposition leaders could afford to include a building devoted solely to African American accomplishments. Booker T. Washington, principal of Tuskegee Institute in Alabama, was invited to deliver the speech marking the opening of the exhibit.

Washington built his introduction around the phrase "cast down your bucket." He began with a story of sailors adrift at sea who were dying of thirst, not realizing they were in the mouth of a large, freshwater river. They needed only to "cast down" their buckets, and they could solve their problem through their own efforts, right where they were. Washington then applied the maxim to African Americans in the South. "No race can prosper," he said, "until it learns that there is as much dignity in tilling a field as in writing a poem. It is at the bottom of life we must begin, and not at the top." This sentiment was undoubtedly music to the ears of white Southerners, but also to white Northerners who had tired of the turmoil caused by the "race problem."

Booker T. Washington delivering his Atlanta Compromise (Cotton States Exposition) speech, 1895. www.myblackhistory.net/atlanta%20speech.jpg.

But then Washington told white Southerners that they, too, needed to cast down their bucket, reaching out to the African Americans who lived among them. Casting down the bucket meant supporting Blacks' education, giving them equal economic opportunities, and treating them fairly. In a most infamous metaphor, giving a nod to the white Southern shibboleth of social equality, Washington said that "in all things that are purely social we can be as separate as the fingers, yet one as the hand in all things essential to mutual progress." Here was the essence of "accommodation"—that Washington would exchange the African Americans' claim to political and civil rights immediately for equal economic opportunities first.

Buried in the middle of Washington's speech was a dire warning. If the proffered compromise was not accepted, he told his white Southern listeners directly by using the second person pronoun, "nearly sixteen millions of hands will aid you in pulling the load upwards or they will pull against you the load downward. . . . We shall contribute one third of the business and industrial prosperity of the South, or we shall prove a veritable body of death, stagnating, depressing, retarding every effort to advance the body politic." The last third of his speech returned to his optimistic message that if African Americans were allowed to begin at "the bottom," it would be for the benefit of all involved, and he affirmed his faith in the belief that "no race that has anything to contribute to the markets of the world is long in any degree ostracized."

Washington's speech was well received by mainstream whites. Accounts in the *Atlanta Constitution*, *New York World*, and the *New York Times* were favorable. Many Black leaders were publicly congratulatory. For example, the Reverend Burwell T. Harvey of Antioch Baptist Church in Atlanta wrote to Washington that "leadership along the vital lines which you so earnestly and manly advocate will carry the race up the sure road to success in all walks of life." W. E. B. Du Bois, then a professor at Wilberforce University in Ohio, sent a telegram saying simply that "it was a word fitly spoken." The *New York Times* coverage was illustrative of the difficulty faced by accommodationist speakers regarding their white audiences, however. The *Times* reprinted significant portions of the speech but omitted the warning about death, stagnation, and depression. Its coverage suggested that the status quo was acceptable to African Americans, if only the "troublesome" speakers among them would be quiet.

Not everyone was so pleased. Bishop Turner attended the speech in Atlanta, and a reporter for the progressive Chicago *Inter-Ocean* wrote that the bishop dismissed Washington's speech out of hand. For his part, the bishop was bitingly critical of white treatment of Blacks. Less than two months later, in November of that year, the A.M.E.'s *Christian Recorder* published an editorial attacking Washington's speech. In February 1896, Professor John Hope, who would later become the president of Atlanta Baptist College (later Morehouse University), famously delivered a stinging rebuke of Washington's compromise. Speaking to a Black debating society in Nashville, he declared, "I regard it as cowardly and dishonest for any of our colored men to tell white people that we are not struggling for equality. . . . If we cannot do what other free men do, then we are not free. Yes, my friends, I want equality. Nothing less."

Two years later, Washington himself would make a speech demanding full equality for Blacks. In his National Peace Jubilee speech of October 1898, delivered to a mass audience in Chicago, Washington demanded full equality. There was a "cancer" of prejudice and discrimination "gnawing at the heart of the Republic," he said, and especially in "the Southern part of our country." The nation would not survive if it did not eradicate this evil. Viciously attacked in the North as well as the South for his outspoken denunciation of race relations in the nation, Washington quickly retreated to his original message of industrial education.

*Protesting the Changes*

It is too simplistic to say that speakers of the era divided into two groups: those who wanted to build the wealth and power of the race gradually through industrial education and those who agitated for an immediate return to the voting, civil, and economic rights that had seemed so close at hand at the height of Reconstruction. In his 1890 address to the NEA, for example, Joseph Price called for white "concession to the negro of all the inalienable rights that belong to him as a man," and in addition to advocating on behalf of better education for Blacks, he also called for better education of whites that would lift the lower classes out of their race prejudice against African Americans. The Reverend Alexander Crummell, in an 1897 address to the American Negro Academy, an association of African American scholars that he helped found, argued that the "industrial education" movement was a "half-truth." Yes, he said, good training could help African Americans who were in the trades to work more efficiently and earn more. By itself, however, industrial education could never be "the grand agency in the elevation of a race." Scholarship within the race and a liberal education were also necessary if African Americans were to take their rightful place as equal citizens of the United States.

For many speakers, African Americans would not be able to take their "rightful place" as citizens until their current status was explicitly acknowledged. "It is a sad reflection for the young colored men of this day," Ohio state senator John P. Green told a national convention of African Americans in 1884, "that, although they are nominally free, they are as a matter of fact so proscribed and hampered by class legislation, unjust decisions and caste distinctions, as almost to produce in their mind the conviction that the term *citizen* is a delusion and a snare." Four years later, speaking at a "celebration" on the anniversary of emancipation in the District of Columbia, Frederick Douglass removed the "almost" qualification. The African American, said Douglass, "is the victim of a cunningly devised swindle, one with paralyzes his energies, suppresses his ambition, and blasts all his hopes; and though he is nominally free he is actually a slave. I here and now denounce his so-called emancipation as a stupendous fraud."

The "cunningly devised swindle" decried by Douglass had multiple facets, which included the Supreme Court's 1883 overturning of the Civil Rights Law of 1875, the sharecropping system, the convict-lease system, the segregated and woefully underfunded schools for Blacks, the erosion of voting rights, and the rise of lynching as a violent tool of social and political control. Many speakers advanced specific proposals to attack these various manifestations of de facto and de jure discrimination.

At an 1887 meeting in Selma, Alabama, the Reverend M. Edward Bryant posed this question in the title of his speech: "How Shall We Get Our Rights?" He answered his question with a seven-point plan.

1. Join the Knights of Labor and any other union that would integrate in order to agitate for and protect the rights of the workingman.
2. Organize "leagues" that would bring court cases to challenge any abridgment of civil and voting rights.
3. Organize defense leagues to protect themselves from lynching and violence perpetrated by whites.
4. Patronize Black-owned businesses in order to build capital in the community.
5. Boycott the sharecropping system. Farm only that land where the landlord will treat Blacks fairly.
6. Read only Black newspapers in order to know the truth about the race.
7. Build private schools for African Americans. Blacks will never be taught equally in public, white-controlled schools.

"Physical slavery has fallen," Reverend Bryant concluded, but "let us unite to break the chains of prejudice, ostracism, deprivation of civil, political and social rights, and the sins that are worse than physical slavery."

Speaking to the National Afro-American League in 1890, T. Thomas Fortune, the editor of the *New York Age*, advanced a similar program that blended political agitation with community self-help. In "It Is Time to Call a Halt," Fortune embraced the notion of "agitation." In the nineteenth century, "agitation" had become a pejorative term in the vocabulary of white Americans. In his Fourth of July oration, Frederick Douglass had strategically named the Founding Fathers as "agitators" and embraced the term whites used to condemn him and his fellow abolitionists. By the 1880s, agitation was still a term with negative connotations, often associated with union organizers and the rise of socialism and anarchism "brought" by recent immigrants from Eastern Europe. Like Douglass, however, Fortune argued that "agitations are inevitable" and that they are the fount of new vigors, new hopes, and political change.

Fortune enumerated seven particular evils of the present system: the suppression of voting, the rise of lynching, the segregation of schools, the convict-lease system, Jim Crow transportation, Jim Crow public accommodations such as inns and theaters, and discriminatory wages. In answer, Fortune advanced a five-point program: create an Afro-American bank in order to "centralize earnings"; establish a bureau of emigration to help African Americans leave those parts of the country where their lives and livelihoods are most in danger; establish a committee on legislation to agitate for better laws and against those that would additionally discriminate against Blacks; establish a bureau of industrial education to increase the number of "trained artisans, educated farmers and laborers"; and establish a cooperative that would provide both a market for Black-produced goods and also be a supplier of reasonably priced, high-quality goods.

African American speakers did not restrict their appeals to Black audiences only, however. At the 1893 World's Congress of Representative Women, where Fannie Barrier Williams and Anna Julia Cooper had also appeared, Frances Watkins Harper spoke under the heading "Duty to Dependent Races." Harper began by challenging the heading that had been assigned to her portion of the program. "I deem it a privilege," she told her audience, to speak on behalf of the African American "not as a mere dependent... but as a member of the body politic who has a claim upon the nation for justice, simple justice, which is the right of every race, upon the government for protection, which is the rightful claim of every citizen, and upon our common Christianity for the best influences which can be exerted for peace on earth and good-will to men." Basic human rights demanded that the government provide protection from death and bodily harm by lynchers. As loyal U.S. citizens, African Americans were entitled to the right of suffrage, civil rights, and a quality education. As coreligionists and fellow human beings, Harper reminded her audience that Jesus Christ had commanded that "whatsoever ye would that men should do to you, do you even so to them." "What I ask of American Christianity," she concluded, "is not to show us more creeds, but more of Christ."

*Answering the Violence*

Without doubt, the greatest challenge for African Americans during the post-Reconstruction era was the widespread use of violence by which whites reasserted political, economic, and social control. Lynching was the most obvious of these tools, but force was manifested in a variety of ways, including whites rioting through Black neighborhoods, such as the Wilmington Riot of 1898.

Many antilynching speakers followed the lines of argument set out in Bishop Henry McNeal Turner's 1893 speech "Justice or Emigration Should Be Our Watchword," delivered to the National Council of Colored Men. By its very definition, lynching was illegal and demonstrated the breakdown of law and order. The "theory of civilization," said Turner, is that a person suspected of committing a crime is arrested, tried, and convicted by a deliberate, impartial process. In contrast, those who lynched and took the law into their own hands were "bloody-handed murderers."

The most typically alleged cause of lynching was the charge that a Black man had raped a white woman, and Turner very directly addressed that issue. He offered no comfort for those who had actually committed such an outrageous crime, but he noted the absence of such crimes during the Civil War when white Southern men were away fighting and African American men had far more ample opportunity to commit such crimes. Turner pointedly reminded his audience how Southern white men had raped their Black female slaves with impunity. He also noted that white Southerners "have all the judges, and all the juries, and virtually all the lawyers, all the jails, all the penitentiaries, all the ropes, all the powder and all the guns." If there were the remotest possibility that an African American man were actually guilty of the crime he was charged with, who could doubt that he would be punished under "the law"?

In 1892, Ida B. Wells (later Wells-Barnett) emerged as an active voice who unwaveringly advanced a different argument against lynching. While many speakers couched their response conditionally—even *if* the allegations were true, lynching was itself still a crime—Wells attacked the very charge itself. Part owner of a newspaper in Memphis, Wells saw three of her friends lynched because they were the middle-class owners of the "Peoples Grocery" who had resisted the coercive actions of a white rival, a man whose illegal pressures were backed up by local law enforcement. Shortly thereafter, Wells published an editorial condemning lynching broadly. In the direct style that marked her public speaking as well, Wells wrote that "nobody in this section of the country believes the old threadbare lie that negro men rape white women." She went further, suggesting what she would later document, that many sexual relations between Black men and white women were consensual: "If Southern white men are not careful they will overreach themselves. . . . A conclusion will then be reached which will be very damaging to the moral reputation of their women." Incensed by the editorial and stirred up by local white-owned newspapers, looters ransacked and burned the offices of Wells's paper, the *Free Speech*. Wells was fortunately away in Chicago, and she never returned South.

Instead, Ida B. Wells began publishing and speaking about the issue of lynching. Her writings and speeches were remarkably similar. Both were journalistic in style. She spoke plainly, recounting the simple facts. She usually began with her own story of the Memphis lynchings of the grocery store owners and the destruction of her newspaper office. She would then recount the stories of other lynchings in intricate detail. She reported names, dates, places, times, witnesses present, and the reason given for why the mob lynched the victim. Her language was not particularly emotional, especially for the nineteenth century when flowery appeals were the norm for men as well as women. But her detailed descriptions of the tarring, feathering, burning, shooting, and hanging of the victims were gut-wrenchingly emotional. She painted a journalistic picture of the lynchings in an age before technology could readily capture the images in moving pictures.

Ida B. Wells also compiled voluminous and impeccable statistics about lynching. Using only reports from white-owned newspapers, she tabulated the number of lynchings over the previous decade and the offenses with which the victims had been charged. Of the 728 cases counted—clearly underreported—only one-third of the victims had been charged with sexual assault on a white woman. Despite the Southern white claim that the lynchers must be excused for their actions because of the "incendiary" nature of the crime, such was clearly not the case in most instances. Thirteen victims had been lynched for "quarreling with white men," ten for "making threats," and five for miscegenation. Will Lewis, reported Wells, was lynched in 1891 because "he was drunk and saucy with white folks." In testimony designed to provoke white prejudice, Wells described cases where Black men were lynched even when the sexual relations were consensual.

Wells lectured throughout the North during the remainder of the century as well as in the United Kingdom from 1893 to 1894. Her work yielded two results. First, her speeches and writings influenced other antilynching speakers to move from conditionally couching their arguments to asserting confidently that even the *charge* of rape—often unproven—was not the cause of the rise of lynching. Frederick Douglass's lecture "The Lessons of the Hour," delivered several times in 1894, is one such case. The claim that lynchings were a reaction to the crime of rape, said Douglass, was "utterly groundless, . . . a mere pretense, a sham, an excuse for fraud and violence, for persecution and a cloak for popular prejudice."

Second, through her speeches and writings, Wells lobbied other reform organizations to adopt antilynching platforms. Her argument with Frances Willard, president of the Woman's Christian Temperance Union (WCTU), was particularly public. When the WCTU passed an antilynching resolution that did more to condemn the alleged crime of rape than it did to say that the lynchings should be stopped, Wells criticized Willard about the organization's obvious prejudice. Although Willard never publicly admitted the WCTU's racial bias, the following year the group passed a resolution that removed the qualifying language and unequivocally condemned lynching. The organization renewed the resolution at each annual convention up through World War I. For her part, Wells remained the most outspoken voice of the antilynching cause and would be instrumental in the founding of the National Association for the Advancement of Colored People in 1909.

While Ida B. Wells campaigned for legal and social pressures to be put on the practice of lynching, other speakers advocated that African Americans resist violence with physical force. As noted above, speakers like Rev. Bryant advocated the formation of "defense leagues." In his 1889 speech "Organized Resistance Is Our Best Remedy," the journalist John E. Bruce argued that "organized resistance to organized resistance is the best remedy" for the problem. "Let the Negro require at the hand of every white murder in the South or elsewhere a life for a life," he told his audience: "If they burn our houses, burn theirs, if they kill our wives and children, kill theirs, pursue them relentlessly, meet force with force everywhere it is offered."

Other African American speakers urged emigration. After outlining the case against lynching and Southern white mob violence, Bishop Turner argued that because power was so concentrated in the hands of Southern whites—and white Americans generally for that matter—"talk about physical resistance is literal madness. Nobody but an idiot would give it a moment's thought." Yet "to passively remain here and occupy our present ignoble status" was "the submission of cowardice." The bravest course of action was to emigrate and make a new life elsewhere. Although he himself was partial to Africa as a destination, he held that any place—Africa, Canada, the Caribbean, Central America—was better than the United States. Others, like T. Thomas Fortune, proposed emigration away from the South but to "friendlier" regions of the United States. Where Kansas and Oklahoma had been the destination of choice for the Exodusters in the 1870s, as the century came to a close, the first major wave of migrations of Blacks to Northern cities was beginning.

The reassertion of almost total control by whites, supported through legal and illegal exertions of force, fueled the emigration of Blacks from the South. It also spelled the imminent demise of those who, like Booker T. Washington, sought cooperative progress with Southern whites. Although Washington would remain a force until his death in 1915, agitation would become the watchword of the day for almost every African American speaker in the new century.

# 4

# Lifting as We Climb

## Advancing the Cause

THE HISTORIAN JOHN HOPE FRANKLIN wrote that in 1896, there were 130,344 African Americans registered to vote in Louisiana. In 1900, after the adoption of a new state constitution, only 5,320 Blacks were still registered. Speaking to the National Negro Conference in 1909, Ida B. Wells-Barnett reported that while the number of Blacks lynched had appeared to crest in 1892, in the first decade of the twentieth century more than 800 African American men, women, and children had been lynched, and those numbers were surely undercounted.

With the new century came what has been called the "Great Migration," when many Blacks moved from the rural South to the urban North. From the census data, it appears that about 200,000 Blacks moved North between 1890 and 1910, and then some 300,000 or more over the next decade, although some estimates put the number as high as one million. Most Blacks continued to live in the South, but even there many moved from their farms to the city to find industrial jobs and escape the poverty of sharecropping. The Black population of Birmingham, Alabama, for example, increased by over 200 percent during these two decades.

African Americans could find jobs in the Northern cities during World War I, when young men Black and white were away in the army and foreign immigration had reduced to a trickle. However, many of those jobs were taken away from Blacks once the war was over. White Northern workers had never welcomed Black competition, preventing most African Americans from joining labor unions and creating de facto segregation of neighborhoods. Tensions flared and race riots broke out across the nation. The Chicago riot of 1919, for example, began when white youths stoned Eugene Williams, a Black youth swimming in Lake Michigan who had crossed the unofficial segregation line at Twenty-Ninth Street. In the end, twenty-three African Americans were killed, more than five hundred had been injured, and some one thousand African American homes had been burned.

In broad terms, two streams of African American public speaking dominated the first half of the twentieth century. One group of speakers continued the work of agitating for equality. They focused on organizing African Americans and lobbying white America for voting rights, civil rights, and equal protection under the law. The second group consisted of speakers who were less interested in speaking to white America but focused instead on the Black community itself. In general, these were charismatic speakers, individuals who could energize the mass audiences that new communication technologies now made possible.

## ORGANIZING AND AGITATING FOR EQUALITY AND INTEGRATION

With the dawn of the new century, African American leaders increasingly coalesced around the need for political agitation and organization. Although calls for industrial education and reforms within the Black community would continue, African American public speaking was largely characterized by those who demanded equal rights, equal justice, universal suffrage, and equal economic opportunity.

No figure better represented the emphasis on organization and agitation than W. E. B. Du Bois. A Harvard-trained PhD, Du Bois was a professor of history, sociology, and economics at Atlanta University at the turn of the century. Although he had earlier congratulated Booker T. Washington in 1895 on the latter's Cotton States Exposition speech, by 1903 he had written *The Souls of Black Folk*, which included a chapter, "Of Booker T. Washington and Others," that sharply criticized Washington's abandonment of claims to equal rights and suffrage. Instead, Du Bois called for the kind of agitation that had been advocated by Fortune, Crummell, Hope, and others.

Du Bois became increasingly active politically, delivering many speeches to audiences Black and white. His speeches usually read like papers delivered at an academic conference, with an emphasis on principles, reason, and evidence. In 1905, he helped found the Niagara Movement, often considered the precursor for the National Association for the Advancement of Colored People (NAACP). In speeches promoting the organization, Du Bois argued that the new association had learned from the failures of the past. He recognized that African Americans were too diverse a people to come together in one mass organization, so he focused on simplicity and "definiteness of aim" among the officers at the top of the organization. Du Bois set forward eight ideals, focused on universal rights, freedoms, and privileges.

"This is a large program," Du Bois acknowledged, as he said that the goals of the movement were to regain suffrage, stop lynching, improve education, open union doors, increase employment, gain access to public accommodations, and support a free and unbiased press. To the objections that other associations had previously adopted these goals and failed, Du Bois replied that it was all the more reason to try again. To the objections of those who said the United States would never admit equal treatment for Blacks, Du Bois replied that those equal rights would never be secured if African Americans did *not* try. He closed his speech in terms reminiscent of Henry Highland Garnet, by challenging the manhood of his audience. "Are we not men enough to protest," he asked, or will it be "proven true that out of ten millions of us there are only a baker's dozen who will follow these fifty Negro-Americans [who signed the Niagara declaration] and dare to stand up and be counted as demanding every single right that belongs to free American citizens?"

There were, in fact, many African Americans who supported Du Bois's organizing and who spoke in support of his program. Those who addressed these issues at meetings with white, Black, and mixed audiences were the Black intelligentsia of the day: ministers, professors, editors, lawyers, and authors. William Monroe Trotter, editor of the *Boston Guardian* and first African American to earn a Phi Beta Kappa key at Harvard, cofounded the Niagara Movement with Du Bois. William Pickens, a Yale graduate and dean of Morgan College in Maryland, was the field secretary for the NAACP. Archibald Grimké, a graduate of Harvard Law School, was a vice president of the NAACP. His brother Francis Grimké was another prominent activist of the day. Francis had graduated from Princeton Theological Seminary and served as pastor of the Fifteenth Street Presbyterian Church in Washington, D.C. James Weldon Johnson, author of *The Autobiography of an Ex-Colored Man* and the first Black professor at New York University, was the first executive secretary of the NAACP. Mordecai Johnson earned his doctorate of divinity at Howard University and served in a variety of academic posts before becoming the first Black president of Howard University in 1926, a position he held until 1960.

Nor was it only men who answered the call. Maria Baldwin, principal of the Agassiz School in Cambridge, Massachusetts, and Mary Church Terrell of Washington, D.C., attended the 1909 conference and were appointed to the Executive Committee. Josephine St. Pierre Ruffin, editor of *The Woman's Era*, was a charter member of the NAACP, as was Fannie Barrier Williams. Ida B. Wells-Barnett addressed the conference on "Lynching, Our National Crime," a speech that was shorter than her normal lecture but reiterated the "three salient facts" that her lectures usually put forward: "First: Lynching is color line murder; Second: Crimes against women is the excuse, not the cause; and Third: It is a national crime and requires a national remedy." To her considerable frustration, neither she nor Du Bois were initially named to the executive committee because they were considered "firebrands" who were fiercely opposed to Booker T. Washington. The lead organizers were concerned about alienating the many powerful white financial backers whom Washington had acquired. Significantly, however, both Du Bois and Wells-Barnett were soon appointed to the executive committee. Washington's hold was waning amid a commitment to political and legal action.

These were educated speakers who spoke in an educated fashion. Their vocabulary was large and their speeches well organized. Like Du Bois, they grounded their arguments in principles and the learned writers of the day. Although most did not include the voluminous evidence typical of Ida B. Wells-Barnett's speeches, they usually provided evidence for their claims. For example, in Du Bois's speech "Politics and Industry," delivered to the 1909 convention, he made the claim that placing workers who had unequal rights and political power in the same jobs would always lead to conflict. As evidence, he pointed to the strike by white Georgia railroad workers who tended the boiler fires on the steam locomotives. The white firemen were striking because Black firemen who had greater seniority with the railroad were being assigned the more profitable runs. In a politically segregated culture, Du Bois pointed out, the white firemen, even if they had just been hired, found this situation intolerable. While the specific arguments and evidence might change depending upon whether these speakers addressed a Black, white, or racially mixed audience, the style of speaking remained consistent—at least in the recorded speeches still available.

In general, African American women spoke about the same issues as Black men, with some special attention in support of education for girls and boys. As noted above, many of these women were by profession educators, and so they often evidenced a particular interest in improving educational opportunities for African Americans. Women also agitated for better job opportunities for African American women. The new century saw new employment opportunities for women, such as typing, stenography, and nursing, but those positions were rarely open to African American women. In "What It Means to Be Colored in the Capital of the U.S.," Mary Church Terrell told her women's club audience about the African American department store clerk who had been light enough to "pass" as white but had been "found out" to be African American. At first, Terrell said, the Jewish store owner had refused the protests of his employees who did not want to work alongside an African American. But when they threatened to tell his customers and foment a boycott, the owner said he was "forced" to let the young worker go. Can't those of you who are employers provide more and better positions for African American women? Terrell asked. It was the same question Maria Miller Stewart had asked her audience in 1832.

African American women also spoke on behalf of universal and woman suffrage. Often marginalized within the mainstream woman suffrage organizations, they were still afforded some opportunities to take the platform at national meetings. At the 1900 biennial session of the National American Woman Suffrage Association (NAWSA), for example, Mary Church Terrell spoke on "The Justice of Woman Suffrage," a lecture she would give in various forms over the next decade and that appeared in essay form in a 1912 issue of *The Crisis*, the national publication of the NAACP. In her speech to NAWSA, Terrell reminded her audience of how men have all the advantages in financial opportunities and control, outside the home and in the marriage laws.

Like those agitating for the restoration of African American voting rights, Terrell observed that "these unjust discriminations will ever remain, until the source from which they spring—the political disfranchisement of woman—shall be removed." Similarly, Terrell ironically noted the gap between the nation's principles and its practices: "Before the world we pose to-day as a government whose citizens have the right to life, liberty and the pursuit of happiness. And yet, in spite of these lofty professions and noble sentiments, the present policy of the government is to hold one-half of its citizens in legal subjection to the other, without being able to assign good and sufficient reasons for such a flagrant violation of the very principles upon which [the nation] was founded."

For Terrell as for all these speakers, the relationship of woman suffrage with voting rights for Blacks was clear. The national irony of refusing to grant women the right to vote was the same irony as its systematic discrimination against African American suffrage. In her 1912 essay in *The Crisis*, Terrell noted that on her recent lecture tour, she had frequently discussed woman suffrage, arguing that the two suffrage reforms were identical in purpose. "What could be more absurd," she asked rhetorically, "than to see one group of human beings who are denied rights which they are trying to secure for themselves working to prevent another group from obtaining the same rights? For the very arguments which are advanced against granting the right of suffrage to women are offered by those who have disfranchised colored men."

Yet the arguments of African American women did not gain much traction among white women suffragists. African American women's organizations were not allowed to affiliate with the NAWSA, and in many states whites-only chapters were sanctioned. W. E. B. Du Bois, an outspoken supporter of woman suffrage, characterized the NAWSA position as "Do not touch the Negro problem. It will offend the South." But in November of 1912, Du Bois spoke to the association, attempting again to attract white women's support for universal suffrage. Echoing Elizabeth Cady Stanton's famous "The Solitude of Self," Du Bois argued that the reason a democracy is the most just form of government is because nobody can speak for anyone else; each individual alone knows his or her sufferings and wants. Throughout the speech, Du Bois raised the objections that were raised against women getting the vote—they are not educated enough, others can vote for them, they do not want the ballot. Those are the same objections to giving the right to vote freely to all African Americans, he noted. The changing world presented the engaged citizen with many important and perplexing problems, but "the cure for the ills of democracy," said Du Bois, "is seen to be more democracy."

*The First Postwar Period*

Although African American speakers were never able to fully bridge woman suffrage and universal suffrage in the minds of their white audiences, World War I amplified their appeals to the principles of democracy. The war experience also spurred the work of organizing, political agitation and legal action, and the public speaking that accompanied those efforts.

The union leader A. Philip Randolph was one of the most prominent speakers who promoted the idea of organization within the Black community. The son of an A.M.E. minister, Randolph initially pursued an acting career in New York City, but there he became involved with the Socialist Party. In 1917, at the age of twenty-two, he cofounded *The Messenger*, which he described in its inaugural issue as "the first voice of radical, revolutionary, economic and political action among Negroes in America." At the same time, Randolph began working as a union organizer, beginning with elevator operators in 1917 and organizing Black dockworkers in 1919 into the National Brotherhood of Workers in America. After *The Messenger* experienced financial difficulties, Randolph moved into labor organizing full time. In 1925, he became president of the Brotherhood of Sleeping Car Porters (BSCP). For twelve years, the BSCP battled the corporate giant Pullman Company for better pay and working conditions for its members, and in 1937 the company finally agreed to a deal that significantly improved the compensation it paid to the porters. This signal victory provided Randolph with stronger leverage to promote the integration of unions across the trades and to agitate broadly for equal rights.

In his speeches to white-controlled labor unions, Congress, and other predominantly white audiences, Randolph appealed to their sense of justice and self-interest. "You can't [build a stronger labor movement] by putting your foot down on one worker, because he happens to be Black or white," he told the American Federation of Labor (AFL) in 1936. To Black audiences, Randolph stressed the need for them to actively fight discrimination and prejudice. "Securing [our rights]," he told the National Negro Conference of 1937, "is the task of the Negro. Freedom is never given; it is won. And the Negro people must win their freedom. They must achieve justice. This involves struggle, continuous struggle." More than just a will to fight was needed, however. To be successful, the struggle for equal rights, like labor representation, must be organized: "True liberation can be acquired and maintained only when the Negro people possess power; and power is the product and flower of organization—organization of the masses."

Organizing and fighting could not be done without passion, however. Whether the cause was better pay and better hours, the integration of a union or equal rights, those who agitated would meet resistance, and that resistance was often physical, accompanied by violence. Randolph was an ideal speaker to bring the necessary emotion to the moment. Biographer Paula Pfeffer wrote that Randolph was physically impressive, with a powerful speaking voice. His early training in acting and as a political speaker on the street corners of New York City had given him commanding skills as a speaker. At key moments, he emphasized short, staccato sentences that encouraged and urged on his audience. As he declaimed in "Call to the March" in 1941, "What shall we do? What a Dilemma! What a runaround! What a disgrace! What a blow below the belt! Though battered and bruised, we are not beaten, broken or bewildered."

While some speakers like Randolph concentrated on organizing African Americans, others focused on political agitation. President Wilson's arguments in support of fighting the Great War, or World War I, provided principles that African American public speakers sought to use as levers for securing their rights. Wilson had declared that the war was being fought to "make the world safe for democracy," and a controlling principle of his proposed Fourteen Points for Peace was that national boundaries should be determined by the "historic" peoples who occupied a region and that any national government should represent the "autonomous" population of the nation. This was the principle of "self-determination"—for example, that the Arabs should govern Arabia and the Serbians should govern Serbia. Through self-determination, Wilson hoped to resolve the ongoing conflicts in the Balkans, in Eastern Europe, and in the European-controlled colonies around the world.

Speaking to the NAACP national conference in 1919, James Weldon Johnson gave voice to the frustrations common to the assembled African Americans. During "the great war for democracy," Johnson said, "there were those in my own race who thought and taught" that if African Americans fought in the war and supported the war effort, "the war would do the rest" about securing them their rights. After all, "we have just finished the great war for democracy." But "the war is over, and no miracle has happened." Johnson advised pragmatism: "Miracles of that kind never happen. If loyalty to the nation and fighting its battles could give the American negro his full rights he would have had them long ago."

Although the bulk of his speech was devoted to the advancement of American Blacks, at the start of the speech Johnson discussed the Pan-African movement. All Blacks should unite in demanding that the principle of self-determination be extended to Africa, he argued. The European colonization of Africa must end, just as the Versailles peace talks were ending the Turkish colonization of Arabia and the Austrian colonization of the Balkans. Johnson said he was under no illusion that the peace negotiators would address self-determination or democratic rights for African Americans in the United States South, but to treat the African peoples with equality and dignity would be an important step in the right direction.

While Johnson laid out the case for voting rights and against Jim Crow segregation, the issue of lynching remained a salient point of agitation for political rights and protection. While white and Black soldiers were abroad, fighting together for democracy, he noted that in 1918 fifty-eight African Americans were lynched, including five women. They were not simply killed or hanged, he pointed out; they were often burned, even tortured with red-hot irons. Johnson reported that when he discussed a recent case of a Tennessee torture and lynching with President Wilson, the president remarked that he "had not heard of it." How, Johnson asked ironically, could it be "that in this great, free, enlightened democracy a human being could be burned alive at the stake and the head of the nation not even hear about it"? "But," Johnson vowed, "we are going to make them hear about it, not only the head of the nation, but we are going to put the raw, naked, brutal facts of this question before the conscience of the whole nation until we make it sick." *Thirty Years of Lynching in the United States* was published and distributed by the NAACP, and the Dyer Anti-Lynching Bill was introduced in the U.S. Senate, but it was never voted upon.

In speech after speech during the interwar period, speakers like the Grimké brothers, Terrell, Du Bois, Mordecai Johnson, James Weldon Johnson, Bethune, and others put before Black, white, and mixed audiences the case for equal rights and equal protection. Mordecai Johnson's "The Faith of the American Negro," delivered at Harvard University in 1922, was a haunting history of African Americans' contributions to the United States, their persistent hope for better days to come, and their continued, crushing disappointment in their government and their fellow citizens. James Weldon Johnson's "Our Democracy and the Ballot," given at a 1923 dinner honoring then-Congressman Fiorello La Guardia of New York, put forward yet again the claims of African Americans on the bases of citizenship, Christianity, and basic humanity. "The Negro," Johnson told his audience, "stands as the supreme test of the civilization, the Christianity, and the common decency of the American people."

Mary McLeod Bethune, the founder of Bethune-Cookman Institute in Florida, made a similar case throughout the interwar period. In her speeches as an education leader, president of the National Association of Colored Women (NACW), and member of Franklin Roosevelt's "Kitchen" Cabinet, Bethune emphasized the importance of education. Education for African Americans would help them secure a better place in America, and education for white Americans was the key to eliminating race prejudice. Cooperation and integration were the keys to improving the condition of African Americans, and she argued in support of both throughout the interwar period. However, only a firm commitment to speaking out against race prejudice would secure such cooperation. "It is our duty to stand against segregation and discrimination," she told the NACW in her 1926 presidential address: "Denied equal share in the fruits of our sacrificing and suffering, we have protested. We shall protest, and protest again."

Preeminent among those who spoke on behalf of legal rights and integration was Thurgood Marshall. In 1933, Marshall graduated from Howard Law School, and while he began his career in private practice, in 1934 he began working pro bono with the Baltimore chapter of the NAACP. The NAACP had formed the Legal Defense Fund (LDF), a unit that sought out

Phyllis Wheatley Club, Buffalo, New York, 1905. Library of Congress.

and prosecuted cases involving civil rights and discrimination. Speaking to the NAACP national convention, Marshall summarized the philosophy of the LDF:

> We must not be delayed by people who say "the time is not ripe," nor should we proceed with caution for fear of destroying the "status quo." Persons who deny to us our civil rights should be brought to justice now. Many people believe the time is always "ripe" to discriminate against Negroes. All right then—the time is always "ripe" to bring them to justice. The responsibility for the enforcement of these statutes rests with every American citizen regardless of race or color. However, the real job has to be done by the Negro population with whatever friends of the other races are willing to join us.

Marshall's public speaking during this era pursued three ends: to secure emotional and financial support for the NAACP's pursuit of legal cases, to recruit individuals who were willing to stand as test cases, and to make the case, both inside and outside the courtroom, that African Americans were being denied their legal rights. In time, Marshall became the preeminent attorney for the NAACP, and he would ultimately argue thirty-two cases before the Supreme Court. He would win twenty-nine of those cases.

Behind the legal scaffolding of discrimination, however, there always lurked racial prejudice, and those who spoke for equal rights invariably found themselves confronting, either implicitly or explicitly, the race prejudices of most white Americans. In 1929, W. E. B. Du Bois accepted an invitation from the Chicago Forum Council to debate Lothrop Stoddard on the question "Should the Negro Be Encouraged to Seek Cultural Equality?" Stoddard, who had earned a PhD in political science from Harvard University, was the highly popular author of books such as *The Rising Tide of Color*. Stoddard argued that the white, European race was culturally superior to all other races and that the Nordic "sub-race" was the highest tier among whites. He argued that the Nordic sub-race needed to protect itself from the growing populations of colored peoples and needed to assert white control over the world. Stoddard was a Social Darwinist, arguing that Darwin's principle of "survival of the fittest" could be applied to races as well.

Social Darwinism was a pernicious philosophy that argued that if an ethnic group was poor or politically disenfranchised, it was because they *should* be poor or politically disenfranchised. The philosophy provided a pseudo-scientific justification of the racial status quo and was promoted by many white academics such as Stoddard. Du Bois began his refutation by commenting upon the absurdity of the topic. Why shouldn't everyone be encouraged to pursue the best education and culture that they can? Only in America, with its obsession about keeping the colored peoples down, he said, would the question even be asked.

Du Bois reminded the audience how far African Americans had advanced since slavery, despite all their impediments. He pointed to African American intellectual achievements, both present and historical. He noted that the "science" of Social Darwinism was completely unproven. He also returned to the absurdity of the question by noting that he himself, with his mixed-race heritage, could just as well stand in front of the audience as a representative of the "Nordic" race. Regarding the shibboleth of social equality and Stoddard's demand that the white race be kept "pure," Du Bois sharply summarized the hypocrisy of that position:

> [The "Nordic" race has] been responsible for more intermixture of races than any other people, ancient or modern, and they have inflicted this miscegenation on helpless, unwilling slaves by force, fraud and insult; and this is the folk that today has the impudence to turn on the darker races when they demand a share of civilization, and cry; "'You shall not marry our daughters!' The blunt, crude reply is: Who in hell asked to marry your daughters? If this race problem must be reduced to a matter of sex, what we demand is the right to protect the decency of our own daughters.

Du Bois concluded his remarks with a confrontational challenge. Stoddard's position was that the "white nations" of the world must control the "darker" nations. "If you are going to keep them in their place," Du Bois observed, "you are going to do it by brute force." "Remember," he warned, "you are standing before the whole world, with hundreds of darker millions.... Have you got the force?"

Two political speakers embodied the shifting eddies of the interwar environment. In 1928, Oscar Stanton De Priest became the first African American representative to Congress elected from outside the South. De Priest had been born in Alabama, raised in Ohio, and made his wealth in Chicago as a contractor and real estate investor. He served three terms as a Republican member of the U.S. House representing the Illinois First District, centered in Chicago. Meanwhile, Northern Democrats, with Eleanor Roosevelt in the forefront, were wooing African American voters. In 1934, De Priest lost his reelection bid to another African American, Democrat Arthur Mitchell. Mitchell, too, had been born in Alabama. He had attended Tuskegee Institute and Columbia University and passed the Illinois state bar. In 1934, he had switched from the Republican Party to the Democratic Party. He would be elected to four terms, choosing not to run again in 1942.

During their fourteen years in the House of Representatives, De Priest and Mitchell were the only African Americans to serve in the U.S. Congress. Historian Kenneth Mann wrote that De Priest recognized that he was an important symbol for African Americans, and so he accepted many of the numerous speaking invitations he received. When he spoke at Bethel A.M.E. Church in Harlem, New York, in 1929, the *Chicago Defender* reported that "thousands lined the sidewalks" and were keenly disappointed when they had to be turned away. De Priest advocated broadly for equal rights, calling for enforcement of the Fourteenth and Fifteenth Amendments, but also on behalf of specific issues that carried important symbolic weight, such as the appointment of a Black cadet to West Point and pensions for ex-slaves. "America never will be what it was intended to be," he told the House in 1934, "until every citizen in America has his just rights under the Constitution."

De Priest's message to Blacks echoed other mainstream African American speakers. "Learn to stand on your own feet, if you want Race leadership," he told his audience in Harlem because "the day is past when the white man will fight your battles." At a speech in Providence, Rhode Island, his message was like that of Randolph, as he told his audience that "the only way you will ever do anything or get anywhere is by organizing and standing together." In a pragmatic move, the Republican congressman urged his Southern Black audiences to switch to the Democratic Party because the Republicans had no political power in the South.

De Priest's successor, Arthur Mitchell, was cut from a different cloth. A member of the Democratic political machine in Chicago and mindful that the First Ward still had a majority of white voters, Mitchell pledged to faithfully represent his district rather than the African American race as a whole. In his first two terms in office, Mitchell's public speaking was characterized by an accommodationist stance in the tradition of Booker T. Washington. He urged Southern Blacks not to migrate to the Northern cities, sponsored an antilynching bill that competed with the NAACP's more aggressive bill, criticized Howard University as being too welcoming to radical—that is, "Communist"—political voices, and attacked A. Philip Randolph and the National Negro Congress for their radical political stance. Only toward the end of his political career, as African Americans once again went to war for the United States, did Mitchell begin criticizing Southern Democrats and their web of racial discrimination.

*World War II and the Second Postwar Period*

With the outbreak of World War II, African American speakers once again faced the dilemma of fighting for a country that denied them their own rights. They remembered the promise of World War I and the crushing disappointment of coming home to a segregated nation. On the other hand, Adolf Hitler was the most powerful and virulent social Darwinist the world had faced. Most African American speakers once again supported the nation in its hour of military need, but they did so more warily than they had in World War I.

A. Philip Randolph spearheaded the move to leverage the war into tangible gains for African Americans. In 1941, before U.S. entry into the war but while the nation was rapidly increasing military spending to serve as munitions supplier to England and the Allies, Randolph combined his calls for mass action with his drive for labor equality by lobbying President Franklin Roosevelt for equal job opportunities for African Americans in the defense industry. To secure concessions from Roosevelt, Randolph threatened to call on African Americans to march on Washington. Federal defense money, he argued, should not be spent to uphold discriminatory employment practices. Adapting Franklin Roosevelt's own language from the "Four Freedoms" speech, Randolph declared in his "Call to the March" speech that African Americans were also demanding "freedom from want! Freedom from fear! Freedom from Jim Crow!"

Randolph's threatened march came at a time when Roosevelt was fending off the "America First" isolationist movement, and the union leader's agitation yielded the creation of the Fair Employment Practices Commission (FEPC) in 1941. The purpose of the FEPC was twofold: to ensure fair hiring practices that would not discriminate against African Americans and to guarantee fair treatment in the workplace once they were hired. Yielding to pressure from Southern congressional leaders, in 1942 Roosevelt assigned the FEPC to the War Production Board, which severely limited the power of the commission. Randolph again threatened a mass demonstration and strike in Washington.

In September of that year, he delivered the keynote address to the policy conference of the March on Washington movement. "Rights must be taken," he told the audience, "we must develop huge demonstrations because the world is used to big dramatic affairs." Like Gandhi's movement against the British colonial power in India, the march and coordinated demonstrations around the nation would be nonviolent. "The Negro masses will be disciplined in struggle," Randolph said, "some of us will be put in jail and court battles may ensue, but this will give the Negro masses a sense of their importance and value as citizens and as fighters in the Negro liberation movement." This was a call to march in mass protest against the continued practices of unequal treatment. "Our feet are set in the path toward equality," he declared, "economic, political and social and racial. Equality is the heart and essence of democracy, freedom and justice."

Once again, President Roosevelt responded to the pressure applied by Randolph, organizations like the NAACP and the Urban League, and individuals who had access to the White House such as Mary McLeod Bethune. He now made the FEPC an individual agency within the cabinet, and by the end of the war, African American employment in the defense industry had more than doubled, increasing to 8 percent. In 1946, the FEPC was disbanded, but the model of mass action—even though only threatened in the 1940s—had proven successful. In 1946, the same year the FEPC was abolished, President Harry S. Truman finally yielded to the argument that Blacks could not fight for democracy around the world in segregated military units. In 1963, it would be Randolph's March on Washington organization that provided the structure that coordinated the August 28 March on Washington for Jobs and Freedom.

Post–World War II public speaking by African Americans was especially influenced by international affairs. The worldwide destruction of World War II, the threat of nuclear war, and the rise of Communism in Russia and China invited a rise of internationalism in the United States, unlike the spirit of isolationism that had followed World War I. In 1946, speaking to the integrated Southern Youth Legislature in Columbia, South Carolina, Du Bois highlighted the incoherence of having the state's native son James Byrnes serving as the secretary of state. Du Bois noted that Byrnes was promoting freedom and democracy around the world as an antidote to Communism, yet neither of those was being practiced in the U.S. South.

"The concern about American racial practices seems especially strong among the two thirds of the world that is darker-skinned," Thurgood Marshall said in a 1953 lecture on "Segregation and Desegregation," as *Brown v. Board of Education* was being argued before the Supreme Court. America's internationalism allowed Marshall to approvingly quote white leaders like ambassador to India Chester Bowles and Vice President Richard Nixon, both of whom argued that American foreign policy would not be effective if racial discrimination continued at home. "Almost invariably," Marshall quoted Bowles as saying, the number one question he heard abroad was, "What about America's treatment of the Negro?"

Speaking the next year at the same lecture series hosted by Dillard University in New Orleans, Ralph Bunche made a plain case for the relationship between U.S. internationalism and equal rights for African Americans. Bunche earned his PhD in political science at Harvard University, taught at Howard University, and then served as a U.S. diplomat with the United Nations. In 1950, he had received the Nobel Peace Prize for his work negotiating a Mideast peace treaty.

Bunche argued that "blind prejudices—racial, religious, national and cultural" were "poison" that had been and would be exploited by "political demagogues" in order to acquire and maintain control. These prejudices were the root causes of the misery and destruction wrought by World War II and the rise of totalitarian governments. "It is in the minds and hearts of men and women that wars are born," he said, "and it is only through the minds and hearts of men and women that peace can ever be won."

Prejudice is cultural, he said, nurtured by ignorance. We can only be prejudiced against that of which we have no knowledge. Knowledge would come from personal experience, and so breaking down racial barriers was imperative. In support of this claim, Bunche recounted a series of personal experiences, ranging from his time on the college basketball team to recent state dinners. In this way, the purpose of racial integration was not simply to treat African Americans as equal citizens but to engender tolerance and respect for each other, and thus fulfill the principle of equality that sat at the heart of the American creed:

Our nation is a union of peoples more diversified in origin than any society in history. . . . We have set out on a great experiment on these shores, the greatest, I believe, in that peoples of all races, colors, creeds and cultures can live and work and play together and be welded into a firm unity by the sheer force of a great and compelling ideal—the democratic way of life. . . . I believe that differences in race, in religion and in culture enrich the society, . . . coming together as free men in a common cause and with common interests, ideals and objectives.

For Bunche as for many speakers of this and later eras, the integration of individuals from diverse backgrounds and ethnicities was the foundation upon which American greatness would be built. Integrating African Americans into society—through schools, employment, neighborhoods, the voting booth, and political office—would be the driving force of the modern civil rights movement.

## SPEAKING WITHIN THE COMMUNITY

While many speakers agitated for integration and equal treatment across the broader American community, an important group of powerful speakers emerged parallel to the "establishment" speakers like Du Bois, Bethune, Randolph, and Marshall. These were important speakers who were more inwardly focused on African Americans. They sought to inspire the Black community and thus help African Americans pull together and rise up together. Typically, these were energetic speakers. Although not all of them were religious leaders, most drew on the traditions of Black preaching, employing irony, humor, imperative demands, call-and-response, and a compelling style of delivery to build an enthusiastic response from their audience. Through the new mass communication technologies of newspapers, radio, and loudspeakers, and with the increasing concentration of African Americans in urban areas, the most successful speakers could attract large and loyal audiences, and through their speaking they built charismatic bonds with their followers.

The best known example of this type of speaker was Marcus Garvey, who rose to prominence early in the interwar period. Born in Jamaica in 1887, Garvey was a printing shop foreman who ran afoul of management when he sided with his workers during a strike. He immigrated first to Central America and then to London. In each new home he became politically active, either starting or working for a race-oriented newspaper. In 1916, he embarked on a year-long speaking tour of the United States that included visits to thirty-eight states. The following year, he settled in Harlem, and on June 12 of that year, in New Bethel Church, he delivered his famed Liberty League address, a speech that catapulted him to the attention of African Americans. In that speech, Garvey called for new leadership that would liberate the race through a militant assertion of control over its own destiny. Garvey was a Pan-Africanist, a Black nationalist speaking in the tradition of Delany, Chief Sam, Blyden, Turner, and Crummell. Garvey argued that Blacks could never be fully liberated and equal until they returned to their homeland in Africa and reestablished their own government there.

Building on the attention his Liberty League address drew, Garvey formed the Universal Negro Improvement Association (UNIA), which rapidly grew to a membership of hundreds of thousands. He launched the successful and influential *Negro World*, and his speeches at UNIA functions drew widespread attention. Committed to a platform of Black self-help and separatism, UNIA was part business operation, part social organization, and part political agitator, and Garvey was the face of the organization in speech and print. Its most famous business operation was its cargo and passenger steamship corporation, the Black Star Line. The line was envisioned as a highly visible business that would connect Blacks around the world, demonstrate their economic acumen, and provide the means to help them move back to Africa, their homeland.

*Negro World* played a significant role in the rapid growth of UNIA and in the popularity of Garvey's speeches. Distributed worldwide, the paper had an audience of about a half million readers. In contrast to the cultural drumbeat from the white media that the African continent was "backward" and "uncivilized," the readers of the *Negro World* were provided with articles that described Africa's storied past and great accomplishments. They were also treated to stories that condemned European colonization of Africa and attacked those of African descent who cooperated with whites or who promoted integration. Each week, a column written by Marcus Garvey appeared on the front page. Through this forum, Garvey advanced his ideas of race pride, the economic uplift of the Black community, and the necessity of reclaiming the African continent, themes he regularly developed in his speeches as well.

Marcus Garvey's speeches were thus opportunities for his followers to come together and hear in person the ideas and programs they already believed. His speeches were celebrations of community, and the UNIA meetings were spectacular events. The organization purchased Liberty Hall, a massive auditorium that could hold six thousand people, although sometimes they held their rallies outside in order to accommodate even larger crowds. Loudspeakers now made these mass meetings possible.

Marcus Garvey speaking at Liberty Hall, 1920. Library of Congress.

Preceding his speech, a band played, marchers entered in uniform, and songs were sung. James Weldon Johnson gave this account of the regular Sunday evening meetings of UNIA:

> Meetings at Liberty Hall were conducted with an elaborate liturgy. The moment for the entry of the Provisional President into the auditorium was solemn; a hushed and expectant silence on the throng, the African Legion and Black Nurses flanking the long aisle coming to attention, the band and audience joining in the hymn: "Long Live Our President": and Garvey, surrounded by his guard of honor from the Legion, marching majestically through the double line and mounting the rostrum; it was impressive if for no other reason than the way in which it impressed the throng.

Garvey was not eloquent in the tradition of a Frederick Douglass or Frances Harper, but his energy and arguments in support of African American interests were enthusiastically received. One observer from outside UNIA thought Garvey was "one of the most powerful personalities" he had ever seen on the public speaking platform. The audience's enthusiasm was captured in a 1920 *New York Times* headline that read, "Cheering

Negroes Hail Black Nation." The reporter wrote that the crowd's "applause shook the building."

Garvey reminded his audience that they were powerful. In his editorials and his speeches, he recounted stories of Africa's historic greatness and he drew attention to African Americans' strength. In his 1922 "The Principles of the Universal Negro Improvement Association," for example, he told his audience seven times that Blacks were "four hundred million strong" and that together they could achieve the "redemption of our own country, our motherland, Africa." He reminded them that the Black soldiers in World War I had been called by their enemy "Black hell fighters," and he declared that Blacks were ready to fight for control of Africa. "If it takes manpower," he said, "if it takes scientific intelligence, if it takes education of any kind, or if it takes blood, then the four hundred million Negroes of the world have it." Black pride meant that Garvey could confidently demand first-class citizenship: "Why should [the white man], because of some racial prejudice, keep me down and why should I concede to him the right to rise above me and to establish himself as my permanent master? . . . I refuse to stultify my ambition, and every true Negro refuses to stultify his ambition to suit any one."

Full citizenship was only possible, however, if Blacks controlled their own destiny as a race and as a community. Speaking from his experiences in Jamaica, Central America, London, and the United States, Garvey argued that "when our [Blacks'] interests clash with those of the ruling faction [whichever race is in control of a nation] then we find that we have absolutely no rights." The philosophy of self-determination that had permeated the World War I experience applied to Black nationalism as well: "We are not engaged in domestic politics, in church building or in social-uplift work, but we are engaged in nation building."

Along with this positive message of pride and self-determination, however, Garvey wove a lesser, but critical, theme that challenged Blacks to do better. Like a good sermon that chastises the congregation's sins, Garvey was critical of the recent past: "We have been satisfied to allow ourselves to be led, educated, to be directed by the other fellow, allowed ourselves for the last five hundred years to be a race of followers." His criticism of Black leadership did not endear him to most of the established leadership, but his followers were enthusiastic and loyal. Those who were proud to be "Garveyites" continued long after his imprisonment for mail fraud in 1925 and deportation from the United States in 1927. As biographer Edmund David Cronon argued, Garvey's major contribution was fundamentally personal: "More than any other single leader he helped to give [Blacks] everywhere a reborn feeling of collective pride and a new awareness of individual worth."

Garvey was not the only such speaker to build a mass audience, and it should be remembered that, as historian Wilson Jeremiah Moses noted in *Black Messiahs and Uncle Toms*, what Garvey did was not new. Moses observed that Garvey "preserved and popularized a variety of Black thought that had been popular with the Black masses" since at least Reconstruction. Other speakers, like Garvey, also attracted large followings as they blended criticism of current behavior with exhortative appeals to Black pride and self-worth. Most came from backgrounds as religious leaders, like Noble Drew Ali, J. M Gates, A. W. Nix, "Sweet Daddy" Grace, Father Divine, and C. L. Franklin, but their speaking was no longer confined to churches, auditoriums, and street corners. Records of abridged sermons or parts of sermons were immensely popular in the 1920s and 1930s. According to Simmons and Thomas, one-quarter of all the recorded sermons sold prior to 1943 were recorded by Reverend J. M. Gates.

These speakers primarily employed the Black folk-preaching style. Their speeches were emotionally evocative, alternately bringing consternation and joy to their audiences. The speeches were usually built around stories, and the stories were used to illustrate the speaker's points and to apply those points to the hearer's life. There was a great deal of repetition used, so that the audience could follow along and begin to anticipate what the speaker would say next. Some of the repetition was in the specific phrase—such as at the beginning of the sentence (anaphora) or at the end of the sentence (epistrophe). Other repetition was created by structuring the speech into parallel structure or parallel contrasts, like antithesis. Sometimes the drawn-out delivery would become singing; other times it would become whooping, a more chant-like sound. Sometimes the call-and-response in the background of the sermon would morph into the choir singing the response. Other times the choir would be singing a countermelody.

When these speakers were heard live, with an extended time to work with, they typically developed a series of climactic, emotionally evocative "runs." Each one would build higher than the last until the speech reached a grand climax. Because the records could only run around three minutes, the sermon typically "began" at what would normally be the "end" of a live performance. On these recordings, the speaker and "audience" would re-create the dramatic climax.

As was usual in an oral tradition, ideas for sermons and speeches were often shared and imitated by these speakers. In 1927, A.W. Nix recorded "The Black Diamond Express to Hell," while J. M. Gates released "Hell

Bound Express Train." Both sermons were structured similarly. In each there was a train bound for Hell that was picking up passengers at a variety of stations, each station named for some type of sin. In his sermon, Gates began by naming the sinners who were getting on board the Hell Bound Express: lawyers, gamblers, drunkards, highway robbers, and smokers. He then took the train to particular locations associated with sin, particularized to his African American audience. The train stopped at Fourth Street in New Orleans, Beale Street in Memphis, and Eighth Street in Birmingham, Alabama. It continued on to similar streets in Atlanta, Chicago, Detroit, and Harlem. "I can hear the damnation passengers when they cry: *Woe is me*," he told the audience. There was no escape for those passengers, however, because eternal damnation was waiting for them on a new street, in "the burning city of hell."

For his Black Diamond Express sermon, Nix recorded three discs, front and back, and so the composite recording ran for over twenty minutes. On the first four sides, Nix described each station the train came to, with each stop featuring a particular sin. The train began at Drunkardsville and from there moved on to Liars Avenue, Deceiversville, Conjuration Station, Confusion Junction, and so on. Many of the sins he listed—lying, drinking, gambling—were staples of such sermons. Nix, however, also applied some of the sins specifically to his church-going audience. For example, one station was "Fight Town." There, the train was picking up "a big crowd of church fighters." These were the people who, he said, never went to prayer meeting, Sunday school, morning service, and the like, only showing up when there was a church business meeting, where they simply caused trouble. Similarly, at "Stealin' Town" the train for hell was picking up the "church thieves" who were always begging money from the church and showing up for church dinners, but never supporting the church with their own money when they had some.

Nix's Black Diamond Express sermon addressed the needs of the broader community as well. "Murder's Row" included passengers who would "murder your feelings and destroy your reputation." At the "Cheating Town" stop, Nix preached the golden rule for doing business in the neighborhood. To avoid being picked up at the "Dishonest Camp" station, his audience needed to pay their debts, and the "Gossiping Town" station was self-explanatory. Toward the end of the "station stops," Nix shifted to geographic stations as, like Gates, he listed streets in cities like Memphis, New Orleans, Atlanta, Chicago, and Detroit where the nightclubs were located. The last third of the sermon was in dialogue form, as Nix gave voice to sinners who were resisting his message, only to find themselves pleading for a way off of the train at the very last minute. Nix then called his hearers to answer the call of salvation and come down to the altar to confess their conversion.

Particularly notable among these speakers were Noble Drew Ali, Sweet Daddy Grace, and Father Divine. Few sermons of Noble Drew Ali were recorded, although he published his theology in *The Holy Koran of the Moorish Science Temple*. He founded the first African American Islamic Society temple in Newark, New Jersey, in 1913, and until his death in 1929 he toured cities preaching race pride and Black nationalism and establishing Moorish Scientist temples. He rejected the label "negro," arguing that African Americans should be called "Moors." One of his followers was Elijah Muhammad, who would later establish the Nation of Islam.

Marcelino Manoel da Graca, better known as Sweet Daddy Grace, was a widely influential Pentecostal preacher. His sermons featured bands, choirs, singing, and members of the congregation speaking in tongues. Healing and full-immersion baptisms were also important elements of the audience's experience. Daddy Grace's extravagant lifestyle was often criticized, but for many of his followers such wealth represented the prosperity to which they could aspire, and like many of the Black churches and Garvey's UNIA, Daddy Grace's United House of Prayer for All People churches were part local-business operation, part social services provider. Through his inspirational preaching and his church's everyday involvement in the people's lives, his public speaking helped create and foster community in the growing cities like Charlotte, North Carolina; Washington, D.C.; and Los Angeles.

There were also some speakers, like Father Divine, who consciously promoted racial integration. Born somewhere in the deep South as George Baker, by 1917 he had moved to Harlem, where he was preaching race harmony, peace, self-help, and prosperity in the here and now. His places of worship were called Peace Missions, and his sermons invariably began with the salutation "Peace, everyone," and ended "I thank you, Peace." Father Divine denounced racial and ethnic prejudice and argued that only an America built on true equality and democracy could bring heaven to earth. In the interim, prosperity was available for those who believed and gave themselves to God. He also preached that his followers should not marry and ultimately argued that he himself was divine. His Peace Missions provided social services to the community, especially free meals, and they also established businesses in the community that supported the church's work and provided followers with employment. In 1919, he moved to Sayville, New York, on Long Island, and by the Depression-era 1930s, his followers around the world were estimated to number more than twenty million.

Outside critics sometimes argued that these populist speakers developed cult-like followings, a charge fueled in large part by the number of followers a compelling speaker could attract. The style of speaking was not itself new, however. Its roots lay deep in the tradition of folk preaching. With the rise of radio and expansion of the press, however, such folk preaching spoke especially loudly to the hopes and frustrations of many newly urbanized African Americans.

## GIVING THEM HELL: ADAM CLAYTON POWELL JR.

The line separating the speakers working through the political system for equal rights and the populist speakers who focused on building community was not so sharply drawn in practice. Du Bois, for example, was a Pan-Africanist as well as a leader in the NAACP seeking to secure African Americans' legal rights in the United States. A. Philip Randolph's union meetings often looked and sounded very much like Garvey's rallies. One speaker in this era especially illustrated how the two styles could merge into a single representative. Adam Clayton Powell Jr. was both a minister and a politician, and he could speak like either.

In Congress, Chicago representative Arthur Mitchell had been replaced in the House by William Dawson, who initially served as the "political" voice of all African Americans. Dawson attacked the Southern use of poll taxes to discriminate against African American voting, and he supported President Harry Truman's 1946 executive order that desegregated the U.S. military. Dawson also spoke widely across the United States to encourage African American involvement in politics. The standard rallying cry he used in his speeches was "Don't get mad! Get smart. Vote!"

In 1944, Dawson was joined by a second African American representative, Adam Clayton Powell Jr., the first Black representative elected from New York City. While Dawson was a political careerist from Chicago, the thirty-five-year-old Powell was minister of the largest African American church in the country, the Abyssinian Baptist Church in Harlem. In the 1930s, Powell had gained attention in New York as he helped lead boycotts and demonstrations against stores, companies, and political agencies that discriminated against African Americans. As biographer Lenworth Gunther noted, Powell used his Abyssinian Baptist Church as an instrument of protest, social work, and community organizing, as well as having it function as a political machine.

Powell's public protests helped force department stores, utility companies, and the bus company to hire African Americans, and he opened opportunities for Blacks in city and federal agencies, such as the trash services, post office, and police force. In 1941, he became the first African American elected to the New York City Council, and in 1944 he was elected to the U.S. House of Representatives. There, he worked politically for equal rights. For example, he became known for proposing that the "Powell Amendment" be added to every piece of funding legislation that came up. Like Randolph's agitation for the FEPC, the Powell Amendment required that federal money could not be used to purchase goods or services from any company that discriminated on the basis of race. Some political allies were frustrated when the amendment was successfully added to a social spending bill, knowing that the amendment would doom the legislation when it got to a vote in the full House. Time and again, however, Powell introduced the amendment as a matter of principle.

Powell brought to mainstream politics the style of speaking more typically heard from the pulpit or on the street corner. His speaking was evocative and direct, and his speeches were participatory. As he asked one audience, "Is this the land of the free and the home of the brave?" The audience shouted no. "Is this the land of liberty and justice for all?" he asked. Again, the audience shouted no. "Is this one nation, indivisible, under God?" he asked. As the audience once again yelled no, Powell could be seen mouthing the word "no" and shaking his head sadly. The speaker and audience shared a moment in common. "Either let us practice the democracy we are preaching," he demanded, "or shut up."

More moderate advocates lamented Powell's strategy of confrontation, but his constituents and many others in the African American community were exhilarated. As Wyatt Tee Walker, a fellow Baptist preacher, observed, African Americans might not always know if Powell was right or wrong on a particular issue, "but he gave white folks hell, and they'd been giving us hell for so long, we were glad to find someone who was in a position to give white folks hell." This was a different political style than what the nation had seen from De Priest, Mitchell, or Dawson. African Americans found Powell's angry speaking both "scary" and "exhilarating." In his autobiography, *Adam by Adam*, Powell described his speaking in similar terms: "There was only one thing I could do—hammer relentlessly, continually crying aloud even if in a wilderness, and force open, by sheer muscle power, every closed door. Once inside, I had to pierce the consciences of men so that somewhere someone would have to answer, somewhere something would have to be done."

Many white Americans had never heard the chastising cadence of a Black populist speaker until Powell arrived in the U.S. House. With the rise of modern civil rights protest and the long reach of American television, however, Powell would be followed by many who sounded very much like him.

# 5

# Waves of Reform and Revolution

## The Modern Civil Rights Movement

IN MAY OF 1954, the U.S. Supreme Court issued a nine to zero decision in *Brown v. Board of Education of Topeka* that struck down public school segregation. It was a major legal victory for the NAACP and other organizations that had supported the lawsuit. Change was slow in coming, however, as may schools across the South refused to integrate. In August of 1955, fourteen-year-old Emmett Till, visiting Money, Mississippi, from Chicago, was murdered for allegedly whistling at a white woman. His body was found in a river three days later, and his mother insisted that his mutilated body be displayed in an open casket so that the world "could see what they did to my boy." The white press did not publish photographs of Till's body, but African American publications did. Less than a month after he had been lynched, the two men accused of the murder were found not guilty, in a jury deliberation that lasted sixty-seven minutes.

A little over two months later, Rosa Parks was arrested and fined for failing to move to the back of the segregated bus in Montgomery, Alabama. The Women's Political Council called for a bus boycott to begin December 5, the day of Parks's trial. That evening, at a community meeting, the Montgomery Improvement Association (MIA) was formed for the purpose of extending the boycott. One of the leaders who emerged at that meeting was the Reverend Martin Luther King Jr., the new pastor of Dexter Avenue Church.

As the MIA began holding nightly meetings to organize and rally support for the boycott, Dr. King became admired as an energetic and eloquent speaker. His style brought to prominence the blend of preaching and politics that had marked Adam Clayton Powell Jr.'s work on boycotts and in the U.S. Congress. King would be joined by other preachers on the national stage, as well as many who were not formally prepared for platform speaking but who emerged from demonstrations and protests as individuals worth listening to. Parallel with this movement dedicated to nonviolent protest and civil disobedience came speakers who took a far more militant line. The next fifteen years saw radical changes in U.S. culture, and African American speakers played a central role in catalyzing those changes.

## PREACHING FOR REFORM AND PROTEST

The foundation for preaching as a form of protest had been established long before King's first address supporting the Montgomery bus boycott, but his speaking embodied that style in its strongest form. On December 5, the first night of the boycott, he spoke at a rally held at Holt Street Baptist Church. The audio recording of his speech conveyed the close interaction of the speaker and his audience. Almost every line of King's included a thought that was phrased so that it invited an echoed response from one or more of his listeners. The first prolonged applause came just five minutes into his fifteen-minute address, when King tapped into the audience's long and deep frustration: "And you know, my friends, there comes a time when people get tired of being trampled over by the iron feet of oppression."

King strategically used repetition to highlight key ideas, and his repetition provided an additional invitation for audience response. For example, he reminded the audience that Rosa Parks's only offense was the color of her skin. He began three successive sentences with a slight variation of "Nobody can doubt," as a method of highlighting her integrity, her character, and her commitment to the Christian faith. Similarly, he used repetition in order to underscore the moral principle of their protest, arguing that their boycott was justified by American democracy and Christian ethics:

> We are not wrong in what we are doing. If we are wrong, the Supreme Court of this nation is wrong. If we are wrong, the Constitution of the United States is wrong. If we are wrong, God Almighty is wrong. If we are wrong, Jesus of Nazareth was merely a utopian dreamer that never came down to earth. If we are wrong, justice is a lie. Love has no meaning. And we are determined here in Montgomery to work and fight until justice runs down like water, and righteousness like a mighty stream.

King brought his run to a climactic close with a quote from the Book of Amos that he would use for the same purpose in "I Have a Dream" eight years later.

King did not begin his speech by condemning segregation—that would come later in the speech—but with an affirmation instead. The audience, he said, had gathered that evening "because of our love for democracy." He quickly moved to the particular injustice that had catalyzed their meeting, however, as he reminded his audience of the intimidation and humiliation they had all experienced on the Montgomery buses. He then personalized that injustice with the case of Rosa Parks. Through the person of Rosa Parks, King asserted the dignity of all African Americans. "Last Thursday," he said, the city arrested "one of the finest citizens in Montgomery—not one of the finest *Negro* citizens—one of the finest *citizens* in Montgomery." After asserting her integrity and character, he again broadened his message by saying that there would be a time when the oppression, humiliation, and intimidation of all Blacks must end.

King reiterated the rightness of the protest in part by distinguishing it from the violence used to maintain segregation and white supremacy. African Americans would not emulate the Ku Klux Klan or the White Citizens Council, he said, nor would they lynch anyone who opposed the boycott. "We believe in the teachings of Jesus," King vowed, and so "the only weapon we have in our hands this evening is the weapon of protest."

Religious themes were woven throughout King's speech, but especially in his discussion of love and justice. The principle of love demanded that the protests be nonviolent, and King observed that "love is one of the pivotal points of the Christian faith." However, he said, "there is another side called justice" because justice is simply love in "calculation." While love demanded that the protests be nonviolent, justice demanded that there be protests. Yes, King said, there is the God of Hosea who tells his people that he loves them, but there is also the God who demands justice or else he will "break the backbone of your power and slap you out of the orbits of your national and international relationships." Here King was invoking the message of the jeremiad in support of his audience. African Americans would serve as God's instrument in bringing justice to Montgomery.

King brought the speech to a climactic close as he described the historic nature of the times. The community must "stick together ... [with] grim and bold determination." Like the Children of Israel, history would be shaped through their deeds. "We are going to work together," King declared. "Right here in Montgomery, when the history books are written in the future somebody will have to say, 'There lived a race of people a Black people, "fleecy locks and Black complexion," a people who had the moral courage to stand up for their rights. And thereby they injected a new meaning into the veins of history and of civilization.' And we're gonna do that."

Over one year later, on December 20, 1956, the city of Montgomery agreed to end segregation on the city buses, but that did not end the underlying issues of racial discrimination. Church bombings and lynchings in the area continued, on December 22 King's house was shot into, and in the spring the city passed new segregation ordinances that were not related to bus travel. Church bombings were particularly common because just as in the Montgomery bus boycott, churches were the places where protests were organized and speakers heard. Powell's Abyssinian Baptist Church had been fundamental to the Harlem boycotts. So, too, for example, was Rev. T. J. Jemison's Mount Zion Baptist Church in Baton Rouge, Louisiana. In 1953, Rev. Jemison had organized a bus boycott that had resulted in a partial success.

During the Montgomery bus boycott, meetings were held virtually nightly in African American churches. While Martin Luther King became the best known of the speakers, in reality he was one among many who helped rally the community and maintain the organization. In early 1956, at the urging of Bayard Rustin, a New York–based activist, King called for a meeting of Black Southern preachers at Ebenezer Baptist Church in Atlanta, where King's father was pastor. Attendees included Rev. Ralph Abernathy, who had worked with King in Montgomery; Rev. Fred Shuttlesworth of Birmingham; Rev. C. K. Steele of Tallahassee; Rev. Joseph Lowery of Birmingham; and Rev. Jemison of Baton Rouge.

From these meetings emerged the Southern Christian Leadership Conference (SCLC), an association that organized local ministerial activists into a regional network that promoted nonviolent protest. These were ministers whose tradition of preaching was represented well by King. As Simmons and Thomas wrote in *Preaching with Sacred Fire*, King and the SCLC "opened up Black preaching to a national white audience." White audiences who had never attended a Black church now heard the distinct rhythms and cadence of Black preaching. At first, it would be heard by those whites who became active workers for civil rights, but as civil rights speakers began appearing on television, even if only in brief clips, their preaching style of public speaking reached a wider audience.

As Simmons and Thomas noted, not all African American preachers embraced the nonviolent, direct-action approach of King and the SCLC. Many thought that direct action would backfire, accomplishing nothing but further oppression of Blacks. The Rev. Joseph H. Jackson, president of the predominantly Black National Baptist Convention, argued that the Black church could not be built on the "hate, envy and revenge" embodied by civil disobedience. The Rev. Wyatt Tee Walker, executive director of the SCLC, estimated that during these early years as many as 90 percent of African American ministers would not collaborate with the SCLC. It is also important to note that the "high church" preaching style used by earlier clerical leaders, such as Alexander Crummell, Francis Grimké, and Mordecai Johnson, was still practiced as well. But the "modern civil rights" movement of the 1950s and 1960s was primarily characterized by the prominent role assumed by those who, like King, employed the more energetic style of public speaking associated with "Black preaching."

Many other community-based organizations were active during this era as well. In Tennessee and then South Carolina, the Highlander and Citizenship Schools were organized by educator Septima Clark to teach literacy and organizing skills to Blacks so they could register to vote. Fannie Lou Hamer, a sharecropper who was fired when she attempted to register to vote, was a prominent speaker who had attended Clark's workshops. Established groups, such as the NAACP, the Brotherhood of Pullman Car Porters, and the Congress on Racial Equality (CORE), were also active community organizers during this time. CORE had begun in the 1940s specifically as an association to support nonviolent direct action.

## YOUNG REFORMERS AND PROTESTORS

Initially, desegregation was the focus of these protests led by preachers and community activists. Despite federal court orders and local victories in some cities and towns, the segregation of buses, schools, eating establishments, parks, and other community amenities was still widespread. In 1957, in the face of a bus boycott, the Rock Hill, South Carolina, bus company chose to go out of business rather than integrate. In the same year, President Eisenhower was forced to federalize the National Guard to ensure the court-ordered school desegregation in Little Rock, Arkansas.

Out of the desegregation campaign emerged the lunch counter sit-ins of 1960 and the Freedom Rides of 1961. On February 1, 1960, four students from North Carolina A&T University organized a sit-in at the Woolworth lunch counter in Greensboro, North Carolina. The students were refused service but continued to occupy their seats until closing. Over the next days and weeks, more students joined them and more lunch counters in Greensboro were effectively closed. Across the South, students at historically Black colleges organized similar efforts, and so the sit-in movement spread to Charlotte, Raleigh, Richmond, Nashville, and other towns.

As with the Montgomery bus boycott, these protests were accompanied by rallies and speeches, many times held at local churches. Preachers, community leaders, and student leaders addressed the gathered audience, securing support from the community and organizing additional means of applying pressure. Ministers exhorted their congregants to boycott all the counters in the department stores until the students had been served at the lunch counters. When Charlotte was hit with a snowstorm, the finest cars in the community, including Cadillacs from the local funeral home, arrived to ferry the students downtown so that the sit-ins could continue. Student leaders emerged as important speakers, as they led meetings and spoke at rallies.

According to reports of these meetings, the speeches were characterized by patriotic appeals, a commitment to Christian ethics, and reports about the conduct of the students as well as that of the whites who showed up in opposition and the response of law enforcement. In short, the speeches provided updates on the protests and reinforced the principles upon which the protests were founded. Although "We Shall Overcome" became the well-known anthem of the movement in this era, church rallies were accompanied by the singing of many songs, such as "America" ("My country 'tis of thee, sweet land of liberty") and "Onward Christian Soldiers" ("Onward Christian soldiers, marching as to war"). Both songs captured the ideals and the spiritual resolve of the speakers and their audiences.

In April of 1960, students who had been participating in these sit-ins met at Shaw University in North Carolina, where they created the Student Nonviolent Coordinating Committee (SNCC). Although supported financially by the SCLC and assisted by Ella Baker, the executive director of the SCLC, this was an independent group from the start. Three speakers took center stage at the conference: James Lawson, Martin Luther King Jr., and Ella Baker.

Lawson was a thirty-one-year-old student at Vanderbilt University's Divinity School who had served as a mentor for the students conducting the Nashville sit-ins, which had been violently resisted. As a conscientious objector, Lawson had been imprisoned in 1951 on charges of draft evasion. He had worked as a missionary in India where he had studied Mahatma Gandhi's principles of nonviolent resistance. Lawson delivered the keynote address at the conference. His speech was a blend of instruction regarding nonviolent protest and criticism of those who counseled patience. "Love," he said, "is the central motif of nonviolence. Love is the force by which God binds man to Himself and man to man. Such love goes to the extreme; it remains loving and forgiving even in the midst of hostility. It matches the capacity of evil to inflict suffering with an even more enduring capacity to absorb evil." Biographer Taylor Branch wrote that Lawson also denounced the NAACP for its "preoccupation with fund-raising and lawsuits." Between his deep-seated commitment to nonviolence as well as the urgent need for change now, Lawson "swept away the crowd," as did King.

King was more political and muted in his criticism of the NAACP, although he did praise the students for "moving away from tactics which are suitable merely for gradual and long term change." In his speech he focused on the immediacy of the students' protests. He urged them to organize in communities across the country, congratulated them on their "revolt" against the upper-class mores that stifled protest, and promoted the "Jail—No Bail" strategy that would clog the jails. Branch claimed that the students' response to King's speech was enthusiastic, although historian Thomas Jackson has argued that both Lawson and Baker exerted far more influence at the conference.

At the conference, Baker advocated for the decentralization of the movement. According to Jackson, Baker told students they needed to resist the "adult attempts to 'capture' their movement." Indirectly but clearly criticizing King and other ministers leading the SCLC, Baker warned the students against blindly following the spellbinding orator "when the prophetic leader turns out to have heavy feet of clay." She said then and wrote later in a report on the conference that the students understood that the rights at issue were "bigger than a hamburger." Jackson later wrote that Julian Bond, a founding member of SNCC and later U.S. representative from Georgia, thought that Baker's speech was an "eye opener" and a "big leap" for the students. Baker's speech was educational, as she helped the students see how they could take control of the whirlwind they had started and build upon that momentum. The next year they would organize the Freedom Rides to integrate interstate bus travel and from there moved on to voter registration drives across the South.

Regardless of whether they heard her words directly or not, youth across the nation answered Baker's call to action and became important public speakers during the early 1960s. In addition to Lawson and Bond, young leaders like John Lewis, Eleanor Holmes (Norton), Robert Moses, Marian Wright (Edelman), Stokely Carmichael, and Jesse Jackson would take center stage at various points during the decade. These speakers differed from the ministerial leaders in that they did not speak from an official position of power, but just as Baker had advocated, their abilities as speakers and leaders influenced the movement. Like their backgrounds and their personalities, these leaders' speaking styles and public appeals varied widely, but all sought to speak to and for the common person.

Despite his youth, John Lewis, one of the original Freedom Riders from the spring of 1961, had been preaching since turning sixteen and had attended seminary for his bachelor's degree. SNCC photographer Danny Lyon recounted the first time he heard Lewis speak, at a SNCC meeting in 1962. Lyon recalled that Lewis was extraordinarily quiet and reserved, until he came to the podium to speak. "Delivered in a heavy, rural Alabama accent," Lyon wrote, the speech "seemed to come up out of him, out of centuries of abuse, and explode from this unassuming young man. His voice was high pitched and trembling with emotion." Lyon had never heard the Black preaching style in person, and he was deeply moved by the experience: "John's speech would have converted anyone, and it converted me."

Robert Parris Moses, another young leader in the SNCC as well as the Council of Federated Organizations (COFO), had a contrasting style. An intellectually gifted student from Harlem, Moses came to Mississippi in 1961 at the age of twenty-six to work on voter registration drives. His speaking style was quiet and thoughtful, and audiences often needed to strain to hear him. He used careful, slow enunciation of his words. His speaking, said those hearing him, was "poetic, [and] his moral stance defiant." He "managed to communicate a soothing, spiritual depth." Reflecting on his own speaking, Moses expressed confidence in the power of ideas and information to persuade people, and his speeches made use of literary analogies, ranging from Albert Camus's *The Plague* to J. R. R. Tolkien's *Lord of the Rings.* Listening to Moses speak at Stanford University in 1964, antiwar activist David Harris recalled that "each word had clearly been considered and was said with the rhythms of a man crossing a stream, hopping from rock to rock." As Moses proceeded with the speech, the audience "grew increasingly intent," and when he finished, the auditorium was "absolutely quiet for almost a minute" before erupting into a thunderous standing ovation.

Eleanor Holmes also worked with the Mississippi Freedom Summer voting drive, where she was profoundly influenced by Fannie Lou Hamer. Attending Yale University Law School at the time, Holmes's speaking was a blend of incisive legal reasoning and heartfelt passion. Her speeches focused on confronting people's assumptions about race and the possibility of change, while she grounded her appeals on core principles, such as family, individual worth, and equality. Marian Wright, too, was a Yale law student who worked in Mississippi's voter registration campaign, although through the auspices of the NAACP. Much of her speaking focused on mounting the legal challenge to discriminatory laws and practices. Her speaking style was brisk and forceful, a staccato delivery of facts and statistics that demonstrated that inequality violated the avowed principles of freedom and equal protection under the law.

## THE RISE OF MILITANCY

An overwhelming number of the young speakers who led the lunch counter sit-ins, the Freedom Ride, and the Freedom Vote movements adhered to the nonviolent approach to civil disobedience that was advocated by Martin Luther King Jr. Many agreed with Ella Baker that the adult leadership was moving too slowly, and speakers like Lewis, Holmes, and Moses wanted the tactics of nonviolence to be used more aggressively, but they still subscribed to nonviolence and integration as the core principles of the movement. Alongside this group, however, were those who believed that the violent forces that supported and maintained racial discrimination—North as well as South—needed to be resisted more aggressively. Although this period is often characterized as a "rise" of militancy, it is important to remember that speakers who advocated militant methods were always present in the community. The family background of Malcolm X, a leading spokesman for separatism and forceful resistance, is a case in point.

Malcolm X had been born Malcolm Little in Omaha, Nebraska, in 1925. He was slightly older than the militant speakers who immediately followed, such as Stokely Carmichael, H. Rap Brown, Bobby Seale, James Forman, and Eldridge Cleaver. Malcolm's father, Earl Little, was a follower of Marcus Garvey and member of the Universal Negro Improvement Association. In 1929, the Little's home in Omaha was burned down in retaliation to his separatist message, and so the family moved to East Lansing, Michigan. In 1931, Earl Little died after falling from a trolley car.

Deprived of their chief provider, the family became impoverished, and Malcolm's mother became mentally ill and eventually institutionalized. Living alternately in Boston, then Harlem, and then Boston again as a teenager, Malcolm was drawn to street crime—numbers running, procuring, burglary, and narcotics peddling—as a way to support himself. At the age of twenty, he was convicted of burglary and sentenced to eight to ten years in prison. There he became interested, once again, in intellectual pursuits, and by all reports he devoured the books in the prison library. He also became a convert to the Nation of Islam, taking "X" for his last name as a reminder that his family had been torn from their ancestors by slavery. Upon his release from prison, Malcolm X became an activist for, and then a minister of, the Nation.

Due in part to his excellence as a speaker, Malcolm X quickly became the face of the Nation of Islam (NOI). When he spoke during the 1950s and early 1960s, Malcolm always stipulated that he was speaking according to the teachings of Elijah Muhammad, the leader of the Nation. "Messenger Muhammad teaches us," Malcolm X would begin, or "Mr. Muhammad says." In the name of Elijah Muhammad, Malcolm X taught the theology of the Nation, which blended traditional Islamic beliefs with mythology and principles unique to the NOI. The NOI preached that whites were devils who had taken power by force, but that God's order—which would bring down the white race—would soon be reestablished. Like Marcus Garvey, the Nation preached self-discipline and hard work. Living a life of discipline included abstention from drinking, smoking, drugs, extramarital affairs, and unclean food, such as the meat from pigs.

Malcolm X and the Nation of Islam also preached separatism, but while most separatist speakers had advocated emigration back to Africa or to somewhere else outside the United States, Malcolm X argued that the U.S. should cede some group of states to those of African descent. African Americans, he told an audience at Yale University in 1962, needed a "separate territory." Such a provision of land, he said, would be "just compensation" to those who had labored "as your slaves for over 300 years without one payday." "If the white politicians have agreed that the Indians should be paid for their lands," he asked, "what price of payment will the GOD OF JUSTICE demand for 20 million Black people who were robbed of our labor, lives, identity, culture, history . . . and even our human dignity?"

Besides casting the issue as one of justice, Malcolm X also justified race separation biblically. Although the Nation of Islam took the Koran (or Quran) as its holy book, like traditional Islam, the Nation honored Jesus and the prophets of Israel as holy predecessors of the Prophet Mohammed. Referencing the Old Testament, he argued that Noah's solution to the sin that surrounded him was separation from the sin, as was Lot's separation from the towns of Sodom and Gomorrah. Moses, he said, separated the Hebrew people from their Egyptian captors, and Jesus preached that the sheep must be separated from the goats. African American leaders were wrong to seek integration. Americans of African descent were already a "nation within the nation." Like Marcus Garvey, Malcolm X argued that only when those of African descent had their own land would peace truly arrive. "Give us some land," he told his Harvard audience in 1961, "some SEPARATE STATES, so we can separate ourselves from you . . . then everyone will be satisfied, and perhaps we will all be able to then live happily ever after, as your own Christian bible says . . . 'every one under his own vine and fig tree.'"

Separation and justice could only come, however, when African Americans recognized the truth of their plight and God's way forward for them. In support of this cause, Malcolm X used what rhetorical scholar Robert Terrell called an emancipatory rhetoric, a style of speaking that places emphasis on renaming as a way of challenging the status quo and of liberating oneself by changing one's perspective. "You are deaf, dumb, and blind," journalist Louis Lomax recorded Malcolm telling his audience at the Mosque, and so "you are lost in the wilderness of North America, and the Black man's new day has been delayed because of you. Now I am here to get you ready." Lomax also reported that the NOI audience frequently called out, urging Malcolm to "make it plain."

So, for example, Malcolm argued that African Americans were not "Negroes," for "Negro" was a white person's term, fashioned to mean someone of an inferior race. We are African Americans, Malcolm said, or Americans of African descent, and that is what we should be called. In his speeches, he qualified the term "Negro" by saying, "the so-called Negroes." The college campus speech he gave on a variety of occasions during 1961 and 1962 was representative:

> Before we heard the teachings of Messenger Muhammad, we (American so-called Negroes) were in the grave of ignorance. We had been taught by our Christian slave master, as well as by our own ignorant religious leaders, that God had cursed us Black and sentenced us to a lifetime of servitude to the Christian white race.... Such religious teachings were purposely designed to make us (so-called Negroes) feel inferior to the white Christian slave master.

To hear the "WORD" of the Messenger, Elijah Muhammad, was to be "able for the first time in 400 years to SEE and HEAR."

To see the truth and hear the word, Malcolm argued, one must see the white man for what he was: the devil. Malcolm had a simple response to those who charged him with being racist himself. Is there any doubt, he would ask, that African Americans are living in a hell of poverty and discrimination? And who made that hell? Certainly, the person responsible would be, by definition, the devil. African Americans needed to have their eyes opened, to see that whites were "tricksters," "rattlesnakes," and, even in modern times, "slave-masters." Speaking at Harvard in 1961, Malcolm held that "a kidnapper, a robber, an enslaver, a lyncher is just a common criminal in the sight of God, and criminal acts as such have been committed by your race on a mass scale for four hundred years against your twenty million so-called Negroes."

Malcolm X was equally unforgiving when talking about African American leaders like Martin Luther King Jr., who wanted integration and were interested in collaborating with white Americans. Such leaders were "Uncle Toms," Malcolm said, "Negro puppets" who "sound like professional beggars, as they cry year after year for white America to accept us as first-class citizens." "The race problem cannot be solved by listening to this white-minded [brainwashed] minority," he told his Yale audience. He continued:

> We have accepted your invitation to come here to Yale University Law School this evening to let you know first hand why 20 million so-called Negroes cannot integrate with white America.... Why white America, after 100 years of religious hypocrisy and political trickery will never accept us as first-class citizens here.... The handwriting is on the wall for America.... Will America now accept an ambassador from God, a Divine Messenger, a Warner, to read the handwriting for her and tell her what solution she must accept? ... Or, will America blindly reject God's Messenger [Elijah Muhammad], and in so doing bring on her own Divine Destruction?

In these early speeches, Malcolm X articulated a consistent position: Elijah Muhammad was a visionary prophet, African Americans must understand the correct use of words in order to see the world plainly, and it was a world in which Blacks and whites must go their separate ways.

Malcolm X's message of militant resistance and separation appealed primarily to younger African Americans, who were frustrated by the very slow pace of change since the 1954 *Brown v. Board of Education* decision and the 1955 Montgomery bus boycott. Boycotts, demonstrations, meetings, and even civil disobedience seemed to achieve only incremental gains. A new generation of militant speakers, such as Floyd McKissick of the Congress of Racial Equality and Stokely Carmichael of the Student Nonviolent Coordinating Committee, began to emerge in the early 1960s and would take center stage by the middle of the decade.

## THE MARCH ON WASHINGTON

In the summer of 1963, mainstream civil rights movement leaders attempted to bring to Washington the pressure that, until now, had been focused on the state and local level. A confederation of groups, including the SCLC, SNCC, NAACP, and Randolph's March on Washington association, organized the March on Washington for Jobs and Freedom to gather demonstrators on the National Mall. The program began at 10 a.m. in front of the Washington Monument, with musical performances by Odetta, Josh White, and the SNCC Freedom Singers, as well as folk singers like Joan Baez, Bob Dylan, and Peter, Paul, and Mary. From there the crowd of about one-quarter million marched to the Lincoln Memorial, where they heard from a series of speakers, including Randolph, Rustin, McKissick, Whitney Young of the Urban League, and Roy Wilkins of the NAACP. Additional musical performances between the speeches were provided by Marian Anderson and Mahalia Jackson.

Leading up to the March, a great deal of behind-the-scenes attention was devoted to the speech of John Lewis, the national chairman of the SNCC. A draft of his speech had been distributed to a number of the March's leaders, both white and African American, and they were concerned about its militant tone. In the draft, Lewis condemned the pending Civil Rights Bill as "too little and too late." He also declared that civil rights activists would "march through the South, through the heart of Dixie, the way Sherman did. We will pursue our own 'scorched earth' policy." According to various accounts, on the day of the March itself, frantic and often volatile negotiations took place back stage at the Lincoln Memorial, as King and other leaders persuaded Lewis to change some of his most fiery language.

Still, Lewis's speech voiced the frustration many felt about the slow progress of change, and he called on the nation to march against discrimination. He recounted the trials, tribulations, beatings, and jail time that civil rights activists had endured in the South, often with the acquiescence or even complicity of the federal government. Like Malcolm X and others who had grown frustrated at the Kennedy administration's equivocations, Lewis dismissed the platitudes and promises that had been made by both parties: "But what political leader can stand up and say, 'My party is the party of principles'? For the party of Kennedy is also the party of Eastland. The party of Javits is also the party of Goldwater. Where is *our* party? Where is the political party that will make it unnecessary to march on Washington? Where is the political party that will make it unnecessary to march in the streets of Birmingham?"

Lewis rejected "those who have said, 'Be patient and wait.'" Echoing the famous declaration by Mother Pollard during the Montgomery bus boycott that "my feets is tired, but my soul is rested," Lewis declared that civil rights marchers were tired: "We are tired. We are tired of being beaten by policemen. We are tired of seeing our people locked up in jail over and over again. And then you holler, 'Be patient.' How long can we be patient? We want our freedom and we want it now."

Although Lewis agreed to remove the reference to marching like Sherman, he still referred to the civil rights movement as a "revolution," and he concluded the speech with a warning that if Blacks did not receive their freedom now, they would take the march to all of the South, from Jackson, Mississippi, to Birmingham, Alabama, until "we shall splinter the segregated South into a thousand pieces and put them together in the image of God and democracy." Unlike Malcolm X, Lewis argued in support of integration, but his denunciation of all politicians and his call for revolution echoed the NOI minister's speeches. In *Parting the Waters*, Taylor Branch noted that of all the speakers that day, Lewis alone eschewed the term "Negro," instead using the term "Black." Despite these militant undertones, however, many members of the SNCC remained bitter that the older leaders had coerced Lewis into changing his speech.

The climactic speech of the program was the address by Martin Luther King Jr., which came to be known as "I Have a Dream." Carried live on national television by CBS, for many Americans it was their first opportunity to see an entire speech by the famous minister from beginning to end. The beginning of the speech was a simple but eloquent declaration that America had not lived up to its promises of freedom and equality

Rev. Martin Luther King Jr. at the 1963 March on Washington. National Archives.

for all. King began the speech by referencing the Lincoln Memorial, "in whose symbolic shadow we stand today." He reminded his audience that Lincoln's Emancipation Proclamation had been signed "one hundred years ago," but "one hundred year later, the Negro still is not free." Using metaphors of slavery, he decried the "manacles of segregation and the chains of discrimination."

King then developed an extended money metaphor, likening the promises of the Emancipation Proclamation and the Declaration of Independence to a "check" that had been given to African Americans but upon which the U.S. had defaulted. The metaphor did double duty for King, as it vividly captured the chasm between the principles the U.S. avowed and what it actually delivered, but it also reminded the audience that a lack of equal rights carried an enormous economic cost for African Americans. Although King was explicitly asking for equal rights at this point of the speech—to break the manacles of segregation and the chains of discrimination—the March on Washington was still a march for jobs as well.

After having confronted America with the irony of its hypocrisy, King demanded change now. "This is no time," he said, "to take the tranquilizing drug of gradualism." King emphasized the "fierce urgency of now," as he termed it, through two series of repeated phrases. Four times, he told the audience that "now is the time" for change. In the first and fourth item in the series, the demand was literal: "To make real the promises of democracy." In the middle two, the demands were stated through metaphors of moving from darkness, valleys, and quicksand, to sunlit paths and the "solid rock of brotherhood." Shortly thereafter, King put words into the mouths of critics, saying that they ask the "devotees of Civil Rights, 'When will you be satisfied?'" Five times King repeated the opening phrase that "we will never be satisfied" until African Americans are given their full rights and freedoms. In a climactic crescendo, King paraphrased from the Book of Amos as he brought the series to a close: "No! no, we are not satisfied, and we will not be satisfied until justice rolls down like waters and righteousness like a mighty stream."

Through repetition, King made clear the demands of the marchers: now was the time, and they would not be satisfied until the freedoms and equality that America had promised them had been made real. Typically, these repetitions are transcribed as *anaphora*, phrases that are repeated at the start of a sentence or paragraph. However, King's delivery often made the phrase an *epistrophe*, a phrase that is repeated at the end of a sentence or paragraph. In this regard, his style here was typical of the "folk" style of Black preaching—where the repeated phrase sometimes starts and at other times finishes a thought. King would repeat this pattern in the speech with his repetition of "I have a dream" and "let freedom ring."

King's preaching style of delivery was critical at this point of the speech because he ended the "run" of "we will never be satisfied" with the paraphrase of Amos. The phrase was enthymematic—that is, the audience brought to it their understanding of the biblical phrase. As a prophet, Amos preached that ethical deeds were more important than religious rituals and that Israel would wither if the Hebrews did not treat those less fortunate with kindness and generosity. The audience understood here that King the preacher had elegantly married his declarative run that they "will not be satisfied" with a perfectly matched quotation from the Bible, and they responded enthusiastically.

According to biographers such as Taylor Branch, and as evidenced by the film of the speech, King responded to the audience's enthusiasm by going off his manuscript. Reportedly, singer Mahalia Jackson prompted King to "tell them about the dream," an idea he had developed in earlier speeches and sermons. King's memory was simply that he knew he could not continue with what he saw as a stilted manuscript, but rather that he needed to preach.

And so the speech moved from an indictment of America's shortcomings to a vision of what America could be if the nation's promise was fulfilled. In what has since become the featured element of King's speech, he described his vision as a dream. As King said in the speech, the metaphor alluded to "a dream deeply rooted in the American dream," but it also evoked Langston Hughes's famous poem "A Dream Deferred." In his vision, King referenced the Declaration of Independence: "That one day this nation will rise up and live out the true meaning of its creed, 'We hold these truths to be self-evident, that all men are created equal.'" Like the communal and spiritual act of breaking bread, King dreamt of a day when "the sons of former slaves and the sons of former slaveowners will be able to sit down together at the table of brotherhood."

In the most often remembered line from King's vision, he used the parallel structure of antithesis, reinforced by alliteration to again contrast America's failures from the first portion of his speech with the ideals of the dream: "I have a dream that my four little children will one day live in a nation where they will not be judged by the color of their skin but by the content of their character." After one more articulation of the dream, King again brought his run of preaching to a close by quoting a Hebrew prophet from the Old Testament. This time, however, he drew from Isaiah, the prophet most closely associated with the coming of the messiah. King's dream was thus implicitly connected with Christ's message of peace and love.

And so it was "with this faith" that King told his audience that "I go back to the South." Through their continued struggle of equal rights, the ideals voiced in the song "America" would become reality. Still in a full preaching style of delivery, King half sung the first verse of the song and then used the phrase "Let freedom ring" as anaphora/epistrophe to call for equal rights ringing from a series of mountains, from Pennsylvania to Colorado to California and back to Georgia and Tennessee, ironically concluding with "every hill and mole hill of Mississippi." When the ideals of America are thus fulfilled, King intoned, then all Americans would be "able to join hands and sing in the words of the old Negro spiritual: 'Free at last. Free at last. Thank God Almighty, we are free at last.'" Through song, King thus joined African American music—the spiritual—to a mainstream national anthem, "America," symbolically uniting the nation through music. By referencing a spiritual that had been sung during slavery, King also returned his speech back to its beginning: that one hundred years after the Emancipation Proclamation, African Americans were still not free.

Two other messages in King's speech deserve attention. The first was that throughout the speech, King expressed the problem of equal rights as a national, and not a uniquely Southern, issue. His passages about "We will never be satisfied," included segregation in the "hotels of the cities," the restricted mobility of African Americans to move "from a smaller ghetto to a larger one," and an analogy that equated the inability of Southern Blacks to vote with the condition that "the Negro in New York believes he has nothing for which to vote." When King urged marchers to "go back" and work for equal rights, after listing several Southern states, he expanded the geography to include "the slums and ghettos of our Northern cities." As previously noted, King's call to let "freedom ring" included non-Southern states such as Pennsylvania, Colorado, and California. It would not be long before King and the SCLC would formally expand their work northward, especially to Chicago and its suburbs.

The other important message was King's cautionary warning to those who were being persuaded to a more militant stand by speakers like Malcolm X. Early in his speech, King opened up his rejection of violent resistance by saying that those advancing equal and civil rights must not be "guilty of wrongful deeds," should not "drink from the cup of bitterness and hatred," and should not let the movement "degenerate into physical violence."

But after he rejected violence as a tactic, King moved swiftly to embrace the spirit, or what he called "the marvelous new militancy." In stark contrast to Malcolm X's separatist views, however, King argued that the militants should recognize that there were white allies with them at the March, and that all Americans must realize that "their freedom"—that is, the freedom of white Americans—"is inextricably bound to our freedom"—the freedom of African Americans. Significantly, however, King's cautionary warning was bookended by his two attention-grabbing anaphora-led sections that were stridently demanding. His careful rejection of force came immediately after he had declared that "now is the time," and was followed closely by his refrain that "we will never be satisfied" as long as inequality and injustice persisted.

In a White House meeting that day between President Kennedy and the leaders of the March, the president complimented King on his outstanding speech, but Kennedy did not move away from his position about the political difficulties of getting the Civil Rights Bill passed. Many mainstream newspapers paid no special attention to King's speech, although the *New York Times* ran a feature story on it. The *Times* reporter observed that it was Dr. King who "brought [the audience] alive in the late afternoon with a [speech] that was an anguished echo from all the old American reformers." King was "both militant and sad" and, when combined with the March itself, "was able to invoke the principles of the founding fathers to rebuke the inequalities and hypocrisies of modern American life."

Whatever uplift may have been provided by Martin Luther King's vision of the future was tragically dashed less than three weeks later when the Sixteenth Street Baptist Church in Birmingham, Alabama, was bombed, killing four young girls aged eleven. Since the late 1940s, Birmingham had experienced repeated bombings of homes, churches, and businesses along Center Street, as African Americans had slowly been integrating into traditionally white neighborhoods. The area had become known as "Dynamite Hill." Three days after the fatal bombing, on September 18, Martin Luther King delivered a eulogy for the four victims. His sermon was two speeches in one. The first half voiced the community's anger and called America to account for the deaths of the four girls. The second half was a message of Christian hope and God's love, directed specifically to the girls' grieving families.

In the first, political half of the speech, King introduced his political message with a stark condemnation of the bombing with the most commonly quoted line from the speech: "These children—unoffending; innocent and beautiful—were the victims of one of the most vicious, heinous crimes ever perpetrated against humanity." Yet it was the subsequent paragraph that expressed the most powerful sentiment, as King asserted about the girls that "they have something to say." They have something to say, King repeated, against every "minister of the gospel who had remained silent," "every politician" who had stayed in power through appeals to racism, "to a federal government" that had stood passively by, to every African American who had not joined the struggle, and to "each of us, Black and white alike," that, rather than merely search for "WHO" planted the bombs, needed to question "the system" that "PRODUCED" these murders. "God still has a way of wringing good out of evil," King reminded the audience, but only if those who hear the call would become that "redemptive force," a phrase that echoed his observation at the March that "unearned suffering is redemptive."

## COUNTERCURRENTS

Despite his nod to the "marvelous new militancy," King and other mainstream leaders such as Roy Wilkins (NAACP), Whitney Young (Urban League), and James Farmer (CORE) were unable to bring the more militant voices into a unified coalition. While mainstream speakers promoted nonviolent demonstrations and political lobbying, others were talking about revolution. Two dueling conferences held in Detroit on November 8 and 9, 1963, were representative. The Detroit Council for Human Rights (CHR), chaired by Rev. C. L. Franklin, hosted a National Negro Leadership Conference that was a follow-up to a June 1963 march that had served as a precursor for the March on Washington. The Reverend Albert B. Cleage Jr., a fiery orator, Black nationalist, and fierce critic of mainstream civil rights leaders in Detroit like Rev. Franklin, called his own competing conference to meet at the same time. Adam Clayton Powell Jr. was the featured speaker at the Detroit CHR conference. Malcolm X was one of three featured speaker at Cleage's Northern Negro Grass Roots Leadership Conference, and on the second day Malcolm delivered "Message to the Grassroots."

Malcolm's "Message" was much more political, and less religious, than his earlier Black Muslim speeches, with little to no mention of Elijah Muhammad (a full transcript is not available, although much of the speech has been preserved in audio and transcription). He still called white people the "common enemy," but he appealed to Blacks of all religious and political affiliations to recognize that they faced a common foe. "You don't catch hell" because you are a Baptist, Methodist, Democrat, or Republican, he asserted, "you catch hell 'cause you're a Black man." He pointed to the Bandung Conference of 1955, out of which came the Non-Aligned Movement (NAM), as a turning point, where the people of color around the world recognized that "where the dark man was being exploited, he was being exploited by the white man," and thus they had unified in the face of a "common enemy." African Americans' enemy was "the same man—blue eyes and blond hair and pale skin—same man." In the face of this common enemy, African Americans needed unity.

African Americans also needed a Black revolution, Malcolm said. As with his earlier speeches, Malcolm focused on the meaning of words. Large social change—of the type advocated by the integrationists—was not revolution. Revolution, he said, always incurred bloodshed and always involved the acquisition of land because land provided the means for independence. Running through a series of examples, Malcolm cited the American, French, Russian, Chinese, Kenyan, Algerian, and Cuban revolutions. "You haven't got a revolution that doesn't involve bloodshed," Malcolm said, and then challenged his audience: "And you're afraid to bleed."

African Americans were content to bleed when sent abroad to fight in America's wars but then peacefully marched for their rights at home. Here Malcolm distinguished the "Negro revolution" from a "Black revolution": "You don't have a turn-the-other-cheek revolution. There's no such *thing* as a nonviolent revolution. Only kind of revolution that's nonviolent is a Negro revolution." In contrast, Black nationalism was about gaining independence by acquiring land, land that could only be gotten through bloodshed, and so Black nationalism was synonymous with Black revolution.

At this point in the speech, Malcolm turned to what became a famous analogy about the "house Negro" and the "field Negro." The house Negro, he said, lived in the mansion, got a little better clothing and food, and his loyalty was thus "bought" by the master. As a result, the house Negro only wanted to keep his place in the house and would do his master's bidding. In contrast, the field Negro barely got scraps to eat and rags to wear, "was beaten from morning to night," lived in a shack, and "hated his master." The masses of Blacks were, of course, "field Negroes," and they wanted nothing more than to "separate" from the white master. The house Negro was an Uncle Tom; the field Negro was a revolutionary.

By analogy, the mainstream civil rights leaders—King, Wilkins, Young, Randolph, and Farmer—were modern-day house Negroes. "The same strategy that was used in those days," Malcolm said, "is used today, by the same white man. He takes a Negro, a so-called Negro, and make him prominent, build him up, publicize him, make him a celebrity. And then he becomes a spokesman for Negroes—and a Negro leader." He said that

Minister Malcolm X, circa 1959–1960. *No Easy Victories: African Liberation and American Activists over a Half Century, 1950–2000*, Eds. William Minter, Gail Hovey and Charles Cobb, Jr. (Np: Africa World Press, 2008).

white leaders, spurred by Kennedy, provided funding for the civil rights organizations and the March on Washington and in that way "bought them off." Whites "infiltrated" the March and "it lost its militancy." They "ceased to be hot; they ceased to be uncompromising." And so "it became a picnic, a circus. Nothing but a circus with clowns and all. You had one right here in Detroit—I saw it on television—with clowns leading it, white clowns and Black clowns. I know you don't like what I'm saying, but I'm going to tell you anyway."

Why did the white man buy out these "house Negroes"? Because Birmingham had "exploded" with Black protest, and the protestors "began to stab the crackers in the back and bust them upside their head." "It was the grass roots out there in the street," Malcolm observed, and "scared the white man to death, scared the white power structure in Washington, D.C., to death." Malcolm's "Message to the Grassroots" was that it was in the grassroots—in his audience—that true revolution would be found, and only a revolution could effectively fight their "common enemy." It was this message of revolution that would propel the Black Power movement in the last half of the decade.

Thirteen days later, on November 22, President John F. Kennedy was assassinated. Despite strict orders from Minister Elijah Muhammad to refrain from criticizing the president by name, on December 1, Malcolm X answered a question about the assassination by saying that he "never foresaw that the chickens would come home to roost so soon." His speech at the Manhattan Center that evening, delivered to an African American–only audience—with the exception of the reporters allowed to attend—was titled "God's Judgment of White America." The speech was part theology—that Elijah Muhammad had prophesied that the end of white rule was near and that the signs of the coming judgment were unmistakable. The speech also included the elements of the "Message to the Grassroots" that had condemned integration and those Black leaders who were cooperating with the "tricky" white liberals—like Kennedy—to keep the Black masses quiescent. Against this backdrop, Malcolm X interpreted Kennedy's assassination as one more sign portending the end of white domination. By December 4, Elijah Muhammad suspended Malcolm X from public appearances, saying that Malcolm had disobeyed a direct order of the leader.

When Malcolm fully returned to the public eye in 1964, he would speak as a Muslim and political leader independent from Elijah Muhammad. He established the Muslim Mosque as a religious organization and the Organization of African American Unity as a political association. On April 3, 1964, Malcolm delivered what became known as "The Ballot or the Bullet" at a meeting hosted by CORE. Like many of his speeches, Malcolm would deliver variations of the speech throughout the following months.

At the beginning of the speech, Malcolm urged African American unity. He declared that he was not speaking as a Muslim or a minister but as an African American. As in his "Message to the Grassroots," he reminded his audience that "we are all going to catch hell from the same man." Throughout his speech he paid close attention to the meaning of words. In his opening remarks, he said that if you are invited to a dinner and there is nothing on your plate, you cannot be called a "diner." In the same way, he said, "being here in America doesn't make you an American."

One way to exercise Blacks' unity was through the ballot, and Malcolm then turned to politics. A ballot is like a bullet, he told his audience: don't use the ballot until you know exactly what you are shooting at. At this moment in time, he said, neither the Republicans nor the Democrats offered anything worth their ballot. Malcolm largely ignored the Republicans in his speech, as that party had by now abandoned any attempt to retain the African American vote. The Democratic Party, however, included a liberal wing that wooed the African American voters in the North, and Lyndon Johnson had made the pending Civil Rights Act a centerpiece of his presidential agenda.

This Democratic Party, however, had historically been the party of the Solid South, where white Democrats had maintained power and segregation since the end of Reconstruction. The Northern Democrats and the Southern "Dixiecrats" were "in cahoots" said Malcolm: "A Democrat is nothing but a Dixiecrat." The Southern Democrats, Malcolm pointed out, maintained their power by being reelected term after term in elections that disenfranchised African Americans. In Congress, the seniority system and the rules on filibustering—where a few senators could prevent a bill from ever being voted on—had concentrated power in the hands of these old white segregationists. But, said Malcom, the Democratic Party—the supposed white Northern liberals—could change the rules if they wanted. "We need some new allies," said Malcolm. So hold onto your vote, until some new allies will actually do something for you.

In the latter half of the speech, Malcolm outlined his new vision of Black nationalism. He was no longer demanding land for a separate Black nation but instead defined Black nationalism politically, economically, and socially. Political Black nationalism meant controlling "the politics and the politicians" in their own community. Here he returned to the analogy that a ballot was like a bullet and should be targeted carefully. Malcolm's economic Black nationalism echoed Marcus Garvey's: keep Black money in the Black community. Individually, African Americans were poor. Collectively, they had considerable wealth. Once you control your economy by supporting Black businesses, Malcolm told his audience, "you don't have to picket and boycott and beg some cracker downtown for a job in his business." Malcolm's "social philosophy of Black nationalism" emphasized the same work that the Nation of Islam had done: to remove vices like alcoholism and drug addiction from the community.

In "The Ballot or the Bullet," Malcolm X addressed two themes that would become increasingly important during the 1960s. The first theme was the emerging war in Vietnam and the anticolonial movement that had been spreading in the post–World War II period. Malcolm argued that African American agitation in the U.S. was not an issue of civil rights but human rights. African Americans were not leading the movement; they were behind the times and needed to think in more fundamental ways about their condition and their goals. The issue was power and not simply access to integrated schools or the right to be served at a restaurant. Malcolm did not mention Vietnam specifically, but he did praise the courage of those who were willing to wage guerilla war, and he again chastised Blacks who were willing to fight in foreign wars but then preached nonviolence at home. "Here you are," he told his audience, "walking around in America, getting ready to be drafted and sent abroad, like a tin soldier," and who are you then fighting for? The white politicians work their "political chicanery" and "make you look like a chump before the eyes of the world."

The second, related theme was nonviolent protest versus the threat of violence. "The only thing I've ever said," Malcolm argued, is that when the government cannot defend African Americans, they must defend themselves. Malcolm walked a fine line regarding guns and self-defense: "This doesn't mean you're going to get a rifle and form battalions and go out looking for white folks, although you'd be within your rights—I mean, you'd be justified; but that would be illegal and we don't do anything illegal." But after his cautionary warning, Malcolm reminded his audience of the four girls who were killed in Birmingham and how their killers had not been captured. And now he did link the violence in Vietnam to violence in America: "Let two or three American soldiers, who are minding somebody else's business way over in South Vietnam, get killed, and he'll [the government] send battleships." Change needed to come, said Malcolm, and he concluded with the phrase he developed across the course of the speech: "In 1964, it's the ballot or the bullet."

Militant speakers like Malcolm X were not the only public speakers who contested the mainstream leaders of the movement—predominantly preachers—like King, Wilkins, and Farmer. The grassroots movement Malcolm X had referenced in 1963 included speakers who came up through the "ranks" of the activists, speakers like Bob Moses of SNCC or the student leaders of the lunchroom sit-ins and Freedom Rides. One such speaker was Fannie Lou Hamer, a Mississippi sharecropper who rose to prominence as she campaigned for the right to vote.

In 1962, Fannie Lou Hamer had attended some of the meetings where SNCC speakers were working to encourage voter registration. On August 31 that year, Hamer and seventeen other African Americans from Ruleville were bused to Indianola, the county seat, where the group tried to register to vote. Only Hamer and one other person were allowed to even attempt the literacy test, which both failed. Upon her return to Ruleville, the plantation owner evicted Hamer and her two children from their home on the farm because she had tried to register to vote. At the end of the growing season, her husband, "Pap" Hamer, was also evicted and their car and belongings confiscated by the plantation owner in "payment" of their debt.

Because of her courage and willingness to speak out against the white segregationists, the SNCC recruited Hamer to work with the organization, where she received some training and a very small stipend. In the summer of 1963, she attended Ella Baker's citizenship school in Charleston, South Carolina. On the return bus trip from Charleston, Hamer and others were arrested at a lunch stop in Winona, Mississippi, and then severely beaten at the jail. Hamer suffered damage to her eyes, legs, and kidneys from which she would never fully recover. While they were in jail, NAACP field secretary Medgar Evers was shot and killed in front of his home in Jackson, Mississippi.

Over the next year, Hamer and the SNCC challenged the state's Democratic Party. Like most of the South, Mississippi was still solidly Democratic. However, these Democrats, unlike some of their Northern brethren, were staunch segregationists, and through the congressional seniority system and the long political careers guaranteed by their safely Democratic seats, the Southern legislators held immense power on the national stage.

In spring 1964, Mississippi's Council of Federated Organizations (COFO), which included SNCC, CORE, and the NAACP, organized the Mississippi Democratic Freedom Party (MFDP) to challenge the mainstream party's stranglehold on statewide politics. In several House and Senate districts, the MFDP recruited and supported candidates to challenge the incumbents. Hamer, for example, ran against Representative James Whitten in the House Second District. As expected, Hamer lost the primary, but in the summer of that year, hundreds of young civil rights activists came to Mississippi to organize voter registration drives. Through her speaking, Hamer was one of the civil rights leaders who helped recruit, train, and organize those activists into what was called Freedom Summer. As artist and activist Tracy Sugarman recorded in *Stranger at the Gates: A Summer in Mississippi*, preaching for voting rights at Black churches in the state, Hamer "rose majestically to her feet.... Her magnificent voice rolled through the chapel as she enlisted the Biblical ranks of martyrs and heroes to summon these folk to the Freedom banner. Her mounting, rolling battery of quotations and allusions from the Old and New Testaments stunned the audience with its thunder." Sugarman's description was strikingly similar to what observers had written about Sojourner Truth a hundred years earlier.

On June 21, the bodies of three young activists—John Chaney, Andrew Goodman, and Michael Schwerner—were discovered shot and buried in Neshoba County. In August that year, the MFDP sent a slate of sixty-eight alternate delegates to the Democratic National Convention (DNC) in Atlantic City, New Jersey. The MFDP argued that because African Americans had been illegally deprived the right to vote in the Democratic primary, the national party should seat these alternate delegates, who had been elected at open meetings held across the state throughout the summer. The Credentials Committee held hearings to determine which delegation should be seated, although the foregone conclusion dictated by President Lyndon Johnson was that the MFDP would not be given any voting seats on the floor. Because he had pushed through the Civil Rights Act of 1964 earlier that summer, Johnson did not want to alienate Southern Democrats further.

Fannie Lou Hamer gave the most powerful testimony provided that day to the committee. Her speech was not elegant, nor did it include the many religious allusions typical of her speeches as reported by Sugarman and others. In three stories, however, Hamer recounted the efforts made by white Mississippians to prevent African Americans from registering to vote. She told the story of her attempt to register and then being evicted from her home, about the night shortly after when sixteen bullets were fired into the home in which she was staying, and then about her return from the Citizens School when she and her fellow attendees were arrested and beaten in Winona.

Although Hamer's stories were simple, she included details that were emotionally powerful. When the plantation owner told her she was now evicted from her sharecropping home, she said he told her that if she withdrew her application to register to vote, he might or might not still evict her because "we are not ready for that in Mississippi." Hamer's often-quoted reply to him was that "I addressed him and told him and said, 'I didn't try to register for you. I tried to register for myself.'"

Hamer recounted the beatings they had experienced at the Winona jail. Ivesta Simpson, a teenaged girl, was beaten because she would not say "sir" to the policeman. In response to his repeated demands, Simpson's simple response was to say, "I don't know you well enough." Hamer said that as Simpson was beaten, the girl prayed that God would have mercy on her jailers. As to Hamer's own beating in the jail, she told about how two African American men were forced by the police to beat her with a blackjack and how she attempted to roll away from the blows in order to protect her left side that had been affected by polio when she was a child. She also told of how, when her dress had gotten worked up during the thrashing and beating, she attempted to pull it back down into place. A policeman promptly pulled her dress back up, adding emotional insult to her physical injuries.

Hamer's testimony served as a powerful indictment of the status quo. As she recited her street and city address in her opening words, she pointedly mentioned that she lived in Sunflower County, "the home of Senator James O. Eastland, and Senator Stennis," the state's two outspokenly segregationist Democratic senators. As she told of the harassment, imprisonment, and beating that she and others endured, she poignantly observed that those individuals who were depriving her and the others of their rights were the "city police" or "state highway patrolmen." The very individuals charged with protecting citizens were the instruments of the state that were confiscating African Americans' rights. These were not Night Riders or the Ku Klux Klan—these were the tools of the Democratic state government that had sent the "regular" delegates from Mississippi to the convention.

In her concluding remarks, Hamer restated the MFDP's quest as something more basic than even voting rights. If the alternate delegation were not seated by the party, she said, "I question America." In her powerful, almost baritone voice with its strong rural lilt, Hamer asked in a tone that demanded an answer, "Is this America, the land of the free and the home of the brave, where we have to sleep with our telephones off the hooks because our lives be threatened daily, because we want to live as decent human beings, in America?"

The party offered the MFDP two nonvoting seats on the floor of the convention. At a meeting of the delegation, a number of liberal Democrats and civil rights leaders urged the group to accept the compromise, but the MFDP refused. As Hamer said, "We didn't come all this way for no two seats, 'cause all of us is tired." Despite acquiescing to the Mississippi state-Democratic machinery, in the general election Mississippi was one of only six states carried by Barry Goldwater, Johnson's Republican opponent. Four of the others won by Goldwater were also Deep South states; the sixth was Goldwater's home state of Arizona. The next year, the Democratic Congress passed and President Johnson signed the Voting Rights Act of 1965. At the 1968 DNC, no "regular" state delegation could be seated if there had been racial discrimination in the primary voting.

## BLACK POWER

Despite these subsequent gains, many activists, such as the SNCC's John Lewis and James Forman, pointed to the MFDP experience as a watershed moment when many African Americans became disenchanted with the mainstream civil rights movement, composed of organizations like the SCLC, the NAACP, and the Urban League. In contrast, the popularity of more militant speakers like Malcolm X grew proportionately.

Ironically, on the heels of the July passage of the Civil Rights Act of 1964, Martin Luther King Jr. became the second African American to receive the Nobel Peace Prize. The first had been U.N. Ambassador Ralph Bunche in 1950, after he had negotiated the Arab-Israeli peace agreement of 1949. King's December Nobel Peace Prize acceptance speech was a defense of nonviolent protest. In his speech, King declared that he refused to accept the cynicism of force and "despair as the final response to the ambiguities of history." He declared that he had "the audacity to believe" that hope could triumph over evil and other-centered people could overcome the self-centered. "I still believe," he said, "that one day mankind will bow before the altars of God and be crowned triumphant over war and bloodshed, and nonviolent redemptive good will proclaim the rule of the land."

King also rebuked the philosophy of Black nationalism, arguing that whites and Blacks collectively could pave a "super highway to justice" through alliances created to "overcome their problems." Perhaps most importantly, King identified the Nobel award with the civil rights movement. I accept this award as a "trustee," he told the audience, "for in the depths of my heart I am aware that this prize is much more than an honor to me personally." He concluded with a paean to the marchers and protestors who had populated the movement from its inception: "When years have rolled past and when the blazing light of truth is focused on this marvelous age in which we live—men and women will know and children will be taught that we have a finer land, a better people, a more noble civilization—because these humble children of God were willing to suffer for righteousness' sake."

For his part, after his hajj pilgrimage to Mecca, Malcolm X softened his claim that the white man was the devil but continued to promote the idea that people of color worldwide shared a common interest in wresting power from U.S. and European governments and corporations. You cannot understand Mississippi, he told a December 20 audience at the Audubon Ballroom in Manhattan, if "you don't understand what is going on in the Congo." At that appearance, Malcolm introduced Fannie Lou Hamer as a speaker. Noting that he was "interested in one thing alone, and that's freedom—by any means necessary," Malcolm then called Hamer "the country's number one freedom-fighting woman."

On February 21, 1965, Malcolm X was shot and killed while again speaking at the Audubon Ballroom. One week earlier, he had spoken at a meeting in Detroit just hours after his home in Harlem had been bombed, with Malcolm and his family in residence. In addition to his themes of worldwide unity and the need to take control of their own lives and communities, Malcolm addressed the issues of violence and racism. The U.S. government, he said, was violent around the world to suit its own interests but then condemned speakers like Malcolm who said that institutional violence—like lynchings and police brutality—would not be changed through nonviolent protest. Malcolm praised the riots of the previous summer—in Harlem, Philadelphia, and Cambridge, Maryland—as appropriate responses to the "police-state activity" in those cities, and he condemned the white press for labeling the rioters as "vandals, hoodlums, thieves."

"I say again that I'm not a racist," Malcolm said, "but I don't think that we should run around trying to love somebody who doesn't love us." He also offered his audience a prediction for the coming year: "1965 will be the longest and hottest and bloodiest year of them all," not because "you want it to be, or I want it to be, . . . but because the conditions [that created the explosions in 1963 and 1964] are still here."

Perhaps chief among those for whom Freedom Summer and the MDFP's experience in Atlantic City were a "watershed moment" was Stokely Carmichael. In the 1950s and early 1960s, Carmichael had picketed and boycotted in protest, first in his hometown of New York City and then down South with the Freedom Riders and the SNCC. Working in Mississippi in the spring of 1964, Carmichael began to question the effectiveness of nonviolent action. In the summer of 1965, Carmichael organized the Lowndes County Freedom Organization (LCFO) in Alabama as a political association that worked similarly to the MFDP. The Lowndes County group adopted the black panther as its symbol. In May 1966, Carmichael replaced John Lewis as the chairman of the SNCC, and the following month he began speaking about a concept he called "Black Power."

Carmichael's speaking style was extemporaneous, drawing heavily from the tradition of Black folk preaching as well as the impromptu street tradition among Black youth of playing the dozens. Like the preacher, Carmichael spoke with an outline in mind and often repeated his phrases, but he did not deliver his speeches from a manuscript. He also focused on building the speech to a dramatic close, and he incorporated key cultural phrases into his speeches, although they were not usually biblical quotations. He also used a biting sense of irony, a technique found in both preaching and "the dozens." The latter is a quick, conversational interchange that involves humorous insults and clever wordplay. Both Black preaching and "the dozens" invite call-and-response from the audience. Carmichael's style of speaking, often called "rapping with the audience," was characteristic of other Black Power speakers and had marked Malcolm X's speaking style as well.

Recordings of two Carmichael speeches illustrate the style of his speaking and also how he adapted when speaking to predominantly white or Black audiences. In October of 1966, Carmichael was invited to speak at the University of California at Berkeley, a center of antiwar and left-wing activism. An audiotape was made of his speech. In April of the following year, a videotape was made of Carmichael speaking at Tougaloo College, a historically Black college in Jackson, Mississippi. In both speeches, Carmichael addressed the idea of "Black Power."

Both speeches began by putting moral power in the hands of African Americans. In both, Carmichael drew on the Existential philosophers as he argued that self-condemnation is impossible. Condemnation, he said, can only come from somebody else, and so condemnation of white discrimination must come from outside the white community. "So Black people have done it," Carmichael said. "You stand condemned." In this vein, like Malcolm X's idea of Black nationalism, "Black Power" meant African Americans taking control over their language, communities, and sense of identity. In both speeches, Carmichael emphasized that the civil rights movement was *not* about white Americans "giving" African Americans their rights. A person is born free, said Carmichael. The movement was about getting white Americans to *stop denying* African Americans the rights to which they were entitled.

African American reassertion of control sometimes took different forms in the two speeches. In the speech at Berkeley, Carmichael spent considerable time condemning the work of white liberals like those in his audience. Liberal outreach programs like Head Start and Upward Bound were simply modern-day versions of the "missionary" movement in Africa, where whites gave Blacks the Bible and then took their land. White activists needed to stay out of the Black communities and teach nonviolence to the *white* community, he said. If whites wanted to solve poverty in the Black community, the solution was simple: give Blacks money. But, he said, do not come into the African American community with antipoverty programs, for they are simply a new, more disguised way to maintain white control.

For his predominantly African American audience at Tougaloo College, he told them not to listen to their white professors who did not know Black history but were busy preaching nonviolence to the Black community.

Those professors, he said, were turning the college into a "brown baby." Study your own history, he commanded. Whites had made "Black" and "Negro" into words that suggested negative meaning. But, said Carmichael, do not let yourself be put into that "trick bag." In part, Black Power meant being proud to be Black.

Regarding the use of force, Carmichael declared, do not be afraid to tell whites that, when whites "touch one of us, you touch all of us." Like Malcolm X, he preached the need to react to force with force. He praised the violent demonstrations that had broken out in Nashville a few days earlier, coming shortly after Carmichael had spoken at Fisk University there. These were not riots, he said. "Riot" was the term the white press used, but really it was a "revolution." He noted with approval that when a Black church had been burned down in Alabama, immediately afterward a white church had been "burned to the ground." In an antithesis typical of his speaking style, Carmichael declared that "either we will all worship inside, or we will all worship outside."

Like Malcolm X, in both the Berkeley speech and the Tougaloo speech, Stokely Carmichael connected the U.S. civil rights movement to the anti-colonial and human rights movements from around the world. The agitation for equal rights by people of color around the world was far ahead of African Americans' efforts, he argued; the latter needed to catch up. U.S. involvement in Vietnam was an example of how the white power structure in the U.S. opposed any liberation effort by a nonwhite group of people. Ironically, Carmichael told his Tougaloo audience, young African Americans were being sent halfway around the world to shoot at a man they never met and who, he said, "ain't never called you n\*\*\*." For ten minutes in the middle of his speech, Carmichael led the audience in a chant of "Hell, no—We won't go!"

In a closely related theme, Carmichael argued that racism was used institutionally as a device for supporting the monied, capitalist interests. Standard Oil, Chase Manhattan Bank, and General Electric all made money by exploiting people of color around the world and maintained their power by setting poor people against each other on the basis of race, rather than economic class. Vietnam thus served as an example of imperial capitalism. We need to "build a new world," he told his Berkeley audience, which would only come when the old political institutions had been destroyed, so that new ones could be erected. Although Carmichael did not use the term "socialism" in these two speeches, his call to tear down the system and the institutions that supported that system resonated with his earlier solution to the problem of poverty: give the poor people money. In these terms, "Black

Power" signified human rights for everyone. Only with the destruction of the hegemonic white power structure could universal human rights become a reality.

Carmichael was not the only speaker to take up the Black Power refrain. In 1966, Bobby Seale met Huey Newton at Merritt College in Oakland. Seale was a thirty-year-old Air Force veteran working in aerospace manufacturing while taking classes part-time. Newton was six years younger and had been in various brushes with the law throughout his teens. Together, they founded the Black Panther Party for Self Defense. In 1967, H. Rap Brown succeeded Stokely Carmichael as the head of the SNCC. Brown would become famous for his observation that "violence is as American as cherry pie" and for changing the word "Nonviolent" in the SNCC name to "National." In 1967, officials and the mainstream media reported that, after delivering a fiery Black Power speech, Brown was responsible for inciting a riot in Cambridge, Maryland, although the Kerner Commission later cleared him of any wrongdoing. Eldridge Cleaver joined the Black Panthers in early 1967. While in prison during his teens and early twenties, Cleaver discovered the Nation of Islam and the preaching of Malcolm X. After Malcolm X's assassination, Cleaver left the Muslim faith but remained devoted to Malcolm's message of Black unity. Angela Davis was a brilliant academic who had been raised in Birmingham's Dynamite Hill. A young faculty member at UCLA, Davis joined the Black Panthers and the American Communist Party, becoming a prominent spokesperson for both.

These speakers shared several points in common. All of them cited Malcolm X as a major inspirational figure in their development. From Malcolm, they took the message that African Americans needed separate control over their community. H. Rap Brown continued the call for African Americans to be given several states. The Black Panthers issued a Ten Point Program, of which the first point was "We want the power to determine the destiny of our Black Community," while the tenth point was "We want land, bread, housing, education, clothing, justice, and peace."

All of them used Malcolm's form of emancipatory rhetoric that renamed ideas in order to create new understandings. "You cannot equate progress with concessions," Brown told the Free Huey Rally in 1968. For example, token gains like the appointment of Thurgood Marshall to the Supreme Court did not represent permanent, systemic change. At the same rally, Brown repeated his often-quoted dismissal of the idea that African Americans were second-class citizens, saying, "You're either free or you're slave. There's no such thing as second-class citizenship. That's like telling me you can be a little bit pregnant." Newton used Malcolm's "Message from the Grassroots" conception of slavery on the plantation, when Newton said that the Black Panther Party were the contemporary field hands and the Black bourgeoisie was the "house Negro."

The Black Panthers and the Black Power movement also drew upon Malcolm's argument that African Americans were not simply agitating for civil rights, but were part of a larger, worldwide movement for human rights, and that the struggle was a contest between those of European descent and the people of color. At different points, the contest would be called "the liberation struggle," the "revolution," or the struggle against the "genocide" of Blacks and all people of color.

Unlike Malcolm X, however, who concentrated on building Black businesses in Black neighborhoods, these speakers argued that racism was inherently the by-product of capitalism. That is, capitalism used racism as a method to divide and control the working people. As Newton characterized it, "The Black Panther Party is a revolutionary Nationalist group, and we see a major contradiction between capitalism in this country and our interests. We realize that this country became very rich upon slavery and that slavery is capitalism in the extreme. . . . We must destroy both racism and capitalism."

Just as the war in Vietnam became the symbol of white American racism for speakers like Carmichael, by the late 1960s, it had become the primary example of what these speakers saw as an intertwined power triumvirate: imperialism, capitalism, and racism. As Angela Davis described it during a 1969 speech in Oakland:

> It ought to become obvious that if the United States government pulled its troops out of Vietnam that that repression would have to crop up somewhere else. Terror is becoming an everyday instrument of the institutions of this country. Within the whole liberation struggle in this country, the Black liberation struggle and the brown liberation struggle, there has continually been the sentiment against the American imperialist aggressive policies throughout this world because we have been forced to see that the enemy is American imperialism and although we feel it here at home it's being felt [with] perhaps much more brutality in Vietnam, it's being felt in Latin America, it's being felt in Africa; we have to make these connections.

Although Carmichael continued to warn again white infiltration and control of the movement, as Newton concluded: "Black Power is really people power." There was a worldwide, proletarian movement against the "three levels of oppression," said Seale, and the Black Panther Party was a vanguard of the revolution.

## THE MILITANT INFLUENCE ON THE MAINSTREAM

Most scholars have agreed that the Black Power movement pressured the mainstream civil rights speakers to take a more militant stand, particularly in relation to two issues: the Vietnam War and the institutional issue of economic justice. As he had since 1955, Martin Luther King Jr. simultaneously represented and influenced that shift.

On April 4, 1967, King delivered a formal proclamation of his opposition to U.S. involvement in Vietnam. He had informally indicated his opposition in early 1966 but had muted his antiwar stance due to criticism from other mainstream leaders who felt that the movement needed to support President Johnson, since the president had been instrumental in securing the passage of the Civil Rights Act of 1964, the Voting Rights Act of 1965, and the Open Housing Act of 1966. In the spring of 1967, however, King began to include criticisms of the war in his speeches, and on April 4 he delivered "A Time to Break Silence" to a meeting of the Clergy and Laymen Concerned about Vietnam, gathered at Riverside Church in New York.

King's speech repeated many of the antiwar themes that had been sounded by Carmichael and the other Black Power speakers. However, King couched those themes within the ministerial frame of the Social Gospel, which emphasizes Christ's call to care for those who are poor, hungry, imprisoned, and oppressed. King began the speech with a confessional stance. He said that he had "agonized" about whether to speak against the Vietnam War, weighing the political costs against the immorality of the war. "A time comes," he said, "when silence is betrayal," and that time, he said, had now come.

Noting the religious symbolism of the number "seven," King laid out seven reasons why he opposed U.S. involvement in the Vietnam War. He arranged them to reach a climax, beginning with the argument that financing the Vietnam War was robbing funds from President Johnson's Great Society antipoverty programs and ending with the Christian imperative to love thy neighbor. In between he included the paradox that Stokely Carmichael had observed: How could King preach nonviolence at home but not speak against the violence of U.S. foreign policy? In its effect on the poor, King also noted that African Americans were disproportionately drafted to fight in a war eight thousand miles away. King also argued that as a minister and a voice for peace, he could not support the U.S. war effort in Vietnam.

While his opening seven reasons provided the foundational arguments of the Social Gospel, his next section put those beliefs into practice. King asked his audience to put themselves into the proverbial shoes of those who were in the midst of the war. He began with the Vietnamese peasants. What must they think, he asked, as the U.S. bombs their fields, bulldozes their forests, and forcibly removes them from their ancestral farms? Americans had not yet heard "the broken cries" of the Vietnamese, he said, and therefore had not lived out the Gospel in practice.

From the Vietnamese peasants, King transitioned to the Viet Cong, the North Vietnamese, and then on to the American soldiers in Vietnam. For each, he asked his audience to see the "demonic" horror from the eyes of those who were experiencing it. "What must [our opponents] think," he asked, of our alliance with the wealthy oligarchy in South Vietnam or our empty words of democracy and equality? In addition to the "brutalizing" effect that all war has on the combatants, King argued that "cynicism" must be added. Shortly after they arrive in Vietnam, he said, American soldiers "surely realize that we are on the side of the wealthy and the secure, while we create a hell for the poor."

King offered a five-point plan for ending the war that echoed the demands of many antiwar activists, with the exception of those who called for an immediate withdrawal. King supported an immediate, unilateral cease-fire; a commitment to the 1954 Geneva agreement; and recognition of the National Liberation Front (Viet Cong) as a legitimate political entity. In his conclusion, he talked about the deeper, more spiritual meaning of the war. There was, he said, a revolution of values that was taking place across the globe, a movement of human rights of which the U.S. civil rights movement was a part and against which stood U.S. involvement in Vietnam. As King summarized it, the situation required Americans to adopt the perspective of the Social Gospel: "I am convinced that if we are to get on the right side of the world revolution, we as a nation must undergo a radical revolution of values. We must rapidly begin the shift from a 'thing-oriented' society to a 'person-oriented' society."

Outside of the antiwar movement, King's speech was not well received. The *New York Times* wrote that King had fused together "two public problems"—the civil rights movement and the war in Vietnam—"that are distinct and separate." The *Washington Post* editorialized that King's arguments were "unsupported fantasy." The NAACP passed a resolution condemning him, and his antiwar stance was criticized by the Urban League, A. Philip Randolph, and Ralph Bunche among other African American organizations and individuals. From the many "no comments" that were reported, it was clear that many of the ministers in the SCLC did not stand with him either. A Gallup poll released the next month found that 48 percent of

African Americans opposed King's stand, while another 27 percent were "reserving judgment." Only one in four African Americans said that they supported his antiwar message.

Over the next year of his life, however, King continued to speak often against the war. In September of 1967, the National Baptist Convention, with two thousand delegates representing half a million members, became the first African American religious organization to pass an antiwar resolution. By the spring of 1968, newspapers reported that King was receiving "prolonged applause" from predominantly African American audiences when he condemned government spending on the "evil, unjust war." What had started as a militant Black separatist appeal had moved to the center of the movement.

Although he never fully embraced the militant speakers' condemnation of the oppressive system, King increasingly connected racial injustice with systemic economic injustice, and the portrayed Vietnam War as a symptom of that injustice. In the spring of 1968, King and others were planning the Poor People's Campaign, a new march on Washington that would reflect the transition from civil rights to human rights. The Poor People's Campaign he portrayed would seek a "radical redistribution of economic and political power" because those of good conscience were "called upon to raise certain basic questions about the whole society."

On March 31, 1968, five days before his assassination, King delivered a sermon entitled "Remaining Awake through a Great Revolution" at the National Cathedral in Washington, D.C. King had delivered variations of this speech at least since 1959, usually as a commencement speech. What had begun as a speech focused on civil rights and the destruction of segregation was now a speech focused more broadly on human rights and economic justice. King still addressed racial injustice, but as he put it, "There is another thing closely related to racism that I would like to mention as another challenge . . . to rid our nation and the world of poverty." He, too, saw the Vietnam War as a manifestation of an institutional problem: "Our involvement in the war in Vietnam . . . has strengthened the military-industrial complex; it has strengthened the forces of reaction in our nation." There is, he said "a single garment of destiny," and the nation's economic system, racism, and imposition of power abroad were all pieces cut from the same cloth.

The last speech of King's career, given in Memphis the night before he was assassinated, is striking for its religious imagery and prophetic foretelling of his own death. In the speech, he imagined that God had told King that the minister had his choice to "be set down" in any time period in history. As King metaphorically flew through history, he saw many great people and accomplishments. However, he said he would choose to live in "these times." Although they were troubled times, King said that this was a great historical moment in time, filled with opportunity for racial brotherhood and economic justice. At the close of the speech, King analogized himself with Moses. After leading the Hebrews through the wilderness for forty years, Moses was not permitted to enter the Promised Land, but God did allow him to see Palestine from a neighboring mountaintop. King declared that he was not concerned about what might happen to him, for "I've seen the Promised Land. I may not get there with you. But I want you to know tonight, that we, as a people, will get to the Promised Land!"

Although the religious imagery and prophecy were striking, King's speech in Memphis most importantly repeated one last time his call for racial and economic justice. The nation's problems were systemic, for "the world is all messed up. The nation is sick. Trouble is in the land." "The issue," he said, "is injustice," and he referenced the sanitation workers' strike that he was in town to support. The garbage collectors were overwhelmingly African American, and the city's treatment of them illustrated the connection between racism and economic exploitation. "The issue," King continued, "is the refusal of Memphis to be fair and honest in its dealings with its public servants, who happen to be sanitation workers."

King thus echoed the Black Panthers' message that racism, power, and economics were all interconnected. To this argument, however, he continued to yoke the Social Gospel. In his National Cathedral sermon, he paraphrased the Gospel of Matthew, saying that if he and the audience did not act, God would tell them, "But I was hungry, and ye fed me not. I was naked, and ye clothed me not. I was devoid of a decent sanitary house to live in, and ye provided no shelter for me." In his Memphis speech, King told his audience that "it's all right to talk about 'long white robes over yonder,' but ultimately people want some suits and dresses and shoes to wear down here! It's all right to talk about 'streets flowing with milk and honey,' but God has commanded us to be concerned about the slums down here, and his children who can't eat three square meals a day." King was still arguing for a "revolution of values," just as he had at Riverside Church a year earlier.

On April 4, 1968, Martin Luther King was assassinated in Memphis, Tennessee. Between 1967 and 1969, Huey Newtown, Bobby Seale, and H. Rap Brown were arrested and imprisoned, while Stokely Carmichael and Eldridge Cleaver left the country in self-imposed exile. Their speaking had influenced and been influenced by great change, including the Civil

Rights Act of 1964, the Voting Rights Act of 1965, and the Open Housing Act of 1966. Among the many notable events that marked 1968 were three that related closely to African American public speaking: Lyndon Johnson dropped out of the race for president due to the unpopularity of the Vietnam War, the Kerner Commission's Report on the 1967 riots laid the groundwork for affirmative action as an institutional reform to the U.S. economic system, and Shirley Chisholm became the first African American woman elected to the U.S. Congress. Whether militant or mainstream, African American public speaking had borne fruit.

# 6

## "I Am Somebody"

### *Public Speaking in the Age of Integration*

IN 1963, JOURNALIST LOUIS LOMAX addressed a predominantly African American audience in a church basement just outside Los Angeles. In a nod to the poem "I Am Somebody" by the Reverend William Borders, Lomax said that young Blacks needed to believe that they were "somebody." To the adults, Lomax said that "I believe we could tell the young people in this choir and in this audience that they should stay in school because by the time they get out of school you and I will have knocked down every barrier there is." "By the same token," Lomax continued, "I'm saying to you young people tonight, . . . if I get my head kicked in for you; if I get bitten by a dog as I did in Birmingham, Alabama, and knocked down by a water hose as I did in Birmingham, Alabama; if I go through all this hell for you, when the job comes you'd better be ready!"

As integration and affirmative action began to take hold, there was a growing sense that barriers were being knocked down and that opportunities were increasing to "walk through" the door. Andrew Young, an organizer with the SCLC, recalled that many civil rights activists pondered their future after King's assassination. Some, like Young, Julian Bond, John Lewis, or Marion Barry, elected to enter politics and work to advance the cause from inside the system. Others, like Jesse Jackson, Marian Wright Edelman, Benjamin Hooks, or Benjamin Chavis, chose to continue their work as community activists.

POLITICALLY SPEAKING IN THE POST-1968 ERA

Following the 1968 election, ten African Americans were now members of Congress. Three of those had been elected in 1968, while three others had been elected within the previous four years. Among the newly elected representatives was the first African American woman elected to Congress, Shirley Chisholm of Brooklyn, an educator who had served as New York State assemblywoman. After holding her peace for the first two months after taking office, on March 26, 1969 Chisholm delivered her maiden speech on the floor of the House. Her subject was not civil rights but rather the Vietnam War.

Citing the newly elected president's own words, Chisholm noted that Richard Nixon had said during his campaign that "we can delay no longer in launching" new programs that would address the many issues facing the nation's cities. But, Chisholm said, "I have never cared too much what people say" but rather "what they do," and the first set of actions proposed by the Nixon administration included massive new defense spending and a "time-out" from social programs. Chisholm was dismayed that Nixon's secretary of defense had testified that the nation must be prepared to "spend at least two more years in Vietnam." "Two more years of hunger for Americans, of death for our best young men, of children here at home suffering the lifelong handicap of not having a good education when they are young," Chisholm lamented. Two more years "to feed the cancerous growth of a Defense Department budget" that now constituted two-thirds of the federal budget. "It must stop this year—now," she told the House.

Chisholm was quick to say that she was not a pacifist, but she did announce that she was "deeply, unalterably opposed to this war in Vietnam." Instead, she said, "our children, our jobless men, our deprived, rejected, and starving fellow citizens must come first." Chisholm concluded with a stark declaration: "For this reason, I intend to vote 'No' on every money bill that comes to the floor of this House that provides any funds for the Department of Defense—any bill whatsoever—until the time comes when our values and priorities have been turned right side up again . . . and our country starts to use its strength, its tremendous resources, for people and peace, not for profits and war."

In Congress, Chisholm also spoke in support of the Equal Rights Amendment for women, education programs for the poor and the young, day care centers for the working poor, and, in the years before *Roe v. Wade*, she supported providing access to birth control and safe abortions for the nation's poor. In 1972, Chisholm ran for the presidential nomination of the Democratic Party, reusing her political slogan "Fighting Shirley Chisholm." In her announcement speech, Chisholm said that she did not want to run as the African American candidate, nor as the woman candidate, but rather as "the candidate of the people." The central issue of her campaign was economic injustice and the expectation that the richest country in the world could do much better for those who were trapped in a life of poverty. Although Chisholm was never a front-runner, her campaign laid the groundwork for women and African Americans who would later run for president and vice president.

That same year, Barbara Jordan joined Shirley Chisholm in Congress, as one of two more African American women elected to the House of Representatives and the first African American woman elected from the South. Like Chisholm, Jordan had also served in her state's legislature, where she had been elected president pro tempore of the Texas state senate. Jordan maintained a relatively low profile during the first part of her freshman term, but on July 25, 1974, she delivered a speech that captured national attention. As a member of the House Judiciary Committee that was considering articles of impeachment against President Richard Nixon, Jordan gave her opening remarks to a prime-time national television audience.

Speaking in order of seniority, Jordan was one of the last committee members to deliver a statement. She had been gathering notes for the speech over the preceding weeks, but the manuscript itself was drafted over the dinner hour. As Jordan began to speak, it was her voice that first commanded attention. Like Chisholm, Jordan spoke firmly and clearly, albeit with an alto that filled the room. Her minister father had demanded that his daughters learn to speak in a way that enunciated each letter and syllable, and Jordan credited her choir training with teaching her about vocal projection. In college, she had been an award-winning competitive debater, which had further prepared her to deliver forceful and carefully reasoned speeches.

Jordan began by referencing her status as an African American and a woman, saying that she was someone who had been "left out" of the Constitution initially but had come to be included over the years through amendment, interpretation, and court decision in "We, the People." Her faith in the Constitution, she said, was now "whole, it is complete, it is total." "And," she continued, "I am not going to sit here and be an idle spectator to the diminution, the subversion, the destruction of the Constitution."

Citing Alexander Hamilton and James Madison, the Constitutional Convention of 1787, the Virginia and North Carolina ratification conventions, and even constitutional law scholar turned president Woodrow Wilson, Jordan laid out the case for why it was Congress's responsibility to move for impeachment if a president had committed impeachable offenses. In a meticulous review of constitutional law, Jordan argued that Congress

Rep. Barbara Jordan, House Judiciary Committee Watergate Hearings, 1974.
U.S. House of Representatives Photography Office.

could not ignore its duty and take the easy way out. "We are trying to be big," she concluded plainly, "because the task we have before us is a big one."

After dismissing the argument that the committee might want to "wait" to see if there were more evidence forthcoming, in a series of partial syllogisms Jordan juxtaposed impeachment criteria with actions the president had been found to undertake. Each criterion of impeachment was a quotation from an authoritative source, such as James Madison or Justice Joseph Story. After setting forth the standard, Jordan recited the president's actions that implicitly matched the criterion. She then repeated the impeachment criterion.

Jordan repeated the structure four times, beginning with "sheltering" guilty persons, moving through threatening rights and liberties and betraying the public trust, and finally concluding with "if the president attempts to subvert the Constitution." The series was built in climactic order, each charge being larger than the last, but with Jordan never explicitly saying that President Nixon should be impeached. As the anticipation grew that she would finally announce the logical conclusion of the syllogism, Jordan instead posed one more partial syllogism. "If the impeachment provision in the Constitution of the United States does not reach the offenses listed here," she said, "then perhaps that eighteenth-century Constitution should be abandoned to a twentieth-century paper shredder." The suggestion of using a paper shredder was a stark contrast to her introduction, where she had vowed not to be an "idle spectator" to the destruction of the Constitution. It made clear how Jordan felt about the impending impeachment vote, and the analogy brought the speech full circle back to Congress's responsibility to protect and defend the Constitution.

Popular reaction to the speech was overwhelmingly positive. Many who wrote or sent telegrams to Jordan agreed with her that the occasion was momentous. Her vigorous defense of the Constitution in a nationally televised speech embodied for many Americans the final, full "arrival" of Blacks and women on the American political scene. In 1976, Jordan would become the first African American and the first woman to deliver a keynote address to a Democratic National Convention.

Jordan's convention speech was unusual in that she did not address the political issues of the day. Because it was a national convention held on the heels of Watergate and the end of the war in Vietnam, Jordan talked about reforging the national community. Politics was not just about making pragmatic changes but rather "attempting on a larger scale to fulfill the promise of America. We are attempting to fulfill our national purpose, to create and sustain a society in which all of us are equal." Jordan admitted that the Democratic Party had made mistakes but that they had been "mistakes of the heart."

In language that Barack Obama would echo three decades later, Jordan emphasized America's historic pursuit of the democratic experiment: "We do not reject our traditions, but we are willing to adapt to changing circumstances, when change we must. We are willing to suffer the discomfort of change in order to achieve a better future. We have a positive vision of the future founded on the belief that the gap between the promise and reality of America can one day be finally closed." Jordan's speech was well received, and many Democrats urged Jimmy Carter to select Jordan as his vice presidential nominee. He did not do so, however, and following a diagnosis of multiple sclerosis in 1978, Jordan stepped away from politics.

During this decade, other African Americans also assumed positions of political prominence from which they spoke. For example, Tom Bradley served as mayor of Los Angeles from 1973 to 1993, Coleman Young was mayor of Detroit from 1974 to 1994, and Marion Barry served four terms as mayor of Washington, D.C., from 1979 to 1991 and then again from 1995 to 1999. The former SCLC organizer and later U.S. Representative Andrew Young was the U.S. ambassador to the United Nations for the first two years of the Carter presidency and was twice elected mayor of Atlanta, in 1981 and 1985.

Although these local political officials all spoke in their own styles, their multiple reelections suggest that each was a pragmatic politician. Andrew Young is representative, as he advocated a moral pragmatism. His political speaking focused on bringing together diverse groups. "Nonviolence is not one side trying to overcome the other side," he said in one speech at the University of Georgia; "nonviolence is both sides coming together ... where both can be free." In his opinion, African American leaders needed to "be able to get along with the brothers on the street in Harlem and ... in the forums of the Supreme Court or in the boardrooms of corporate America."

When advocating policy, Young particularly emphasized education and economic opportunity. In the kind of statement that might be misunderstood, Young told one audience that "I don't care what you do with race relations; it's economics that are vital." He did care about race relations—sometimes letting his background as a preacher emerge and brashly upbraiding those who would not admit the injustice of their words or actions. What Young argued, however, was that racial inequities would be perpetuated through educational and economic disparities, and in his role as an organizational leader, he prioritized attacking those inequalities. Broadly, these were the two issues that consumed many African American speakers who were in positions of governmental power.

## IN THE COMMUNITY

While Chisholm, Jordan, Young, and many others spoke for change through the authority of their political offices, others spoke as community activists. Many of the organizations that were prominent in the 1960s—such as the SCLC, the NAACP, and the Urban League—continued to be active in the 1970s and beyond, and community leaders such as Ralph Abernathy, Roy Wilkins, and Whitney Young were still active and important speakers. Other organizations and speakers, however, rose in visibility as well.

In 1972, the Reverend Jesse Jackson resigned from the SCLC, for which he had been directing Operation Breadbasket in Chicago, and he founded People United for Saving (later Serving) Humanity. Like Operation

Breadbasket, PUSH had a dual focus. It lobbied corporations to increase employment, management, and franchise ownership opportunities for minorities, and it also provided employment counseling and services in the community to help people take advantage of these and other economic opportunities that arose. Jackson used a high-energy, folk-preaching style, employing many parallelisms, colorful figures of speech, and even rhyme. In the later 1970s, he became known for his inspirational lectures to youth, marked by encouraging them to believe of themselves that "I am Somebody!" Another signature slogan of his was the optimistic "Up with Hope, Down with Dope." Jackson would rise to even greater prominence with two runs for the Democratic presidential nomination in 1984 and 1988.

In 1973, Marian Wright Edelman founded the Children's Defense Fund (CDF). Edelman had previously worked as a lawyer with the NAACP's Legal Defense Fund, suing for voting rights and other legal gains for Blacks in places like Mississippi during Freedom Summer. Like many other African American activists of the 1960s, Edelman was concerned about the history of poverty in the African American community and how the nation could break the cycle of poverty by improving the health, education, and living conditions of the children who were born into that poverty. Although Edelman's work was rooted in her concern about the African American community, her activism lobbied for programs to help impoverished children of any race.

Edelman's public speaking mirrored her style of personal lobbying. She quickly became recognized for her rapid, staccato delivery that packed a great deal of information into a short period of time. Whether speaking to an audience of hundreds or a single legislator, she always spoke as if time was of the essence and the children needed help now. Her speeches were full of statistics, detailing with specific numbers which programs delivered what results and how much they cost. She would, though, occasionally pause for the dramatic story that drove home the urgency of the situation, as when she told her National Education Association audience about the twenty-nine-year-old grandmother she had met. How can we hope to break the cycle when children are having children? she asked. Edelman began the CDF in the 1970s but would rise to special prominence in the 1980s as one of the most severe critics of the Reagan administration and as an influential lobbyist in the 1990s due to her close friendship with First Lady Hillary Clinton.

In 1976, Benjamin Hooks became the new executive director of the NAACP and was widely credited with revitalizing that organization. Hooks had earned a law degree from DePaul University in 1948, had worked as a public defender, and, in 1965, was the first African American judge appointed to preside in a criminal court in the state of Tennessee. In the meantime, Hooks had begun developing a parallel career in the ministry, and by the mid-1960s he was the lead minister for two Baptist churches, one in Memphis and one in Detroit. In 1972, Richard Nixon appointed Hooks to the board of the Federal Communications Commission (FCC). Hooks then led the NAACP from 1976 until his retirement in 1992. In that leadership role, he delivered thousands of speeches to a wide variety of audiences, both inside and outside the organization.

Although Hooks could talk about laws and the statistical results of government policies as well as anyone, his public speaking more generally assumed the gentle but earnest cadence of a minister. Like a minister opening his mind up to his congregation, Hooks often adopted the tone of confiding in the audience. "My mind examines some of the things we face now," he told one audience. Reminiscing about Martin Luther King Jr.'s last speech in Memphis, Hooks admitted that "I must confess that I was a little bit surprised" when King emphasized that there would be "dark and difficult days ahead" for the audience.

Hooks would use his personal tone, storytelling, and ironic humor to modestly chide his audience into changing their ways. Speaking in 1976 to the annual convention of the Association for the Study of Afro-American Life and History (ASALH), Hooks developed three points. The first was that some "limited success" had come to the African American community. There were now more than 4,000 Black CPAs in the United States, and there were more African Americans in college than there were students in all the British colleges combined. But his second point was that there was still too little progress. Drawing on his FCC experience, he pointed out that there were more than 7,000 commercial radio stations in the U.S., but only twenty were owned by African Americans. There were 1,600 telephone companies in the U.S., he said, but not a single one was owned by an African American.

What was needed, therefore, was his third point. African Americans needed to stick together, support each other, and continue to agitate for change. He extolled the ASALH for promoting the proud history of great African Americans like Percy Julian, the inventor of chemical synthetics; Charles Drew, the innovator of blood transfusions; and George Washington Carver of agricultural fame. But he admonished his audience for not applying those lessons of Black pride to their daily lives. He praised young African Americans for embracing their ethnicity with pride, telling his audience about how his nephew had grown his hair into an Afro and how

Hooks told his nephew that he "looked like a fool" with that hair. To which his nephew had responded, "Well, I'll cut it if you insist, but if I'm a fool with this hair, then I'll be a fool without it, too." Appropriately chastised, Hooks had begun growing out his own hair. In turn, Hooks had been asked by the ladies of his church when he was going to "cut his hair." He said that his response was that when they stopped wearing wigs to church, he would cut his hair. Through humor and storytelling, Hooks made his point, that the Black middle class needed to lead the way in agitating for stronger laws against discrimination, in taking greater pride in their community, and in working in tangible ways to lift the community out of poverty.

A major element of the NAACP's legal fight was to protect the few advances that had been attained at great cost. For example, in the late 1970s, some white Americans protested that they were becoming victims of "reverse discrimination," as was alleged in the *Regents of the University of California v. Bakke* case, where the plaintiff sued because he had not been accepted to the UC Davis Medical School. Affirmative action goals, Hooks said, were not quotas:

> All we are asking in this nation is that you give those of us who have planted your corn and picked your cotton and wet-nursed your babies and fought in every war and been loyal to this nation, all we're saying is that we want equality and parity and an opportunity to demonstrate that we can be part of the great American dream. We're not asking you to lower your qualifications because God in heaven knows they're low enough already. All we want is an opportunity.

Historic and systemic discrimination could not be changed without "goals and timetables" and legal mechanisms that would force them to be met.

In addition to change at home, Hooks was one of the African American speakers of the day who made the issue of apartheid in South Africa a touchstone in American politics. Speaking to a college audience in 1978, he used the repetitive style of preaching to arouse the conscience of the audience. There is a "regime in South Africa" that parallels the Nazis of Germany, he said, and yet "so many of us are satisfied." The white government has banned Black-owned newspapers and jailed dissidents, exhibiting "the most massive deprivation of human rights" the world had seen in three decades, and "yet so many of us are unconcerned because it doesn't seem to affect us." But though these are events "6,000 miles away," Americans of all backgrounds "ought begin to pay attention to it and to pay our witness and to do our best to see that the kind of apartheid, the kind of viciousness that exists in South Africa can be brought to a close."

## GROWING POLITICAL INFLUENCE

During the late 1970s and 1980s, African American politicians earned a number of "firsts": the first African American elected governor, the first African American elected mayor of a major city, the first African American elected U.S. senator from the Democratic Party. And finally, in 1984 and 1988, a major party presidential candidate who placed in the top three and top two delegate counts respectively.

Following the footsteps of a Shirley Chisholm or a Barbara Jordan, many of these leaders rose through the political system, elected first to lower, local-level offices before ascending to higher, nationally prominent positions. In contrast to these progressive climbs to power, Jesse Jackson's political career was meteoric, through which he was able to wield great influence. Moving directly from community organizer to a presidential campaign, Jackson became a national force politically.

In his first run for the presidential nomination, Jackson placed third behind Walter Mondale and Gary Hart, well ahead of the next closest candidate. On the second night of the 1984 Democratic National Convention, Jackson delivered his speech "The Rainbow Coalition," which was actually three speeches in one: an apology, a stump speech, and a motivational speech for the youth. The run-up to the speech had been contentious. In the spring, Jackson had been quoted using an ethnic slur to refer to the Jewish voting bloc in New York City. That characterization, along with his public appearances with Palestinian leaders, made many supporters of Israel uneasy. Negotiations between the Mondale and Jackson campaigns were acrimonious, with the former thinking that the latter had not demonstrated appropriate loyalty to the party's nominee and the latter feeling disrespected. The Jackson campaign finally secured the right to debate the party's platform and to have Jackson address the convention during prime time in exchange for his endorsement of Walter Mondale for president.

Although the speech began with an announcement that he would endorse the party's nominee, Jackson quickly made his apologies for the ill-conceived, controversial comment he had made earlier in the campaign. Using a series of antitheses, Jackson said that "if in my high moments," he had done some good, then his campaign was worth it. If he had "caused anyone discomfort, created pain," then, he said, "that was not my truest self." "I am not a perfect servant," he offered; "I am a public servant," and "God is not finished with me yet."

After thus confessing his sin, Jackson advanced his apology by recalling the close bonds between Jews and African Americans during the civil rights campaign and by referencing the religious heritage shared by Judaism and Christianity. He reminded his audience about the Mississippi murders of Schwerner, Goodman, and Chaney—two Jews and one African American. He supposed that "Dr. Martin Luther King and Rabbi Abraham Heschel must be crying out from their graves for us to find common ground." In the process of his historical recollection, Jackson paid his respects to the role the Jewish community had played during the 1950s/1960s civil rights campaign.

In the process of celebrating "our Judeo-Christian heritage, much too victimized by racism, sexism, militarism, and anti-Semitism, much too threatened as historical scapegoats to go on divided from one another," Jackson expanded his reach to include Islam. All three religions, he said, had been born in the holy city of Jerusalem. In this way, Jackson offered an olive branch to Jews even as he implicitly justified his support of the Palestinians.

Once Jackson had thus brought Muslim Americans into the Jewish–African American mix, he transitioned naturally into his stump speech, beginning with a description of his Rainbow Coalition. The coalition was Jackson's term through which he united those whom America had "left behind," including Hispanic Americans, Native Americans, young Americans, disabled veterans, small farmers, and the gay and lesbian communities, among others.

Jackson's discussion of disabled veterans was representative. Although he began by bringing up disabled veterans, he quickly expanded his attention to all of those with disabilities, using an antithesis to deplore the status quo: "The disabled have their handicap revealed and their genius concealed; while the able-bodied have their genius revealed and their disability concealed." "Don't leave anybody out," he commanded his audience, concluding with another antithesis that celebrated the disabled while condemning the incumbent president. Referencing President Reagan's penchant for being photographed at his California ranch, Jackson declared that "I would rather have Roosevelt in a wheelchair than Reagan on a horse."

The policies of the Reagan administration, he said, had not helped those in the Rainbow Coalition, and the stump speech portion of his address moved into a detailed indictment of President Reagan. "Rising tides don't lift all boats," Jackson said in a metaphor, especially "those stuck at the bottom." One passage was particularly memorable. After decrying the administration's cut to school breakfast and lunch programs, Jackson noted that President Reagan was a vocal proponent of prayer in schools. "Apparently he is not familiar with the structure of prayer," Jackson observed wryly; "you thank the Lord for the food you are about to receive, not the food that just left." He also urged the convention audience to pray—not about the food that "just left" but "to pray for the man who took the food to leave."

After indicting the Reagan administration for having abandoned the common person, Jackson promoted the platform of the Rainbow Coalition. Speaking broadly, he called for stronger enforcement of the 1965 Voting Rights Act and a clamping down on gerrymandering, less military spending and a greater emphasis on diplomacy and alliance-building in foreign affairs, and greater spending on jobs, infrastructure, food programs for the poor, education, and health.

Jackson then concluded the speech on a motivational note. Once more employing a series of antitheses, he contrasted the "slummy side" of the status quo with the "sunny side" of his proposed programs. "When I see a missing door," he said, "that's the slummy side," but "train some youth to become a carpenter—that's the sunny side." And so, he told the youth of his audience, "exercise the right to dream" of a "bright tomorrow." "Our time has come," Jackson proclaimed. "Give me your tired, give me your poor, your huddled masses who yearn to breathe free," he said, referencing Emma Lazarus's poem at the Statue of Liberty, "and come November, there will be a change because our time has come."

Jackson's speech was well-received. *Time* magazine wrote that it was a "stem-winder," a "sweaty, moving 51-minute tour-de-force." *Newsweek* magazine reported that his speech "brought a new music to the mainstream of American oratory." Some political reporters grumbled that much of his speech was the stump speech that they had been listening to on the campaign trail for half a year. But most of the television audience had never heard a Jesse Jackson speech from start to finish. Jackson's speech gained him a great deal of respect across the Democratic Party, and when he ran for president again in 1988, he doubled his primary vote total from 3.5 million to 7 million, and he placed first or second in forty-six primary contests. There is little doubt that the speech Jackson gave in 1984 paved the way for Barack Obama twenty-four years later.

At the 1988 Democratic National Convention, Jesse Jackson spoke again. Although that speech did not have the same historic impact, many scholarly observers thought that it was an even stronger speech. Jackson took "Common Ground" as his theme, advocating for unity within the party and across the country. "We meet tonight at the crossroads, a point of decision," he said early in his speech. "Shall we expand, be inclusive, find unity and power; or suffer division and impotence?"

Although he only referenced the Rainbow Coalition twice in his forty-nine-minute speech, the constituency he described was the same as 1984: the middle class and working poor. "What's the fundamental challenge of our day?" he asked, and then answered: "It is to end economic violence." Several times he used narrative to convey the experience of being a victim of "economic violence." In one passage, for example, he talked about hospital orderlies and janitors:

> No, no, they're not lazy. Someone must defend them because it's right and they cannot speak for themselves. They work in hospitals. I know they do. They wipe the bodies of those who are sick with fever and pain. They empty their bedpans. They clean out their commodes. No job is beneath them, and yet when they get sick they cannot lie in the bed they made up every day. America, that is not right.

He again used statistics to indict the Reagan administration, observing for example that taxes on the wealthiest 1 percent of the population declined by 20 percent, while the poorest 10 percent were paying 20 percent more.

A notable difference between his two convention speeches was that in 1988 Jackson twice used his own impoverished childhood to identify himself with his stated constituency. The first time occurred relatively early in the speech, when Jackson proposed a new metaphor for the blended nature of America:

> Common ground. America is not a blanket woven from one thread, one color, one cloth. When I was a child growing up in Greenville, South Carolina, my grandmama could not afford a blanket; she didn't complain and we did not freeze. Instead she took pieces of old cloth—patches, wool, silk, gabardine, crockersack—only patches, barely good enough to wipe off your shoes with. But they didn't stay that way very long. With sturdy hands and a strong cord, she sewed them together into a quilt, a thing of beauty and power and culture. Now, Democrats, we must build such a quilt.

Again, as he headed toward the conclusion of his speech, he became intensely personal, recollecting his childhood. The son of "a teen-age mother who was born of a teen-age mother," Jackson had been born at home, in a house without running water. Born out of wedlock, Jackson's name had changed three times by the time he was twelve. He was bullied and picked on and often had to do without, but "when my name goes in nomination," he told his Rainbow Coalition, "your name goes in nomination."

It was an interesting feature of the speech that he reserved this credibility appeal until he was just about finishing the speech. There may have been two reasons for doing so. The first was that Jackson seemed more interested in creating credibility that would continue after the speech was over, as if his continuing career in politics was more important than building additional credibility for this particular speech. The second reason was that it provided a natural transition into a motivational appeal, a nonpolitical section of the speech that echoed the conclusion of his 1984 DNC speech.

"I was born in the slum," he concluded with one more antithesis, "but the slum was not born in me." Youth still needed to "dream," and youth and partisans alike must "never surrender." Adversity would simply make them stronger. "Suffering breeds character," Jackson said, and "character breeds faith. In the end faith will not disappoint." Once again, Jackson was rewarded with a long standing ovation from the enthusiastic, placard-waving convention crowd. Although he did not run for president again, he was elected to serve as the shadow U.S. senator—a nonvoting position—from the District of Columbia from 1991 to 1997.

Jesse Jackson was not alone among African American speakers who were running for or serving in political office or government. In 1989, Lieutenant

Rev. Jesse Jackson, speaking at the U.S. Capitol about the 2000 presidential election, 2000. Florida Memory Project, State Archive of Florida.

Governor L. Douglas Wilder was elected governor of Virginia, becoming the first African American ever elected as governor. Wilder's speaking style contrasted sharply with the preaching style of Jackson. Trained in argumentation and debate at Howard University School of Law, as a state legislator in the 1970s, Douglass was known initially for his confrontational style. By the time of his election to statewide office in the mid-1980s, however, Wilder was using a plainer style, focused more on constructing arguments that bridged the issues that divided voters. As he said to one interviewer, in his speaking he emphasized using "words that are clear and understood by all—not fancy language."

In his arguments, too, Wilder spoke with the purpose of reaching everyone. Regarding abortion rights, for example, rather than frame the issue as one of women's rights, he emphasized the libertarian principle that government should be limited regarding the choices it forced upon the individual. Casting a wide net, Wilder praised Virginia's founders, drew on the state's identity as a "commonwealth," and referenced mythic American figures like Franklin Roosevelt. Within his broad appeal, however, Wilder especially sought to include those who, like Jackson's Rainbow Coalition, had historically been excluded. "In the coming years," he said in his inaugural speech, "we must persist in making every citizen of our commonwealth the subject of our interest and concern. We must insist that every agency of our government utilize every proper and effective instrument to carry out the will of the people.... An administration can only be effective when it works for the people, ... all the people." If his words about freedom and democracy could be made real, he said, then the "young people" of the commonwealth would know that "oppression can be lifted; ... that discrimination can be eliminated; ... that poverty need not be binding; ... that disability can be overcome."

Contemporaneous to Douglas Wilder's rise the 1970s and 1980s in Virginia state government, many major cities elected African Americans to serve as mayor, such as Bradley in Los Angeles, Coleman Young in Detroit, and Andrew Young in Atlanta during the 1970s and Harold Washington in Chicago in 1983. All were more liberal in their politics and public speaking than Wilder, but all of these government officials were also institutionalists. They all used public speaking in order to rally, cajole, encourage, and move the machinery of government to do better for African Americans and other historically disadvantaged and ignored people. This was also a political era when conservative African Americans became more visible in politics. One figure especially assumed center stage in national politics in the late 1980s: General Colin Powell.

Colin Powell first attracted national notice when he was appointed as national security advisor in 1987. Two years later he became chairman of the Joint Chiefs of Staff, and in 2001 he would be appointed secretary of state. Powell's public speaking reflected his military training. His speeches were usually problem oriented, unemotional, and with few stylistic embellishments. When weighing the relative costs and benefits of the solutions, Powell typically turned to history, experience, and traditional values in order to judge which solution would be best. His calm speaking demeanor was authoritative and reassuring.

Colin Powell's style of speaking shifted slightly when delivering a ceremonial speech, such as celebrating a national holiday or speaking for commencement at a historically Black college. In those situations, Powell became a bit more emotional and employed somewhat more stylized rhetorical flourishes. These speeches were still very traditional, adhering to the norms of the occasion, but within those structures he often made them very personal as well. For example, shortly after the Gulf War, Powell gave the featured remarks at the Vietnam Veterans Memorial on Memorial Day. To those who were apologetic that the Gulf War veterans were being celebrated in a manner the Vietnam veterans had never experienced, Powell took a defiant perspective on the issue, a view fashioned by his own two tours of duty in Vietnam.

> The parades and celebrations are not needed to restore our honor as Vietnam veterans because we never lost our honor. They're not to clear up the matter of our valor because our valor was never in question. Two hundred and thirty-six Medals of Honor say our valor was never in question. Fifty-eight thousand, one hundred and seventy-five names on this Wall say our valor and the value of our service were never in question.

"On this Memorial Day," Powell eulogized, "we run our fingers softly over the names. We again draw near to feel its grief and its dark pain. We again experience the terror and horror of war—all war."

To predominantly Black audiences, Powell acknowledged the country's shortcomings, but he reiterated a traditional faith in the U.S. "America," he said at Fisk University, grounding his claims in his extensive experience of traveling the world, "is the only country in the world that strives incessantly to make the dream of America the reality of America." Invariably, in speeches to these audiences, Powell would also pay homage to those who came before. Speaking to a convention of the Tuskegee Airmen, Powell asserted that "I never forget for a day, or for an hour, or for a minute that I climbed to my position on the backs of the courageous African American men and women who went before me." Powell exhorted his audience to heed in any manner they chose the NACW's motto of "Lifting as We Climb" and Du Bois's notion of the Talented Tenth. "You face great expectations," Powell told his Howard University audience, "much has been given to you and much is expected from you." Although Powell's political policies were conservative, his message about building the community was a theme that echoed across the political spectrum.

## COMMUNITY ACTIVISM IN THE 1980s

Most African American community speakers in the 1970s were primarily known within their own circles of influence. In the 1980s, however, many African American community activists became prominent nationally. For some, it was by virtue of the organizations they led, but for others it was their public speaking that brought them to national attention.

### *Organizational Leaders*

Marian Wright Edelman, for example, continued to lead the Children's Defense Fund. During the 1980s, she was an especially prominent critic of the Reagan administration. Speaking to the National Education Association in 1985, Edelman began by quoting Martin Luther King's "A Time to Break Silence." King had said, Edelman observed, that "a nation that continues year after year to spend more money on military defense than on programs of social uplift is approaching spiritual death." The president's budget cuts to health, education, and welfare spending was, she announced, a "moral travesty."

As was her habit, Edelman blended statistics, anecdotes, moments of self-reflection, homey phrases, and ironic ridicule to persuade her audience to support her platform. She noted, for example, that a single mother of three earning an annual income of $10,500 in 1984 had paid federal income tax of just under $1,200. Edelman bitingly pointed out that this working mother, who lived below the poverty line, had paid more federal taxes than Boeing, General Electric, DuPont, Texaco, Mobil, and AT&T combined. She went on to attack Reagan's Grace Commission, a committee tasked with identifying waste in government spending. Edelman noted that the company owned by the commission chair, the W. R. Grace Company, had not only *not* paid any income taxes but had received from the federal government a $12.5 million rebate. "If we just brought the W. R. Grace's [federal] tax rate up to *zero*," she observed, "we could pay for nine million school lunches that the president has cut."

Edelman supported a broad array of social programs that supported children: birth control clinics for the young and the poor, school lunch and breakfast programs, tax breaks for the working poor, pre-K education for those unable to afford it, and day care for the working poor. While her policies were liberal, many of the values she espoused were very traditional. Welfare, she argued, could not replace the dignity of work, but government tax policies, day care support, and training programs needed to support that search for dignity. In her mind, family planning was critical. Teenage mothers were too likely to repeat a cycle of poverty: "Children having children is like an engine that is driving new generations of poor children." Prenatal care for those who did become pregnant was an equally pressing need. "It costs us $600 to give prenatal care, including vitamins and nutritional supplements to women," Edelman told an audience of educators, "[but] about $20,000 to care for a premature infant just in the first twenty days of life."

In 1978, Faye Wattleton became the first African American and the first woman to be chosen to serve as president of the Planned Parenthood Federation of America. Wattleton was also the youngest person ever selected for that job. A nurse with an M.S. in maternity and infant care, Wattleton spoke as an organizer and lobbyist on the issues of women's health, birth control, and prenatal as well as postnatal health care in the U.S. and around the world. During the 1980s, Planned Parenthood, too, resisted the conservative political shift under Ronald Reagan. Scholars noted Wattleton's effective organizational leadership, of which her speaking was a vital part. During Wattleton's fourteen years as president, Planned Parenthood became the seventh-largest charity in the nation, with a budget that had tripled to $380 million annually.

Like Edelman, Wattleton was as comfortable using anecdotal evidence as she was using statistics. She would tell stories of her visits to clinics in Asia and Africa, and she would also remind her audience that the fates of "four million people we serve are hanging by a thread." "If Planned Parenthood's program is defunded," she observed, "there will be 400,000 additional unwanted pregnancies, 70,000 additional abortions, and over 1,200 deaths from abortions."

Wattleton's criticisms were, like Edelman's, sharply phrased. "As a woman," she said at a 1989 rally for women's equality, "I know that the power for the government to control women's reproduction is more frightening than any other tyranny, more binding than any other prison." "In a pluralistic society," she argued in the same vein as Douglas Wilder, "private morality must be just that—private!" Her motivation for speaking on behalf of reproductive rights and government funding for women's health services echoed those of many community activists: "To speak out for those who are too weak, too young, too far away—or just too desperate and dispirited—to make their voices heard."

*Ministerial Voices*

After Malcolm X was assassinated in 1965, no powerful new speaker emerged immediately for the Nation of Islam. Elijah Muhammad was always a relatively insular speaker, focused inwardly on the Nation's followers. After his death in 1975, a split emerged between his son, W. Deen Muhammad, and Louis Farrakhan. The younger Muhammad wanted to move the Nation toward the traditional teachings of Islam, and he renamed the organization several times until finally settling on the American Society of Muslims. Farrakhan, who had increasingly spoken as a proxy for Elijah Muhammad, broke with Elijah's son, revived the Nation of Islam under its original name, and brought back to the oratorical vigor it had experienced with Malcolm X.

Public speaking was vital to Louis Farrakhan's work with the NOI. Rhetorical scholar Mark McPhail noted that over the first two decades of his leadership, Farrakhan traveled over 250,000 miles a year to deliver speeches to his followers and potential converts. Like Malcolm X, Farrakhan was a controversial speaker. Many observers saw him as a demagogue who continued the anti-white condemnation of the United States that characterized Malcolm X's early speeches. Like many Black nationalists, Farrakhan has argued that the U.S. is imperialist and colonialist and that white racism fuels that drive. As McPhail noted, Farrakhan used war metaphors and prophecies of Armageddon to unite his followers and to reassure them that the Nation would ultimately triumph.

During the 1980s, Farrakhan allied himself with the Palestinian cause and became a vocal critic of Israel. Combined with reports that he had praised Hitler and characterized Judaism as a "gutter" or "dirty" religion, Farrakhan was widely condemned as being anti-Semitic and a demagogue. In turn, many observers criticized Jesse Jackson for accepting Farrakhan's endorsement and for not sufficiently distancing himself from Farrakhan's anti-Semitic remarks. Others saw him as a powerful and "spellbinding" voice against systemic and institutional racism. Many of Farrakhan's critiques of the U.S. systems of education, economics, and criminal justice were repeated by subsequent speakers, such as Patrisse Cullors, Alicia Garza, and Opal Tometti of the Black Lives Matter movement, or Bryan Stevenson with the Equal Justice Initiative.

Another community activist speaker who rose to national prominence in the 1980s was the Reverend Al Sharpton. Sharpton began preaching at age four, and by ten he was an ordained Pentecostal minister known as the "Wonderboy" preacher, touring with gospel singers such as Mahalia Jackson. In 1969, at age fifteen, he was appointed by Jesse Jackson to be the youth director of the New York chapter of Operation Push. Throughout the 1970s and early 1980s, Sharpton moved fluidly between the worlds of religion, politics, and entertainment, working for a time as the business manager for James Brown and later collaborating with boxing promoter Don King on sporting events and anti–South African apartheid agitation.

In the mid-1980s, Sharpton became the leading activist in a series of demonstrations in New York City. In 1985, Bernard Goetz, a white man, shot four African American teenagers on the subway because he thought they were "threatening." In 1986, three Black men were assaulted by a group of white teenagers. One of the Black men escaped, another was struck and killed as he ran across a highway, and the third was savagely beaten with a bat and tire iron. These incidents were, Sharpton said, "the ugly face of northern racism," and Sharpton's fiery speeches at rallies and press conferences helped fuel community demonstrations. When some observers criticized him as simply being a "showman," Sharpton defended himself: "I was speaking for people who didn't normally have a voice, I was speaking from neighborhoods that didn't normally gain attention, I had to be dramatic, I had to be loud." In 1987, a third event, in which an African American girl falsely accused four white men of raping her, tarnished Sharpton's image among some as he steadfastly and unequivocally supported the girl. Despite these criticisms, however, Sharpton continued to be a popular and very visible speaker.

Another national figure was Benjamin Chavis, who brought his ministerial and activist voice to the issue of racial justice, putting a special spotlight on environmental racism. Chavis had worked in politics, in the civil rights movement, and as a youth leader with the United Church of Christ throughout the 1960s. In 1971, he participated in protests in Wilmington, North Carolina, and was subsequently brought to trial as one of the Wilmington Ten and convicted on charges of conspiracy and arson. In 1980, the Federal Court of Appeals overturned the verdict and Chavis was released from prison. That same year he was ordained as a minister by the

United Church of Christ, having earned his master's of divinity while in prison.

In the 1980s, Chavis was a leading speaker and writer who challenged what he called environmental racism. Racism was systemic, Chavis said, for it was threaded throughout the institutions that controlled the lives of people of color. His charge of environmental racism rested on three elements of environmental injustice. First, corporations found it cheaper and easier to locate their plants and refineries near impoverished neighborhoods, especially those where people of color lived. Corporations also found it cheaper to improperly dispose of waste and, if caught, pay the fine than to take proper care of the contaminants in the first place. Second, Chavis said, a government that has little minority representation would not pass laws to protect those communities nor enforce the laws it did have. Finally, the environmental movement that had sprung up in the 1970s was itself systemically racist, even if not intentionally so. Environmental groups, Chavis noted, were more interested in protecting forest preserves and little-known species than in making sure that the air being breathed by racial minorities was not toxic or that the water they drank was not polluted.

*Intellectual Voices*

Not all community activists were leaders of organizations or members of the clergy. Many writers, academics, and thought leaders spread their influence popularly through lectures and speeches. Angela Davis, for example, remained an active and much-sought after speaker on college campuses throughout these decades and has remained so to the present day. Historically, Black intellectuals like Crummell, Terrell, Du Bois, James Weldon Johnson, Bethune, and Richard Wright spoke widely and publicly and were usually politically active as well. Traditionally, however, their audiences were often limited to African Americans, progressive whites, and Europeans. By the 1970s and 1980s, however, the invitations to speak to integrated audiences became far more plentiful.

One pioneering voice of Black intellectuals in this era was Audre Lorde. A poet and a professor of literature, Lorde, too, used emancipatory rhetoric to challenge what she saw as the prevailing vocabulary of power. To the issues of class, race, and gender, Lorde added concerns regarding sexual orientation. Challenging the status quo, said Lorde, required different words. "The master's tools," she frequently noted, "will never dismantle the master's house." As she confessed in a 1980 talk at Amherst College, this was exhausting work but also a vital effort of survival:

> As a forty-nine-year-old Black lesbian feminist socialist mother of two, including one boy, and a member of an interracial couple, I usually find myself a part of some group defined as other, deviant, inferior, or just plain wrong. . . . [But] to pluck out some one aspect of myself and present this as the meaningful whole, eclipsing or denying the other parts of myself . . . is a destructive and fragmenting way to live. . . . My fullest concentration of energy is available to me only when I integrate all the parts of who I am, openly, allowing power from particular sources of my living to flow back and forth freely through my different selves, without restrictions of externally imposed definition.

Supporters and critics alike observed that Lorde's writing and speaking were often "angry," but Lorde's anger was intentional. Anger against the forces of oppression, she argued, could be a liberating force. After she was diagnosed with breast cancer, Lorde said she examined her life reflectively and discovered that "what I most regretted were my silences. . . . Of what had I ever been afraid?" She concluded, "My silence had not protected me. Your silence will not protect you."

Across the course of the 1980s, Lorde became increasingly frustrated with white feminists, seeing in many of them the continued prejudices of classism, racism, and heterosexism. More and more, Lorde focused on speaking to Black women and in support of Black feminism. She argued that the linear, problem-solving discourse of Euro-Americans was restrictive and confining. The poetic and holistic speaking of African cultures erased boundaries and allowed the individual to draw power from their very nature. Her speeches reflected these beliefs, as they were often free-flowing, creatively oriented, and filled with references to African goddesses, myths, and cultural practices that were often obscure for her audience.

Another important intellectual voice that emerged in the 1980s and beyond was bell hooks (Gloria Watkins). Like Lorde, hooks was a poet and professor of literature who addressed the systemic biases of gender, race, class, and sexuality through her speaking and writing. hooks came to national notice in 1981, with the publication of *Ain't I Woman: Black Feminism and Feminism*. The title was taken from Sojourner Truth's speech of 1853, and hooks emphasized the deep, historical nature of discrimination. The white-capitalist-patriarchy had to be confronted not simply through the redefinition of terms, but through a clearer perception of the historical nature of the forces they were confronting.

Where Lorde used anger to confront the social injustice, hooks argued that feminists needed to break down barriers. Like Lorde, hooks, too, was concerned about the racist structures that persisted among some white feminists, but she welcomed all those—regardless of race or gender—who sought to resist systemic injustice. Put simply, she said "feminism is a movement to end sexism, sexist exploitation, and oppression." Patriarchy, she said, tries to dominate and control, which inherently divides one group from another. In contrast, feminism is an inclusive force. "Positive social equality," she said, "that grants all humans the opportunity to shape their destinies in the most healthy and communally productive way can only be a complete reality when our world is no longer racist and sexist."

Consistent with the content of her message of inclusivity, hooks's speaking was clear and definitively phrased, even while being calm and soft-spoken. She effectively delivered traditional speeches, like lectures and commencement speeches, but a large portion of her public speaking was conversational, conducted as dialogues with an interviewer or in a panel setting with other speakers.

One such dialogue partner was Cornel West, who in 1991 published with hooks *Breaking Bread: Insurgent Black Intellectual Life*, which consisted of a series of dialogues between the two. A theologian by training and a protest activist by habit, West criticized the racism and patriarchy of the U.S. and promoted Christian socialism. A prolific author, he was yet another highly sought-after Black speaker. One of the causes he took up, as did many Black intellectuals of the era, was the issue of apartheid in South Africa. Speakers like West focused on the human rights aspect of apartheid, analogizing it to the system of segregation that had existed in the U.S. They demanded that U.S. companies and universities divest themselves of their economic interests in South Africa. Among universities, the argument was particularly persuasive, as many of these speakers, like West, held appointments at prestigious institutions. These speakers also helped make Nelson Mandela the "face" of issue in the United States. In South Africa, Mandela had been imprisoned since 1962 for having led the resistance to apartheid and had several times refused offers of release because the arrangement would have left the system of apartheid in place.

While West was a theologian who extended his studies of religion into history, philosophy, and economics, Henry Louis Gates was a literary critic who worked on legitimizing the study of African American culture, including forms of discourse such as African American Vernacular English. His 1989 book, *The Signifying Monkey: A Theory of African-American Literary Criticism*, proposed that African American literature should be understood as being highly contextual, where earlier texts and discourses are interwoven with current texts in order to create new meanings. Although he spoke in support of creating academic departments of African and African

American studies, in the larger picture Gates advocated a program of integration and an appreciation for multicultural diversity throughout the academy.

A third important speaker and writer of the era was Molefi K. Asante (formerly Arthur Smith), a communication studies scholar who helped found the Department of Africology and African American Studies at Temple University in Philadelphia. Like Gates, Asante argued that African American works, especially the oral messages, must be understood by contextualizing them within the traditions of African discourse. The author of *Afrocentricity* (1980) and *The Afrocentric Idea* (1987), Asante placed Afrocentrism as the dialectical opposite of Eurocentrism. Like Gates, Asante argued that Afrocentric communication was deeply rooted in oral culture and therefore highly contextual and nuanced in its meanings. Central to Afrocentric messaging was the concept of *nommo*, which translates broadly as "the word," but which focuses on meanings and community brought together by the language rather than on the notion that language is something the speaker controls. *Nommo* entails the creation of a unified meaning that creates and emerges from the community and erases the divide that is created when one person is labeled the speaker and the other is the audience. The call-and-response characteristic of African American speaking is one manifestation of *nommo*, where the speaker and the audience become one and a single meaning emerges. *Nommo* also emphasizes the community-building function of speaking, rather than simply thinking of it as an "instrument" to produce some end "product."

## THE TURN OF THE MILLENNIUM

The two decades that straddled the start of the twenty-first century solidified the role of African American public speakers in the broad life of the nation. As government officials, politicians, ministers, intellectuals, business leaders, community leaders, entertainers, and athletes, African Americans were heard speaking about the full range of issues and opportunities that faced the country.

The 1990s began with African Americans speaking prominently in a wide variety of venues, some familiar, others less so. Colin Powell was named chairman of the Joint Chiefs of Staff in 1989 and was a featured government spokesperson for the U.S. invasion of Panama and the First Gulf War. In 1993, he became embroiled in Bill Clinton's controversial policy regarding gays in the military of "Don't Ask, Don't Tell." Powell defended the traditional military point of view that LGBTQ individuals should not be allowed to serve in the military "at this time," as he tried to qualify his objection. Faye Wattleton was nearing the end of her long tenure as president of Planned Parenthood, defending the organization against renewed attacks by the Bush administration.

Jesse Jackson continued to be a major voice on the political stage, although he resisted calls for him to run for the position of Washington, D.C., delegate to the House of Representatives when Walter Fauntroy was stepping down after two decades in office. In Fauntroy's place, the district elected Eleanor Holmes Norton, a lawyer known for her work with the SNCC, Mississippi Freedom Summer, and later the American Civil Liberties Union. Norton continues to hold that office in 2022. As a congresswoman, Norton is a speaker very much in the tradition of Shirley Chisholm. She carefully marshals her arguments and evidence and expresses her beliefs clearly and forcefully. As Norton herself said about her public speaking, "To undo the handicaps that the slave culture worked on Black family and the Black psyche takes more than just handing out resources"; it takes asserting oneself and one's rights in the public sphere. To do that, Norton argued, requires a forceful presence, and her public speaking embodies that belief.

Marian Wright Edelman continued to be a well-known speaker, in part through her close friendship with First Lady Hillary Clinton and the informal influence Edelman was perceived to have with the Clinton White House. Despite her close association with the Clintons, Edelman continued to take the U.S. government to task for having misaligned priorities, spending too much on defense and corporate giveaways and not enough on children's health, education, and welfare. She reminded audiences that nearly one in five children in the U.S. lived in poverty and that the number was increasing. She attacked the rise of violent deaths in the U.S., as well as the increased incarceration of poor men convicted of nonviolent crimes, which in turn broke down the traditional family structure.

Much to the chagrin of the Clintons, Edelman continued to talk about her statistics in moral terms. As she told an audience in 1995 at a public health conference, "I don't use the word 'evil' very often, but I tell you it is evil what is happening in Washington today. And I tell you, we must stand up with all our might and fight this." When George W. Bush was elected in 2000 and proposed his "No Child Left Behind" program of education, Edelman embraced the phrase and attempted to guide the program's implementation by doing so. "It's time!" she said at Tulane University in 2001. "It's time to build a mighty movement to Leave No Child Behind in the richest and most powerful nation on earth. I hope you will be part of it." When the Bush administration pivoted from No Child Left Behind to the wars in Iraq and Afghanistan, Edelman returned to criticizing the diversion of spending away from children's causes and back to defense.

Minister Louis Farrakhan was another speaker of continuing prominence at the turn of the millennium. In 1995, Farrakhan organized the Million Man March, a call for Black men to assemble in Washington, D.C., as both an act of and a call for atonement. Farrakhan said that African American men had a special responsibility to come together and confess that they had fallen short on their commitments to their families and communities and to physically demonstrate a commitment to do better. Because of his controversial past, many critics, including some African Americans like Colin Powell and some leaders of Black Christian churches, dismissed the March and used the event as an opportunity to again condemn Farrakhan as being racist, anti-Semitic, and patriarchal. In his speech to the marchers, Farrakhan disavowed any such motives, implicitly rejecting the earlier Nation of Islam characterization of whites as the devil:

> Let me say in truth, you can't point out wrong with malice. You can't point out wrong with hatred. So, we ask Muslims, who, in our first stage, we pointed out the wrongs of America, but we didn't point it out with no love, we pointed it out with the pain of our hurt. The pain of our suffering. The bitterness of our life story. But we have grown beyond our bitterness. We have transcended beyond our pain.

As rhetorical scholar Mark McPhail writes, Farrakhan's challenge to white America was to look beyond the Nation's past to the truth of what he was saying now. The message, writes McPhail, is that "*I* have atoned. *We* have atoned. Now *you* should atone."

While Farrakhan remained a controversial figure into the new century, his speeches appealed to many Blacks, as well as some whites. Similar to the trajectory of Malcolm X, Farrakhan moved away from the origin story of the white devil to the more traditional teachings of Islam, and his appeals became more inclusive. Many Jews remained distrustful, seeing his support of the Palestinian cause as a reminder of anti-Semitic remarks he had made, and many women remained skeptical about the patriarchal ethos of the Nation of Islam. However, his calls for self-control and responsibility, as applied not only to each individual but to the U.S. government, appealed to many. Regarding the government, he long condemned the mass incarceration of Black men and called for U.S. reparations to African Americans whose ancestors had been held in slavery.

A similarly militant voice at the turn of the century belonged to Rev. Al Sharpton. He remained a speaker who sharply challenged the status quo. After a car driven by a Hasidic Jew struck two African American children, killing one, in the highly segregated Crown Heights neighborhood of New York City, Sharpton was accused of fanning the flames of division. Preaching at the child's funeral, Sharpton excoriated the "apartheid ambulance service," saying that criticism of Blacks' second-class treatment there was "not anti-Semitism; the issue is apartheid.... All we want to say is what Jesus said: if you offend one of these little ones, you got to pay for it. No compromise, no meetings.... Pay for your deeds."

That year, Sharpton founded the National Action Network (NAN) to fight for social justice, and over the next three decades, he would often appear at meetings and rallies across the country to bring attention to issues of racial and social injustice. He also threw himself into the political ring. In 1992 and 1994, he campaigned in New York for the U.S. Senate, and in 1997, he sought the Democratic nomination for the position of mayor of New York. Although he remained a sharp-tongued critic of social and political polices that disadvantaged African Americans, Sharpton increasingly emphasized the nonviolent legacy of Martin Luther King Jr. In an Inauguration Day speech protesting George W. Bush's 2000 election as illegitimate, Sharpton characterized his audience's protest as a continuation of the civil rights movement: "We have taken an oath today that the blood of Goodman, Chaney, and Schwerner was not shed in vain, ... that Martin Luther King will not be erased from the annals of history, ... that we will turn this nation around."

In 2003, Sharpton began a run for the Democratic nomination for president. He was appalled at the conservative turn the "New Democrats" had taken under Bill Clinton, who had declared in his 1996 State of the Union address that "the era of big government was over." Sharpton objected to the rise of three-strike laws and the severe criminalization of drug use that disproportionately punished Blacks as well as the reduction in social services. He never ran his campaign to win, he said, but rather "to slap the donkey" and take it back to its liberal roots. "When I ran for president," he said later, "I put affirmative action, police misconduct, and racial profiling on the national agenda. These issues never would have been discussed during the campaign, wouldn't have had the chance to become more mainstream, if I hadn't been at the table."

Although Sharpton never placed higher than third in any of the primaries, like Jesse Jackson in 1984 and 1988 his speech at the 2004 convention brought a prominent African American voice to the dais that summer. Fittingly, another African American had delivered the convention's keynote speech the night before: Illinois state senator Barack Obama.

## CHAPTER 6

## THE TALE OF TWO SPEECHES

In their addresses to the convention, both speakers sounded common American themes. Reverend Sharpton talked about the promise of America, the family values of hard work and responsibility, and he concluded by referencing "America the Beautiful" and called for America to be made beautiful again. Sharpton also talked about his candidacy as an example of what was possible to the child in the "ghetto." For his part, Senator Obama quoted from the Declaration of Independence and the U.S. Constitution and held up the U.S. motto *E Pluribus Unum* (Out of many, one) as the representative image of America.

A comparison of the two addresses, however, shows that while both touched on themes common to American political discourse, Sharpton's speech more pointedly raised the issue of where African Americans fit into the twenty-first century U.S.

Throughout his speech, Sharpton touched on issues and themes that were specific to African Americans. He began his address by noting the convention's location in Boston, the site of the 1770 Boston Massacre that set the nation on its path toward the American Revolution. The first American who died at the massacre, Sharpton observed, was "a Black man from Barbados, Crispus Attucks." He then referenced Fannie Lou Hamer and the 1964 Democratic National Convention at Atlantic City, the Bloody Sunday march at Selma, and Jesse Jackson's speech at the 1984 Democratic National Convention. Each of those moments, he said, were endured in an effort to attain and secure the freedom of all citizens.

Sharpton also spent time explaining why African Americans were supporting the Democratic Party but also asking for reparations. The Republican Party of Lincoln, he said, had promised those who were emancipated "40 acres and a mule." While Democratic leaders had helped secure passage of the Civil Rights Act of 1964 and the Voting Rights Act of 1965, and thus earned African Americans' support, neither the acreage nor the mule had ever been realized, and so there was much more to be done.

In his address, Sharpton linked the themes of civil rights to women's rights, gay rights to social welfare programs, and human rights crises abroad to "police misconduct" at home. However, while he evoked broader ideals of American equality and the natural rights of people, he remained focused on the particular circumstance of African Americans. He reminded his audience about the controversial 2000 presidential election vote count in Florida four years earlier and explained why the issue was so important to African Americans. "Mr. President," Sharpton said, "the reason we are fighting so hard ... is [because] our right to vote wasn't gained because of our age. Our vote was soaked in the blood of martyrs, soaked in the blood of Goodman, Chaney, and Schwerner, soaked in the blood of four little girls in Birmingham. This vote is sacred to us."

In contrast, Barack Obama's speech stressed that the United States was fundamentally a single community, albeit one that drew its unity from the value of diversity. He began with his personal biography, which blended the stories of a white mother from Kansas with a Black father from Kenya. While his parents came from diverse backgrounds, he said that they were both bound by a single belief in a "common dream" that in America everyone could live up to his or her potential. He repeatedly touched on what he called "the true genius of America," which was at various turns in the speech "a faith in the simple dreams of its people," "a belief that we are connected as one people," the "belief that there are better days ahead," and a belief in the self-evident "truths" that were expressed in the Declaration of Independence, that "all men are created equal."

Obama touched on points that implicitly referenced his identity as an African American speaker, but unlike Sharpton's speech, these references did not confront the issue of racial disparity. He said that the "Black child on the south side of Chicago who can't read" mattered to him, even if it was not his child, but Obama went on to make similar claims about the senior citizen who could not afford prescription medicine and the Arab American family "being rounded up without benefit of an attorney or due process."

Twice the senator told a story about people from East St. Louis, a city where over 90 percent of the population is African American. The first brief story was about a woman who had the grades, drive, and will to go to college but not the money. The second brief story was about Shamus, a Marine with "absolute devotion" to his country who was being deployed to Iraq the next week. Was the government serving its military as well as its military was serving the country? Obama wondered. In both stories, the race of the person was implied but never explicitly mentioned.

In one of the few specific times that Obama mentioned African Americans, he explicitly discussed an African American in terms of reverse stereotyping. As he talked about taking personal responsibility and asserted that no American expects government to do everything, he condemned "the slander that says a Black youth with a book is acting white."

The conclusion of Obama's speech became famous for his parallel reversal of political stereotypes. He began by declaring that "there's not a liberal America and a conservative America; there's the United States of America." He continued with a disavowal of issues specific to race: "There's not a Black America and white America and Latino America and Asian America; there's the United States of America." After reminding the audience that blue states was the name for those that leaned Democratic and red states were those that leaned Republican, he attacked the idea of issue ownership: "We worship an awesome God in the Blue States, and we don't like federal agents poking around our libraries in the Red States. We coach Little League in the Blue States and have gay friends in the Red States. There are patriots who opposed the war in Iraq and patriots who supported it. We are one people, all of us pledging allegiance to the stars and stripes, all of us defending the United States of America."

The convention was, as many have noted, a tale of two speeches. One speaker drew on the tradition of African Americans who called America to account for the distance between its promise of equality and its treatment of its Black citizens. Martin Luther King had said that America had defaulted on its promissory note. Al Sharpton wondered what had happened to the forty acres and a mule. The other speaker drew on the tradition that ignored the racial disparities and instead emphasized those instances in society where equality had been realized. Senator Obama sounded much more like Colin Powell than he did like Jesse Jackson.

Communication scholar Mark MacPhail argues that while both Sharpton and Obama embraced the "ideals" of America, Sharpton did so in order to call America into account for its failure to live up to those ideals, while Obama did so in order to paint a portrait of "hope." Sharpton was speaking "truth to power," while Obama was promoting "racelessness." Obama's speech, MacPhail says, celebrated the "abstractions of the social contract while ignoring the realities of the racial contract," while Sharpton emphatically reminded the audience about those realities. A part of MacPhail's concern was that, while Sharpton's speech drew longer sustained applause at the convention, many white commentators criticized the minister for "hijacking" the convention with a speech that was "off message" and "incendiary." Notably, while Sharpton's speech was largely forgotten, Obama's lived on in public memory.

The two speeches foreshadowed Senator Obama's successful campaign for the presidency four years later. He would be challenged by some critics for not being "Black enough," while many whites would still see him as "too Black." His election ushered in pronouncements that the "post-racial" society described in his 2004 DNC keynote had arrived, but the realities of race relations in the United States would quickly put the lie to that declaration. In the next decade, African American speakers would address this paradox head on.

# 7

# Barack Obama and the "Post-Racial" Society

WHEN BARACK OBAMA SWEPT TO VICTORY in 2008 with 365 electoral votes to John McCain's 173, and with almost ten million more votes, journalists, historians, and many in the public believed that a post-racial United States had arrived. Even when it became clear that Obama would be the Democratic nominee, many experts had said that it would be very difficult for an African American to be elected president. His overwhelming victory proved them wrong, and many saw his election as a watershed moment in history. The celebration continued through his January inauguration, as officials estimated that 1.8 million people attended the swearing-in, the largest crowd ever to witness a president taking the oath of office.

Other observers were not so sure, however. Many, especially those in the African American community, were quick to say that one presidential election would not erase four hundred years of American history and that their own everyday experiences of prejudice and discrimination had not changed simply because a Black man was in the Oval Office. When examined closely, the election results confirmed the warnings that the optimism had been overstated. In the general election, Obama had been overwhelmingly supported by African Americans, Latinos, and Asian Americans. Among white Americans, however, he had only garnered 43 percent of the vote. Even among Democrats, this was the same percentage Obama had received from white voters in the primaries, when he was running against Hillary Clinton. Race was a contentious issue in the primary, emerged as a factor in the birther conspiracy and Tea Party movement, and, in the last part of

Obama's presidency, took center stage with the Black Lives Matter movement. Through it all, African Americans continued to use public speaking to promote resistance and to mobilize their hearers to action.

## BARACK OBAMA

In large part, Barack Obama rose to national prominence due to his public speaking. He first drew attention with his 2004 speech to the Democratic National Convention, and throughout the 2008 presidential primary, his speaking was called "electric" and "eloquent." Audience members said they were "transfixed and thrilled" by his words. He was typically analogized to John Kennedy and Martin Luther King Jr. His opponents even tried to make his eloquence a liability, suggesting that he was "hiding" a lack of substance because he spoke so well. To be sure, Obama's electoral success owed much to his campaign's ability to harness enthusiasm and financial support through its use of the Internet and social media. Both of his presidential campaigns were models of how to use computer-based communication, but the catalyst for the campaign's energy was the candidate himself.

The power of Obama's speaking could be attributed to his ideas, his style and delivery, and his ability to seamlessly blend those three elements. The content of his speeches drew on the standard American tropes of liberty, democracy, and equality. Scholars noted that Obama was comfortable with and conveyed authenticity as he talked about the American Dream in 2008 and that his election would be just one more step on the American journey. Told this way, the American story is teleological. A telos is an ethical purpose, or goal, that is contained within the nature of the thing itself. For the United States, that telos is told in the story of the Pilgrims searching for religious freedom, the American Revolution, and the U.S. Constitution. In particular the Declaration of Independence frames this approach. The Declaration's phrase "All men are created equal" provides the grounding principle, that inherent in the nation's DNA is the message that each American can enjoy "life, liberty, and the pursuit of happiness."

Barack Obama's 2007 speech announcing his candidacy illustrated his ability to couch his political message in the American teleological story. As a U.S. senator representing Illinois, he selected Springfield, the state's capital and longtime home of Abraham Lincoln, as the setting for his speech. Obama opened and closed the speech with references to Lincoln. Obama also used the national motto, *E Pluribus Unum* (Out of many, one), to say that his candidacy was a message of hope, to bring a divided nation together through the shared principles of justice, equality, and opportunity. The life of Lincoln, said Obama, "tells us that there is power in words. He tells us that that there is power in conviction. That beneath all the differences of race and region, faith and station, we are one people. He tells us that there is power in hope."

A teleological construction is also patient. It argues that, as long as progress toward the goal is being made, then one has been successful and ethical. Like many other speakers, Obama found this aspect of American teleology directly in the Preamble of the Constitution, which identified the purpose of the document as seeking to "form a more perfect union." The goal was not the actual attainment of perfection but the achievement of greater perfection than the present. "It is because men and women of every race, from every walk of life, continued to march for freedom long after Lincoln was laid to rest," said Obama, "that we have the chance to face the challenges of this millennium together, as one people—as Americans." He continued: "In the face of politics that's shut you out, that's told you to settle, that's divided us for too long, you believe we can be one people, reaching for what's possible, building that more perfect union."

In the climactic conclusion of his speech, Obama issued a call of arms to his audience, beginning with a reference to the U.S. Constitution and at the end invoking Lincoln's "Gettysburg Address," which had closed with the "resolve that these dead shall not have died in vain—that this nation, under God, shall have a new birth of freedom—and that government of the people, by the people, for the people, shall not perish from the earth." Said Obama in his speech: "I want to win that next battle—for justice and opportunity. I want to win that next battle—for better schools and better jobs and health care for all. I want us to take up the unfinished business of perfecting our union and building a better America.... Together, starting today, let us finish the work that needs to be done and usher in a new birth of freedom on this Earth."

Obama's language matched the content of his speaking. He used a great deal of parallel structure, as when he repetitively listed the battles he wanted to win, which helped undergird his message of unity. In contrast, he used relatively few antitheses, which place contrasting ideas into parallel structure. He would use those later, when he wanted to underscore the differences between his vision and that of his Republican opponents. For the message of unity, however, paralleled similarities worked better.

Parallel similarities also reinforced the idea that Obama wanted to be part of the long march of American history toward the nation's telos, and his metaphors reinforced that message. Images of a journey, path, march, and quest frequented his vocabulary. The classical theorist Pseudo-Longinus wrote that the eloquent speaker will use "nobility of phrase," that is, language that elevates the discussion rather than demeaning it by using coarse or vulgar words. One must be careful, however, not to do so artificially and thus seem to be putting on an air of superiority. Obama's vocabulary never became coarse, and he seemed to have the ability to sprinkle his speeches with words that were not used in everyday conversation but that also did not seem to show off. He asked his audience to join him on an "improbable quest," to "shake off our slumber" and "slough off our fear." "Let us keep that promise—that American promise," he told the 2008 DNC, "and in the words of Scripture hold firmly, without wavering, to the hope that we confess."

Finally, Obama's delivery was flawless. He invariably placed the emphasis correctly on the words that needed to be stressed. His tone was generally measured, but the particular intonation rose or fell appropriately depending on the emotional content. A comparison of his prepared manuscripts with his actual delivery revealed that he was comfortable changing words extemporaneously to meet the situation and the audience, thus making the speech sound more natural. There was, reported one audience member, "an energy going between us," which was an experience that can only be attained through an effective delivery.

*Race and the 2008 Campaign*

The issue of race surfaced early in the 2008 campaign during the South Carolina primary. After Obama and Bill Clinton traded a series of jabs at each other through the media, Obama won the primary with strong support from the African American community. The ensuing innuendo, which many attributed to the Clinton campaign, was that Obama had become the "Black candidate," a label that some critics of Obama hoped would trigger white backlash. The controversy abated somewhat after Bill Clinton's role in his wife's campaign was reduced but then fully erupted with the release of video excerpts of sermons given by Obama's minister, the Reverend Jeremiah Wright.

Reverend Wright was the minister of Trinity United Church of Christ (UCC) in Chicago, with eight thousand members the largest church in that denomination. Wright's sermons were consistent with the style of Black folk preaching, were full of irony, and built to emotionally climactic endings. His theological points addressed everyday life and in doing so encompassed politics as well. The former Marine and Navy corpsman was critical of the United States, often excoriating it for its systemic racism. After the

September 11 attacks on the World Trade Center and the Pentagon, Wright invoked Malcolm X's famous proclamation, saying that after U.S. violence such as the nuclear bombing of Hiroshima and Nagasaki, the 9/11 attacks were "America's chickens coming home to roost." The other excerpt for which Wright was criticized was a 2003 sermon in which he condemned a government that gives Blacks "drugs, builds bigger prisons, passes a three-strike law, and then wants us to sing 'God Bless America.'" Echoing the Old Testament prophets, Wright called on God to damn America instead.

As a longtime member of Wright's church in Chicago, Obama was criticized for guilt by association. On March 18, Obama defended himself with a speech about race that came to be called "A More Perfect Union." The location of the speech was significant, as Obama delivered it from inside Independence Hall in Philadelphia, where the U.S. Constitution had been written, as well as the Declaration of Independence. Reportedly, the speech was written by the candidate himself, and in fact there were extended passages that were taken from his autobiography *Dreams from My Father*, written thirteen years earlier. Obama began his speech by referencing the setting and the opening line of the Constitution: "We the People, in order to form a more perfect union." From this position, he argued that the United States was continually perfecting itself in a long journey toward realizing its teleological goal: to recognize that all its citizens are created equal and should be treated as such.

In his speech, Obama fashioned three key arguments. First, the U.S. was moving toward perfection but had not achieved perfection. Therefore, it could and must be criticized in order to continue "perfecting" itself. Reverend Wright's criticism—even if incorrect—was a part of that process; in other words, the marketplace of ideas that would help the nation in its journey. While Obama the churchgoer had not agreed with everything that Reverend Wright had preached from the pulpit, Obama the citizen respected the process. Second, although Rev. Wright had recognized that the nation needed to move toward perfection, he had failed to recognize the nation's journey toward racial justice. "The profound mistake of Reverend Wright's sermons is not that he spoke about racism in our society," Obama said, "it's that he spoke as if our society was static, as if no progress had been made." The minister had elevated "what is wrong with America above all that we know is right with America." Third, Rev. Wright's criticisms were "not only wrong, but divisive," which constituted a grievous error in a nation that was working to perfect its "union."

Obama said that he agreed with the motivation for Rev. Wright's comments, saying that as a Black man, Obama understood all too well that prejudice and discrimination remained active, evil forces in America. He also praised the minister's good works in the community, acts that further demonstrated what the nation was capable of when it worked toward perfection. But he balanced those statements with ones in which he expressed empathy with lower-income whites' frustrations about closed-off economic opportunities. He argued that those frustrations were misplaced, however, when they were directed against Blacks, rather than at the government policies that were skewed toward helping the wealthy. The nation needed a candid, but not divisive, discussion about race, Obama said. Such a conversation is "where we start. It is where our union grows stronger."

Obama's speech played well in the mainstream press, which emphasized his condemnation of the minister's "divisiveness." They noted too his "even-handedness" in acknowledging the positions of whites as well as Blacks regarding perceptions of race and how he had grounded his speech in the ideals—the telos—of America. African Americans were more divided in their responses. While some understood the political necessity, or even the desirability, of distancing himself from the minister's condemnation of America, others believed that Obama had betrayed both the minister and himself by saying that there had been anything wrong about Wright's message. To their mind, Wright was a modern Stokely Carmichael, who had declared that the U.S. was the most violent nation in the world and was hypocritical in the extreme when it denounced the violent actions of others. These critics felt that Obama's speech had papered over the racial divide rather than create the space for an honest and candid dialogue about race in America.

Race would be injected into the campaign at several junctures, but it was not addressed again in a major speech by the candidate. Several weeks after giving "A More Perfect Union," more videos of Wright's sermons reignited the controversy and Obama resigned his membership in Trinity. In the general campaign, prejudicial rumors circulated that Obama had been born in Kenya, the home of his father, but the Republican candidate John McCain forcefully rejected that story. It would be resurrected during Obama's presidency by the "birther" conspiracy theorists. As a rule, Obama preferred not to speak about such controversies, for fear of providing such conspiracies with additional fuel.

The timing of Obama's acceptance speech at the 2008 DNC was a poignant reminder of race, however, as it fell on August 28, the anniversary of King's "I Have a Dream" address. Observers and critics waited to see how Obama would speak to the historic nature of his nomination on this particular date. He made no direct reference to the occasion until his conclusion, although halfway through he gave an implicit nod to King's speech by using the phrase "now is the time" six times to call for change on issues such as renewable energy, health care, and equal pay for equal work. King had used that introductory phrase four times in his call for the nation to "rise from the quicksands of racial injustice to the solid rock of brotherhood."

As he concluded his Acceptance address, Obama at last noted the significance of the date, saying that "forty-five years ago today brought Americans from every corner of this land to stand together on a mall in Washington, before Lincoln's Memorial, [to] hear a young preacher from Georgia speak of his dream." They could have heard "words of anger and discord," he said, but instead they heard that as Americans, "our destiny is inextricably linked—That together, our dreams can be one." "We cannot walk alone," Obama said, "the preacher cried, 'And as we walk, we must make the pledge that we shall always march ahead. We cannot turn back.'" Obama then wove that theme into his closing sentences: "America, we cannot turn back. . . . We cannot walk alone. At this moment, in this election, we must pledge once more to march into the future. Let us keep that promise—that American promise—and in the words of Scripture hold firmly, without wavering, to the hope that we confess."

Obama's deft touch regarding race was most prominently displayed in his 2008 election night victory speech, delivered in Grant Park, Chicago. For the most part, the topics of his speech—the financial crisis, health care, equal rights—applied to everyone in his audience regardless of race. Still, he alluded to his election as the first Black president of the United States. "If there is anyone out there who still doubts that America is a place where all things are possible," he said, "who still wonders if the dream of our founders is alive in our time, who still questions the power of our democracy, tonight is your answer." He did not define what he meant by "tonight," but the audience understood. "Tonight," he said, the nation proved once more the "true genius" of American democracy, "that America can change." Once again, it was eminently clear what the "change" was to which he was referring.

"This election had many firsts and many stories that will be told for generations," he remarked, as he led into the story of Ann Nixon Cooper. At 106 years old, Cooper was "born just a generation past slavery," in a time when she could not vote due to her gender as well as the color of her skin. Obama noted that Cooper had witnessed many changes in America, including woman suffrage, the New Deal, World War II, landing on the moon, and the end of the Cold War. Woven through his recounting of events she had witnessed, Obama included references to the Montgomery bus boycott, the Birmingham protests and church bombing, and Bloody Sunday on the bridge to Selma. And now, implied Obama, she had been able to vote for the first Black president. Although he may not have intended this result, Obama's speech suggested that America had become post-racial. "It's been a long time coming," he declared, "but tonight, because of what we did on this day, in this election, at this defining moment, change has come to America."

*The Obama Presidency: The First Term*

In the first two years of Barack Obama's presidency, his oratorical prowess continued to impress observers and seemed to play an essential role in his success. He came to the presidency with an ambitious political agenda, fueled in large part by the idealism contained in his "Yes We Can" campaign slogan, but he now confronted the reality of a major economic crisis. His inauguration speech was satisfying, but memorable mostly for the large, enthusiastic crowds who celebrated the swearing-in ceremony. The tenor of his speech echoed that of Franklin Roosevelt's first inaugural, when the country had also faced a daunting economic future.

While jobs bills and financial reform occupied a great deal of Obama's time and public speaking in the first four years, he was also able to propose and pass a major health care reform bill, which became known as "Obamacare." Where Bill Clinton had been forced to admit defeat, Obama prevailed, and in doing so he devoted many speeches to pitching the program. In foreign policy, he spoke of democracy and collaboration but also defended a troop surge in Afghanistan. In his first term, he also began a string of speeches through which he served as "Consoler-in-Chief," eulogizing victims of gun violence.

In June of 2009, Obama delivered a major foreign policy address at Al-Azhar University in Cairo, Egypt. He had come to Cairo, he said, "to seek a new beginning between the United States and Muslims around the world, one based on mutual interest and mutual respect." Like Jesse Jackson at the 1984 DNC, Obama grounded his argument in part upon the common religious traditions of Judaism, Christianity, and Islam. At several points in the speech, he quoted from the Quran, and in his conclusion, he quoted from the Torah, the Bible, and the Quran. He repudiated the notion that any nation should impose its system of government upon others, although he asserted that certain principles of democracy and human rights should be adhered to by all nations. Those principles, he said, were America's foundational values, but these ideas were universally understood. Leaders should govern with the consent of the governed, with a "spirit of tolerance and compromise" that would respect the rights of the minority.

In contrast with the previous administration's bellicose discourse that supported the wars in Iraq and Afghanistan, Obama's outreach suggested a signal change in foreign policy. Some critics of the speech thought he had gone too far in softening the U.S. tone toward Islamic hard-liners, while others argued that it was still too traditional because it had not renounced Israel or U.S. military involvement in Iraq and Afghanistan. The speech was widely praised, however, for shifting the "attitude and tone" of U.S. foreign policy and for opening up new possibilities for Middle East peace. The speech is often seen as one of the catalysts for the Arab Spring of 2011, when youthful demonstrators in North African and Middle Eastern countries overturned autocratic governments in their countries.

One interesting outcome of Obama's inspirational speaking on foreign policy was that, in October of 2009, it was announced that he was the winner of the Nobel Peace Prize. Even supporters of the president wondered what he had done in nine months that merited his receiving the award. The occasion of his Peace Prize acceptance speech in December was made even more challenging when he announced a major military build-up in Afghanistan just nine days earlier. Obama began his Nobel speech by once again asserting that America's founding principles of human rights and dignity were in fact universal and should be applied to all. From these principles, he developed the idea of a "just war" and a "just peace."

For the former, Obama drew on the long philosophical tradition of the idea of the "just war." Some war would always be thrust upon nations simply because humans were imperfect. Attacks require defense. Obama argued, however, that a just war was not simply one that was unavoidable, but that the means of war must embody the ends. A just war must be fought justly, and a nation could do so if, even in the midst of war, human rights and the dignity of the individual were observed. Obama then argued that peace cannot simply be the absence of war. If in a period of "peace" the rights and dignity of individuals were being viciously denied, then the idea of a just peace required that force be used to protect the rights of the defenseless. "We can understand that there will be war and still strive for peace," he concluded, "we can do that—for that is the story of human progress; that's the hope of all the world, and at this moment of challenge, that must be our work here on Earth."

Obama's speech was widely praised as "eloquent," "magisterial," "visionary," his "most presidential," and "as outstanding as any he has given." In a "scholarly" address that defended his troop surge while it spoke to his idealistic hopes, he had developed what a *New York Times* writer called "the intellectual predicate for the issues that he knows are ahead in the coming year." Even some conservatives agreed with columnist Kathleen Parker that the "Nobel Prize may have been all the things critics have listed, but Obama's response was a triumphant expression of American values and character."

Obama would be similarly praised for his televised speech announcing the death of Osama bin Laden. He was dignified, somber, and resolute, exuding no sense of joy about being responsible for the death of a man, even one so widely reviled by Americans. He took responsibility for the decision but distributed credit for the success to the military, the intelligence community, the previous administration, and the Pakistani government. He particularly took pains to distinguish bin Laden and the al Qaeda organization from other Muslims. "We must also reaffirm that the United States is not—and will never be—at war with Islam." He continued: "I've made clear, just as President Bush did shortly after 9/11, that our war is not against Islam. Bin Laden was not a Muslim leader; he was a mass murderer of Muslims. Indeed al Qaeda has slaughtered scores of Muslims in many countries, including our own. So his demise should be welcomed by all who believe in peace and human dignity."

Early in his speech, Obama took Americans back to September 11, 2001. In our time of grief, he recalled, "the American people came together. We offered our neighbors a hand, and we offered the wounded our blood. We reaffirmed our ties to each other, and our love of community and country. On that day, no matter where we came from, what God we prayed to, or what race or ethnicity we were, we were united as one American family." Obama's nostalgic remembrance did more than help justify the military mission that had killed bin Laden. In elections the previous year, the Republicans had taken control of the House of Representatives. The election campaign had been particularly contentious, as "Tea Party" Republicans demonstrated against Obamacare and the deficit spending designed to help boost the economy. In conjunction with this fiscal concern, however, were racially tinged charges that Obama was "un-American" and the resurgence of the birther conspiracy. Any semblance of a "post-racial" America had disappeared by 2011, but the president was still trying to evoke a spiritual unity across races and ethnicities.

*Race and Obama's Second Term*

Obama's early speeches about gun violence framed the issue universally. Speaking in Tucson, Arizona, at a 2011 memorial ceremony after the shooting deaths of six persons attending a rally for Rep. Gabrielle Giffords,

Obama spoke about the need for civil discourse and the universal principle that a democratic culture requires that all voices be expressed and all voices be respected. "We can question each other's ideas without questioning each other's love of country," so that "our democracy can be as good as Christina [a young victim] had imagined it." He would similarly speak in universal tones as a parent after the Sandy Hook Elementary School shooting in December 2012.

In early 2012, however, the Florida shooting death of Trayvon Martin had brought race relations to the forefront of the president's public speaking. It began small, with some comments at an unrelated announcement in the Rose Garden. Trayvon Martin was a seventeen-year-old Black youth who was shot and killed in Florida by a white neighborhood watch volunteer, George Zimmerman. Answering a reporter's question about the case, the president talked broadly about the emotional toll of the tragedy and the need to investigate the shooting. But then his remarks turned personal. "If I had a son," said Obama, "he'd look like Trayvon. When I think about this boy, I think about my own kids."

Obama offered a similarly personal commentary a year later, in July of 2013, when he spoke about Zimmerman's acquittal. He noted that another way of saying that Trayvon could have been his son was to say that "Trayvon Martin could have been me thirty-five years ago." As with his 2008 speech on race, Obama attempted to convey African Americans' perspective to white Americans. When Black men report the experience of being followed suspiciously around department stores, said Obama, "that includes me." Door locks click when a Black man walks by, the president noted, and women hold their purses a bit more tightly in the elevator, and he, too, had experienced those reactions.

The Martin case marked the beginning of a series of speeches about race and justice that the president would make over the remainder of his second term. The deaths of Michael Brown in Ferguson, Missouri (2014); Eric Garner in New York City (2014); Walter Scott in North Charleston, South Carolina (2015); Alton Sterling in Baton Rouge, Louisiana (2016); and Philando Castille in St. Anthony, Minnesota (2016) at the hands of police officers were just some of the most notable cases to which Obama responded with a speech. In response to these events—all recorded on cell phone video—protests and protest organizations arose, including Black Lives Matter. In each speech, Obama attempted to contextualize the African American community's anger over police use of force and the systemic racism of the criminal justice system, while also calling for nonviolent protest and restraint on all sides.

On July 7, 2016, five Dallas police officers were killed by a sniper as an apparent reprisal for the killings of Sterling and Castille in the previous two days. On July 12, Obama spoke at the memorial service, summarizing much of what he had said over the previous four years. "Scripture tells us that in our sufferings, there is glory," he began, hoping to find common ground by citing Scripture and by highlighting the suffering that was being experienced on all sides of the issue. He then personalized the suffering for those gathered to remember the officers, by noting that policing is a call to service. He memorialized each slain officer individually, beginning with how that person "answered that call" to service and noting something unique about each officer's biography.

Obama was never able to gain much traction on the issue of race through his public speaking, however. That much was apparent in his farewell speech, delivered on January 10, 2017, in Chicago, the site of his election night victory speech in 2008. He devoted most of his speech to talking about four threats to American democracy: lack of economic opportunity, poor race relations, increasing political polarization, and Americans taking their democracy for granted. In many regards, the race portion of his speech echoed his 2008 speech on race. "Race relations are better than they were ten or twenty or thirty years ago," he said, "but we're not where we need to be."

To the disappointment of many, he did not dwell on the cases of Trayvon Martin, Michael Brown, or the other Black men who had died, but instead included the criminal justice system as just one site among others where Blacks faced discrimination on the basis of race. Obama's prescription for change was largely the same as the one he had championed in 2008. In the context of Donald Trump's election to the presidency, Obama connected the issue to other kinds of discrimination, specifically those based on immigrant status and gender. But the heart of his argument was summarized as he quoted the fictional character Atticus Finch about not understanding someone until you "climb into his skin and walk around in it."

Obama's inability to bring his powerful public speaking skills to bear on the issue of race, the police, and the criminal justice system left many with mixed feelings about his legacy. They were proud that the first African American president had conducted himself so well and with such dignity, not only through his policies but through his public speaking. They were discouraged, however, that there was a deficit of policy changes that might have resulted in more tangible progress.

## ACTIVISTS FOR CHANGE

As with the preceding decades, public speaking by African Americans in the "era" of the Obama presidency continued to be marked by a diversity of voices. Politicians, preachers, organization leaders, and intellectuals were in abundant supply as speakers. Many of the voices from the previous eras—such as Jackson, Sharpton, Lewis, Gates, and West—continued to be prominent voices. They were joined by new figures on the political scene, such as Attorneys General Eric Holder and Loretta Lynch; Senators Kamala Harris, Cory Booker, and Tim Scott; and Governor Patrick Deval. Upon her retirement as host of her daytime talk show, Oprah Winfrey became an increasingly prominent speaker addressing a variety of political and social topics.

First Lady Michelle Obama was a somewhat reluctant speaker at first, but by 2016 she had developed a forceful persona as a strong, intelligent advocate for women, children, and military families. Commanding a prominent platform, she combined a deliberate and determined style of delivery with clear organization, arguments, and evidence and managed to disrupt the stereotypes that many had about African American women. Her speeches at the 2008, 2012, and 2016 Democratic National Conventions were widely praised.

A hallmark of Michelle Obama's speeches was her ability to use her personal story to talk about politics in a way that did not seem maudlin or oversentimentalized. In 2008, her convention speech helped humanize voters' perceptions of the cool, sometimes detached personality of her husband. In 2012, she reminded audiences of the president's commitment to improve the economy the right way and to keep America safe. In 2016, she spoke as a character witness for Hillary Clinton and not-so-subtly criticized Donald Trump without ever saying his name.

Her 2016 speech began with her family's story about her daughters' first day of school after moving into the White House and how, as they got into the large SUVs with the Secret Service agents, Michelle and Barack realized that they would need to consider thoughtfully every day about how these foundational experiences were shaping their daughters' futures. This anecdote then became the guiding principle for the speech: How would the 2016 election shape the lives of all America's children? Obama praised Hillary Clinton as a fighter dedicated to improving the lives of women, children, and all Americans and as a role model to all America's daughters as someone who could break the glass ceiling of the presidency.

The strongest application of her principle, however, lay in her implicit message that Donald Trump was unfit to guide America's children. We must insist "that the hateful language they hear from public figures on TV does not represent the true spirit of this country," she said. When Clinton lost her presidential bid in 2008, she "didn't get angry or disillusioned," nor did she sulkily "pack up and go home"—an answer to Trump's pre-voting grousing that the election was already "rigged." Obama said the children's futures must be shaped by a president who knows that issues are complex and "cannot be boiled down to 140 characters"—a reference to Trump's heavy use of Twitter. "You can't have a thin skin or a tendency to lash out," she continued—alluding to Trump's famously quick temper. These criticisms were encapsulated in the most often repeated line from her speech that itself sounded like the kind of counsel a parent would use to teach a child: "When someone is cruel or acts like a bully, you don't stoop to their level. No, our motto is, when they go low, we go high."

Similarly, as the first Black woman to become the vice president of the United States, Kamala Harris also merged her personal story with the teleological telling of American history. She frequently talked about her mother, Shyamala Gopalan Harris, an immigrant from India who married an African American, Donald Harris. In her nomination acceptance speech, then-Senator Harris referenced the women who "inspired us to pick up the torch and fight on," women such as "Mary Church Terrell and Mary McCleod Bethune. Fannie Lou Hamer and Diane Nash. Constance Baker Motley and Shirley Chisholm." She then told the story of her mother, a woman "whose name isn't known, whose story isn't shared," but who dedicated her life to the same purpose as those famous women. Her mother gave her children "a vision of our nation as a Beloved Community—where all are welcome, no matter what we look like, where we come from, or who we love."

In her victory speech on November 7, 2020, Vice President-elect Harris reversed the order of her stories. She started with her mother, saying that when Shyamala Harris "came here from India at the age of nineteen, she maybe didn't quite imagine this moment. But she believed so deeply in an America where a moment like this is possible." She proceeded to enumerate other inspiring women, although not by name. These women were those who fought for the Nineteenth Amendment to give women the right to vote, the Voting Rights Act of 1965, and the "new generation of women" who were so politically active. "I stand on their shoulders," Harris declared.

Like Obama, Harris saw in stories and history the teleological ideal of America. "You are pushing us to realize the ideals of our nation," she told the audience listening to her nomination acceptance speech: "Pushing us to live the values we share: decency and fairness, justice and love." These are ideals to work toward rather than a static state of being. Quoting Congressman John Lewis in her victory speech, Harris said that "democracy is not a process. It is an act." Also like Obama, Harris assured audiences that the process would not be easy. "Make no mistake," she said in her nomination acceptance speech, "the road ahead will not be not easy. We will stumble. We may fall short. But I pledge to you that we will act boldly and deal with our challenges honestly." In her victory speech, Harris again assured her audience that "the road ahead will not be easy." But, she reassured them, "America is ready." And while the struggle would be real, "the vision that our parents and grandparents fought for" was "the vision that makes the American promise—for all its complexities and imperfections—a promise worth fighting for."

*Activism and the Criminal Justice System*

The strongest public-speaking challenge by African Americans to "established" political speakers like the Obamas, Harris, or Booker came from intellectuals and community activists, catalyzed particularly around the Black Lives Matter (BLM) movement, the criminal justice system, and the broader issue of social justice. Developed through social media like Twitter and Facebook and then organized from the grassroots up, the traditional channel of public speaking continued to play an important role. Organizational meetings, rallies, and government hearings were three common venues in which protesters and leaders stood up to speak.

Three women emerged as the primary leaders and spokespersons for the Black Lives Matter movement. Alicia Garza was a community organizer and editorial writer from the San Francisco Bay Area. Patrisse Cullors was a writer, performance artist, and professor from the Los Angeles area. Opal Tometi was a community organizer and writer in New York City. While each had individual interests and speaking styles, common themes emerged from their public statements.

Opal Tometi's address to the United Nations General Assembly on July 12, 2016, succinctly summarized three of those common themes. "First," she told the Assembly, we must "tell the truth." Specifically, that meant that "if there is an issue, name it and create the context for it to be heard. Only when oppressed people are heard can we have an honest, solutions-based dialogue." This idea of *nommo*, or saying the name, is woven throughout these leaders' speeches, just as "Say his/her name" became the most prominent rallying cry at demonstrations protesting police shootings of African

Americans. Speaking at a Citizen University event earlier in 2016, Garza provided a poignant example of the problem. Referencing the experience of African Americans in New Orleans after Hurricane Katrina, she noted that "stuffed in stadiums, abandoned in jails, shot as we were attempting to cross bridges to find safety, we were called looters and rioters, while white families were called finders and survivors." Too often, said Cullors speaking in Australia in 2017, whites "can choose whether or not they will name what is taking place here." Whites must assume the obligation to give voice to the injustices done to people of color: "We need you to name the people who have been killed by this government, name the realities of anti-Black racism and state-sanctioned violence." Such naming should both call out the injustice and honor those who had gone before. "We must say the names of those who have fallen," she told her audience, "because it's through us that they continue to survive. We must say the names of our folks who have fought so we can fight and win."

This mindfulness of history, about ancestors who had struggled against injustice and the injustices against which they had struggled, was an important part of telling the truth and naming the problem. As Garza said at the start of one speech, "It is important to us that we understand that movements are not begun by any one person. That this movement actually was begun in 1619 when Black people were brought here in chains and at the bottoms of boats." Black Lives Matter speeches usually included references to earlier Black leaders and speakers like Nat Turner, Sojourner Truth, Frederick Douglass, and Fannie Lou Hamer. In her Australian speech, Cullors reminded the audience about "blackbirding," the practice of deceitfully or forcefully bringing Black indigenous people to work as indentured servants on plantations in Australia. Like the sharecropping and convict lease systems in the United States, "blackbirding" was a de facto form of slavery after legalized slavery had been outlawed.

Second, Tometi told her United Nations audience, she and the other founders believed that the BLM movement was inclusive. "We advocate with and are led by women, Black immigrants, queer folks, people who are incarcerated, transgender folks, disabled, and people who practice different religions," she explained, because "we see this diversity and complexity as a strength." In another speech, Tometi explained the big tent approach to challenging the system by quoting Audre Lorde, "The Audre Lorde, brilliant queer Black feminist who said, 'There is no such thing as a single-issue struggle because we do not live single-issue lives.'"

Cullors similarly argued that systemic injustice took multiple forms and that this helped explain the larger power of the Black Lives Matter movement, even though the movement was rooted in police killings of Black men. The world view of the BLM movement was "one that looks at the necessity of intersectionality, the recognition of our struggles being interconnected, that our freedoms are intertwined, that this movement is global and has been global. It is the realization that we are all responsible." In this argument, she echoed the message heard so often from African American public speakers. Tometi concluded by echoing Jesse Jackson's argument that the "damned, disowned, and the disinherited" must find common ground, and in doing so, she said, they embrace their own names for their own selves. "What the Black Lives Matter cofounders (Alice, Patrisse, and I) believed when we started this project is that it was time to do away with respectability politics. We will not be blamed for brutality against us—or murder. We won't be blamed for being poor or being a woman or being undocumented, transgender, or queer. We won't be blamed for wearing a hoodie. Or for not being in the right place at the right time."

The third principle that Tometi enunciated in her U.N. speech was that "mobilizing is not enough. You must demand what you need. We are insistent in our demands for transformation. Reform for the current system will not suffice—we must transform it." Tometi argued that anti-Black violence was a "disease" that had taken root in the system and the culture, and that "police brutality, mass incarceration, health disparities, high unemployment, poverty, deportation, education inequality, substandard housing are all symptoms of this disease." The ill was systematic, and therefore so must the cure be: "And we must organize. We must organize culturally and politically against the systems that operate with anti-Black logic and bias and that leave our lives diminished all across the board." As Garza succinctly summarized, "The solution to police violence and police brutality is not to lock up killer cops. The solution is to reimagine what kind of safety do we want and deserve."

What was clear from these women's public speaking was that what began as a protest against police violence had evolved into an organized movement that opposed a wide range of societal injustices, not only against Blacks and people of color, but against all who were discriminated against simply because of who they were. As Cullors concluded in her speech in Australia, "We must organize and build in non-colonial ways and that means centralizing those who are most marginalized, building their capacity in self-determined ways, and putting them in positions of leadership." In this evolution and growth, the Black Lives Matter movement had followed the historic path of many African American movements, and in the evolution of those ideas and the community organizing, public speaking played an integral role.

Among the many voices raised in protest against the criminal justice system, one of the speakers with the longest record was Bryan Stevenson. After graduating from Harvard Law School in 1985, Stevenson moved to Atlanta, Georgia, to work with the Southern Center for Human Rights (SCHR), which paid special attention to providing legal defense for death row cases. Shortly after, he was assigned to direct the SCHR's Alabama office. When federal funding was eliminated, he opened the nonprofit Equal Justice Initiative (EJI) to provide free legal defense for capital cases. In addition to trying cases and filing multiple appeals on behalf of clients, Stevenson became a vocal opponent of the death penalty and the practice of trying children as adults. His advocacy particularly focused on racial bias in capital cases, judicial discrimination against the poor, and the injustice of defining children as adults and sentencing them to life in prison without possibility of parole.

In 1995, Stevenson received the MacArthur Fellowship, a grant that supports creativity and justice, and he donated the sizable cash award to the EJI. In 2014 he published a memoir, *Just Mercy: A Story of Justice and Redemption*, which laid out his case against the death penalty and the discriminatory practices of the justice system through a series of first-person stories. In 2018, EJI opened in Montgomery the National Memorial for Peace and Justice, a six-acre site commemorating by name the more than four thousand victims of lynching. A few miles away, it also opened the Legacy Museum: From Enslavement to Mass Incarceration.

In the tradition of Black intellectuals who brought their message to the public, Stevenson most frequently spoke at the invitation of organizations or on college campuses. These were often fundraising talks, designed to support the work of EJI. Like many such speakers who preceded him, Stevenson spoke with a thoughtful, relatively soft-spoken demeanor. He was passionate without raising his voice because most of the emotional appeal in his speaking arose from his stories and somber manner of capturing the injustice he described through his words.

Stevenson typically began his speeches with numbers that summarized the injustice of mass incarceration that he would later in the speech personalize. In 1972, he told audiences, there were 300,000 people in prison. Today, he said, there are more than 2.3 million. Moreover, he said, race plays a critical role in determining who went to jail. "One in three Black men ages eighteen to thirty," he said in his 2012 TED Talk, "are in prison, jail, on probation or parole." Consider the repercussions of that, he told the audience. "My state of Alabama," he noted, "permanently disenfranchises you if you have a criminal conviction. Right now in Alabama 34 percent of the Black male population has permanently lost the right to vote. We're actually projecting in another ten years that the level of disenfranchisement will be as high as it's been since prior to the passage of the Voting Rights Act. And there is this stunning silence."

Stevenson most often explained the numbers by using the same frame as that which is conveyed by the Legacy Museum: that mass incarceration of African Americans is simply the continuation of slavery, lynching, and segregation in a new form. As he said in 2019 to the Association of American Medical Colleges (AAMC), "I believe the true evil of American slavery was the narrative of racial difference, [the myth] that Black people aren't fully human.... And because of that I don't think slavery ended in 1865—it just evolved." He continued: "Today there is still a presumption of dangerousness and guilt that gets assigned to people of color. It's unhealthy, and it breaks my heart."

Like Garza, Tometi, and Cullors, Stevenson argued that, at least in part, truth-telling would be the cure to the racial myths, harmful narratives, and resulting discrimination. Look at South Africa, Rwanda, and Germany, he would tell audiences, and see how there was a commitment to "truth and reconciliation" because those countries understood that wounds could not heal until they were first exposed. As he said to the American Bar Association (ABA), "I think we're burdened by a history of racial inequality that is so difficult and so painful that it's actually creating a kind of smog." Naming the ills and their causes, through speeches, museums, memorials, and court cases, could clear the smog, but it would require persistence and courage.

But Stevenson expanded his indictment of the justice system beyond its problems of race to its larger discrimination against the poor. As he told his TED Talk audience, "We have a system of justice in this country that treats you much better if you are rich and guilty than if you are poor and innocent." His most common aphorism has been that "the opposite of poverty is not wealth; the opposite of poverty is justice." For the AAMC audience, he used an illness metaphor to characterize the problem: "There's an epidemic of hopelessness in so many of the communities where there's poverty and despair. I go into poor communities and I sit down with twelve-year-old boys and [they say], 'I know I'm going to be in jail or prison by the time I'm twenty-one.' And they see little in their future other than hardship." As he told the ABA, "We've got to find new ways to create justice, to open doors that have been closed for too long, to create opportunities for people who feel marginalized and excluded."

The first step toward creating justice, he said, is to be "proximate." It is easy to ignore problems that are distant. As he told the *Fortune* CEO

Initiative in 2018, "When we allow ourselves to be shielded and disconnected from those who are vulnerable and disfavored," we lose our effectiveness, but "proximity is a pathway through which we learn the kind of things we need to know to make healthier communities." To illustrate his point, he told stories about the death row inmates and prisoners under eighteen years of age who changed his own perceptions about justice. As he said to his fellow lawyers at the ABA, "We need to find ways to get closer to the people who live on the margins of society, to find ways to get closer to the poor, the neglected and the excluded, the disfavored. It's necessary that we see the anguish. It was my proximity to the condemned that radicalized my view of the law. I got close to condemned people, talking about what it's like to struggle for justice." He gave the same advice to the CEOs assembled by *Fortune* magazine, telling them to "find ways to get proximate to the poor and vulnerable."

Through Stevenson's words, audiences have heard the echoes of earlier African American speakers who have argued for equal treatment under the law for all, regardless of race or income. He has also repeated familiar themes about integration: that segregation leads to indifference, fear, and misapprehensions. Society will prosper, he argued, if it lives up to its creed of equality. To these arguments, Stevenson blended a religious message of mercy as well. The message incorporated into the title of his book, *Just Mercy*, infused his speeches as well.

He spoke to the *Fortune* CEOs with a message of stewardship that sounded as if it had been lifted from the New Testament: "I believe that our stewardship, our leadership, our citizenship, our meaning, cannot be reflected just in how we treat the powerful and the privileged. We're going to be judged by how we treat the poor, the excluded, and the neglected. And in that context, there's something meaningful and rich waiting for us." It is not only CEOs who heard this message, however; instead, it was a thread woven into all his speeches. He summarized the point succinctly and powerfully for the health professionals at the AAMC: "It is the broken who can show us the power of mercy and grace and redemption." Although Stevenson did not use the folk preacher's energy and vocal range to deliver his message to his audience, his themes of mercy, grace, and redemption were profoundly religious messages, given voice by a lawyer in the name of justice for all.

## Black Preaching and Activism

Of course, preachers continued to occupy an important place in contemporary African American public speaking. Speakers who honed their skills in the pulpit, like Jesse Jackson, Al Sharpton, and Louis Farrakhan, still played prominent roles on the national stage. Another modern-day heir to the political/preaching tradition was the Reverend Dr. William Barber II. Born in 1963, Barber became politically active with the NAACP while in high school. He originally believed that he would follow a career in the law, but in college he felt the call to follow his father's footsteps into the ministry. After earning a doctorate of divinity from Drew University and working for a time as chair of the North Carolina State Human Relations Commission, in 1993 he accepted a pastorate at Greenleaf Christian Church in Goldsboro, North Carolina. That same year, he was diagnosed with ankylosing spondylitis, an incurable condition that causes bones in the joints and spine to fuse. Barber spoke with a rich baritone voice and the energy of a preacher, even as audiences were reminded visually that he did so in defiance of stiffness and pain caused by his disease. He often contrasted his good fortune at having adequate health care with the hardships faced by those who were uninsured.

Continually active in the NAACP, in 2013 Barber responded to the conservative legislation being enacted by the Republican-controlled state government by organizing what he called "Moral Mondays." Each Monday he led a coalition of activists to occupy the State House Building in protest, which frequently led to his arrest and the arrest of other protestors for trespassing. "We said if they were going to crucify the poor, the sick, the children, the unemployed, the immigrants, the LGBT, and the women, and then on top of that crucify voting rights," Barber would tell audiences, "then every crucifixion, as Billy Kyles [a Tennessee civil rights leader] would say, needs a witness."

As with the preachers of the past, Barber applied the lessons of the Bible to the needs of the present day. Speaking in Memphis on the fiftieth anniversary of Martin Luther King Jr.'s assassination, he reminded the audience that the "the Bible says woe unto those who love the tombs of the prophets," and so they must be careful not to be trapped in the past when they honored Dr. King. "We don't need a commemoration," Barber said, "we need a *reconsecration*," and he recited Social Gospel reforms that he reiterated wherever he spoke: "We've got to hold up the banner until every person has health care, we've got to hold it up until every child is lifted in love, we've got to hold it up until every job is a living-wage job, until every person in poverty has guaranteed subsistence."

Although Barber garnered national attention among activists with his Moral Monday protests, his first appearance before a nationwide audience was with an eleven-minute speech at the 2016 Democratic National

Rev. William J. Barber, II at Moral Mondays rally. Flickr: twbuckner; https://www.flickr.com/photos/twbuckner/9295256177/.

Convention. The first half of his speech established the political principles that he believed should decide the election. In doing so, he indirectly but unmistakably attacked the opposition. He began his speech by challenging the common understanding of what it meant to be a conservative: "It may sound strange, but I'm a conservative because I work to conserve a divine tradition that teaches us to do justice, love mercy, and walk humbly with our God." He then repeated an antithesis that he often employed: "I'm so concerned about those that say so much about what God says so little, while saying so little about what God says so much." The Bible, Barber told his audience, says almost nothing about abortion or homosexuality, but it repeatedly calls for mercy, love, and forgiveness. Focusing on the New Testament and his own Christian faith, Barber argued that "Jesus, a brown-skinned Palestinian Jew, called us to preach good news to the poor, the broken, and the bruised and all those who are made to feel unaccepted."

In the second half of his speech, Barber used a heart metaphor to call the audience to action. He set up the metaphor by saying that "we know that when religion is used to camouflage meanness, we know that we have a heart problem in America." Turning to the key political issues, he argued that when the audience fights for voting rights, fifteen dollar an hour minimum wage, universal health care, public education, immigrant rights, LGBTQ rights, and the legitimate discontent of the Black Lives Matter movement, "we are reviving the heart of our democracy." He concluded:

> When the heart is in danger, somebody has to call an emergency code, and somebody with a good heart will bring a defibrillator to work on the bad heart. Because it is possible to shock a bad heart and revive the pulse. In this season, when some want to harden and stop the heart of our democracy, we are being called like our foremothers and forefathers to be the moral defibrillators of our times. We must shock this nation with the power of love ... mercy ... and fight for justice for all. And so I stopped by this evening to ask, "Is there a heart in this house? Is there a heart in America?"

Barber's speech was widely praised, with the *Washington Post* reporting that "what [Barber] delivered ... was evidence of a long tradition of liberal, religious patriotism" and "just about the most engaging version of everything that every other speaker touched on over the course of the four-day event."

On April 26, 2018, Barber delivered one of his most highly acclaimed speeches at the opening of the Equal Justice Institute's (EJI) Peace and Justice Memorial in Montgomery, Alabama. The memorial commemorates the victims of lynching throughout U.S. history. Each victim is listed by name, on a series of rectangular steel columns hanging from the ceiling, one for each county in the country. In a long historical lecture, Barber used the stories represented by the memorial to contextualize the contemporary challenges the audience was facing. He talked about how violence, enacted through slavery, lynching, chain gangs, and prison, had always been used as a tool to keep the wealthy in control of those in poverty, both Black and white. Implicitly indicting the election of Donald Trump as president, Barber reminded the audience that Reconstruction had ended and Jim Crow resurrected when Rutherford Hayes lost the popular vote but won the presidential election after making a deal with the South. "What we are seeing now," Barber told his audience, "is nothing but the regurgitation of the vomit of racism that we have seen before."

But, Barber said, racial politics is about more than just keeping Blacks poor and powerless; it is about keeping poor whites content to be poor. He redefined lynching to mean the systemic deaths caused by racial politics. Each year, he told the audience, 250,000 people die from "low wealth." Universal health care, environmental and ecological justice, and a living wage are not "Black" issues, he said, contrary to the common stereotype. He pointed out that more whites die from poverty than do Blacks.

After setting the scene with his recounting of history and the meaning of racial violence, Barber told his audience that they must take courage from those who had gone before them and confronted the horrors of lynching. He called on the audience to stand up in honor of those who had died and those who had protested against racial violence.

> Take a few seconds and stand and pay homage to all of those that kept fighting even after they saw the bodies swinging in front of them. Come on. All of those past, all of those that died and gone on. But they never quit. They never stopped. All of the white folk, all of the Black folk, that still stayed together. The ancestors. And, before you sit down, I want you to turn to your neighbor and say, "Neighbor (audience repeats), if they kept fighting (audience repeats), in the face of lynch mobs (audience repeats) I dare you to be scared of Trump (audience repeats) I dare you, I dare you. . . . I dare you to be afraid of modern-day white nationalists. They must not know who we are. We are the sons and the daughters of those who kept on anyhow.

As he concluded, Barber again referenced those who had gone before and used them to energize the audience.

> This is not the worst we've ever seen. It's just our time. Others have stood before, but they're dead and gone. I declare unto you, Harriet Tubman's not getting up out of the grave. William Lloyd Garrison, A. Philip Randolph, Rabbi Heschel, Dorothy Day. I visited the crypt of Martin Luther King and called his name, and he didn't get out of the grave. But America, America needs to know this. They may not get out of the grave, but we are their children.

Jelani Cobb, a writer for the *New Yorker*, reported that Barber was interrupted by standing ovations six times and that it was "the best speech" that Cobb had heard him give.

Another preacher, the Reverend Starsky Wilson, provided a complementary example of contemporary Black preaching. Wilson is the former pastor of St. John's Church (The Beloved Community) in St. Louis and head of the Deaconess Foundation, which focuses its philanthropy on community programs that promote health and children's well-being. Wilson also served as co-chair of the Ferguson Commission, following the police shooting of Michael Brown.

Reverend Wilson's 2015 sermonic speech to Freedom Riders who came to Ferguson to protest police violence illustrated the nuanced continuities and differences in Black preaching. Both Barber and Wilson exhorted their audiences to see the Christian faith as a call to live the Social Gospel and to enact social justice. Both held that Christianity must go beyond personal morality and publicly extend into the community. Both used biblical references to support their points.

Where Barber referred to himself as conservative, however, Wilson called for revolution. In this particular speech, Wilson took as his theme "The Politics of Jesus." "Jesus's political climate sounds eerily similar to the political climate we find ourselves in today," he began. He expanded on that thought, using Jesus's environment as a means to understand what Jesus stood for: "Jesus lived under Roman occupation and a militarized presence in his neighborhoods. The Roman occupation in Jesus's neighborhood seems similar to the police state on the streets of Ferguson that we have seen in the last two weeks.... There are those who have tried to forget,... denying the political setting of Jesus's life, so that you may deny the political nature of Jesus's ministry—suggesting that Jesus was more concerned with individual morality than social justice; that he was more concerned with inward evil than with systemic evil and oppression."

Once Jesus is removed from a private morality and placed in a public and political setting, Wilson defined the essence of politics: "Politics is about who gets what, when, where, and why." Jesus's focus was on the poor and disenfranchised, and therefore he rejected the political system of the day that denied food, housing, and justice to the poor. Wilson's core message, therefore, was that "Jesus's politics are real, revolutionary, radical, and our Christian roots," and "we must not preach Jesus, but preach what Jesus preached."

Two messages in Wilson's speech illustrate the radical nature of his preaching. At one point he sounded the themes of speakers like the Exoduster Pap Wilson or Malcolm X as Wilson condemned the African American "leaders" who came to Ferguson preaching reform rather than revolution. Wilson called it the "HNIC [Head Negro in Charge] syndrome" and likened such "leaders" to King Herod, the Jewish leader who was a puppet of Rome during Jesus's time.

Another graphic image Wilson used was the crucifixion. Like Barber and others, Wilson drew a straight line of comparison between lynching and policy brutality. Lynching, crucifixion, and police brutality were all, he said, tools used by the government to suppress insurrection. Contemporary police shootings, he said, must be used to make the politics of Jesus real and seen in the same way as Jesus's crucifixion had been understood: "[God provided ... ] for wandering Hebrews ... for oppressed Galileans ... for a persecuted people left depressed after his crucifixion ... for a divided

Western world and America, a vision of beloved community that is a multiracial, multicultural community of peace and justice where God is the governing ethics. To put into practice the politics of Jesus, we must magnify this picture of humanity that affirms all people as made in the image and likeness of God."

The audience's response, with multiple "Hallelujahs" and calls of "He is able," suggested the power of Wilson's sermon to move and motivate his hearers. Like the Reverend Barber, Wilson's sermon provided evidence that the preaching style of public speaking still commands attention, even in the highly mediated twenty-first century.

## PROTESTS AND ELECTIONS

The events and public speaking of 2020 and 2021 reflected all of these motifs that centered around the issue of systemic racism. The May 25, 2020, videotaped murder of George Floyd by a Minneapolis police officer sparked widespread, nationwide protests and a multitude of speeches in support of Black Lives Matter. Many speakers' emphasis on intersectionality and grassroots mobilization continued the motifs established earlier by Garza, Tometi, and Cullors. One particularly prominent voice among the many was that of civil rights attorney Benjamin Crump. Earlier, Crump had worked with the families of Trayvon Martin and Michael Brown and on the Flint, Michigan, water case. In 2020, he worked with and spoke on behalf of the families of Ahmaud Arbery, George Floyd, Breonna Taylor, and Jacob Blake, and in 2021 with the family of Daunte Wright.

Like Black speakers traditionally, in speeches and news conferences, Crump appealed to traditional American values even while expressing frustration that those values and principles were not extended to African Americans. As he remarked after the killing of Daunte Wright, families simply wanted to get their "day in court," so that "we can live up to our promise of liberty and justice for all." "We are hurting," he said, and "enough is enough":

> We're just outraged that during the Derek Chauvin trial, during the Derek Chauvin trial regarding the killing of George Floyd, ten miles from where this pivotal case of American jurisprudence has taken place, one of the most important consequential cases in the history of America, dealing with police excessive use of force, you would think that the police would try to do everything in their power to use the best standard of care.

"I know people say, 'Oh, there they go, talking about everything is racial,'" Crump acknowledged, but then answered that critique with a response reminiscent of Malcolm X: "Well, unfortunately and regrettably, we don't see white people being shot and killed like this. So what are we left to conclude?"

Yet Crump also sounded themes similar to those developed decades earlier by Martin Luther King Jr. Crump praised the protestors, saying that "because of those individuals [who protest, we are] raising the consciousness level that our children's lives matter and that Black people's lives matter," and he was hopeful for the future: "Because of that, we believe that we're starting to see a change in America. . . . We are making progress and I want to encourage those protestors, those young people, those activists, that you're making a difference and Minneapolis, Minnesota, right here now, is ground zero for that change." Recalling all the previous and current incidents of Black persons being killed by police or vigilantes, Crump expressed frustration but also a recognition that with criminal charges being brought against officers, some progress was being made. Echoing Martin Luther King Jr's famous observation that the moral arc of the universe is long but tends to bend toward justice, Crump told his audience that "all we can do is say we're making progress. The journey to justice is a long one."

While protestors Black and white voted with their feet in the summer of 2020, Black speakers urged them to vote with their ballots in the fall. Democrats had regained control of the House of Representatives in 2018 and had their sights set on the presidency and the Senate in 2020. Election turnout would be the key, and some states were putting in place policies that would discourage voting, particularly among poorer communities and communities of color. A leading voice in counteracting this effort was Stacey Abrams, who had lost a closely contested race for governor of Georgia in 2018. Following her defeat, Abrams founded Fair Fight Action to combat voter suppression. Speaking virtually to the 2020 Democratic National Convention, Abrams founded her arguments on the traditional principles of democracy: "This nation belongs to all of us and, in every election, we choose how we will create a more perfect union, not by taking sides but by taking stock of where we are and what we need. . . . In a democracy, we do not elect saviors. We cast our ballots for those who see our struggles and pledge to serve, who hear our dreams and work to make them real. To defend our way of life by protecting our right to vote." Many observers credited Abrams's organization and her personal advocacy with winning Georgia's electoral votes for Democratic presidential candidate Joe Biden in November and then, several weeks later, electing two Democrats to the U.S. Senate in extremely close run-off races. In 2022, Abrams continues to lead the opposition to restrictive voting laws proposed by a variety of states.

## CONCLUSION

The history of African American public speaking has been woven from many common threads. Individual speakers, however, have always crafted their message and delivery from their own set of experiences, tailoring their speeches to meet the exigencies they faced and the audience at hand. While there are some motifs that have continued and evolved since colonial times, there is no single style nor message that has defined African American public speaking. However, some conclusions can be drawn from studying its history.

The first lesson is that public speaking has mattered. Many African Americans made their place in history in large part because of their public speaking. Sojourner Truth, Frederick Douglass, Booker T. Washington, Ida B. Wells-Barnett, Marcus Garvey, Martin Luther King Jr., Fannie Lou Hamer, Barbara Jordan, and Jesse Jackson were just a few who gained national prominence through their powerful speaking. But others who were best known for their writings or other historical contributions were also heavily engaged in public speaking because public speaking was always an important medium for reaching audiences of all colors. Prince Hall, David Walker, W. E. B. Du Bois, Mary McLeod Bethune, Thurgood Marshall, and Shirley Chisholm are just some who are known best for other accomplishments, but all were active and important public speakers. What was clear during colonial times and has continued to the present day is that public speaking has been vital to the construction of the African American community, and it has also been a critical means of outreach to the larger community beyond.

A second lesson is that African American public speaking has occupied a prominent place in U.S. history. These speakers were thought leaders in opposing slavery, segregation, and lynching and in promoting civil rights, voting rights, and equal rights for all. Beyond issues of race, however, they participated in every movement and development in U.S. history. African American public speakers embraced the revivals; supported U.S. wars; promoted temperance, suffrage, and gay rights; helped audiences understand the idea of environmental racism; organized labor unions; advanced child welfare and education; and defended women's rights. There is not a social, economic, religious, or political issue in American history that has not been influenced by an African American speaker.

The third lesson is that African American public speaking has often served as the conscience of the nation. The United States was founded on the ideals that all humans are created equal, guaranteed the right to life, liberty, and the pursuit of happiness, and that government is comprised of "we the people" in order to form a more perfect union. Those professed ideals were sharply divergent from much of American practice, however, particularly in regard to U.S. citizens of African descent. African American public speakers often found themselves in the position of affirming the nation's principles of equal rights and democracy and of calling to account the nation's leaders and its everyday practices. The Southern Christian Leadership Conference was not alone in believing that African Americans had a unique role "To Redeem the Soul of America."

That spirit of commitment has lived on in African American public speaking. In December of 2019, speaking to the House of Representatives as it debated the articles of impeachment against President Donald Trump, Representative John Lewis gave voice to the same ideals he had spoken about from the steps of the Lincoln Memorial on August 28, 1963:

> This is a sad day. It is not a day of joy. Our nation is founded on the principle that we do not have kings, we have presidents, and the Constitution is our compass. When you see something that is not right, not just, not fair, you have a moral obligation to say something, to do something. Our children and their children will ask us, "What did you do? What did you say?" For some, this vote may be hard. But we have a mission and a mandate to be on the right side of history.

In February of 2019, less than a year before his passing, Representative Elijah Cummings of Maryland led the House Oversight Committee as it heard testimony from President Trump's personal attorney Michael Cohen. Cummings used the moment to famously challenge his audience about how they were living out the nation's principles: "The greatest gift that you and I, Mr. President, can give to our children is making sure we give them a democracy that is intact. A democracy that is better than the one we came upon.... When we are dancing with the angels, the question will be asked, 'In 2019, what did we do to make sure we kept our democracy intact? Did we stand on the sidelines and say nothing?'" This history of African American public speaking demonstrates that African Americans have never been willing to stand on the sidelines and say nothing, but have instead been vocal, determined, and eloquent in speaking on behalf of American democracy.

On January 21, 2021, the Reverend William Barber delivered an inaugural sermon that called to account the promise of America and the need to address the systemic racism that had stood in the way of achieving that promise. He took as his text Isaiah 58, which he said begins by saying, "This is the kind of fast day I'm after: to break the chains of injustice, get rid of exploitation in the workplace, free the oppressed, cancel debts. What I'm interested in seeing you do is sharing your food with the hungry, inviting the homeless poor into your homes, putting clothes on the shivering ill-clad." Isaiah was telling the Hebrews, he said, that "bad leadership, greed, and injustice and lies had led them into trouble, exile, and economic hardship," and the message of Isaiah applied to America in 2021 as well.

Alluding to his Repairers of the Breach organization, Barber said that the problem in America currently was the "gap," or breach, "in the nation between what is and how God wants things to be." Although initially framed religiously, Barber converted his call into secular language that echoed the Pledge of Allegiance and the Constitution:

> Transposed to our time, the breach is when we say "one nation under God, indivisible, with liberty and justice for all" with our lips while we see the rich and the poor living in two very different Americas. The breach would be knowing the only way to ensure domestic tranquility is to establish justice, but pretending we can address the nation's wounds with simplistic calls for unity. The breach is telling lies when we need truth, greed when we need compassion, fighting one another when we need to find common ground, and hating when we ought to be loving. And every now and then, a nation needs breach repairers to take us forward.

As Black public speakers have historically done, Barber reminded his audience that for its citizens of color, America had not yet fulfilled its promise, but he also reminded them that the need for justice extended to all of its citizens regardless of color or economic status: "If we want to come out of this jam and move forward together, we cannot accept the racial disparities, violence, and breaches that impact Black, brown, Native, and Asian Americans while offering collateral damage to our poor white brothers and sisters and ultimately our entire democracy." "America has never yet been all that she has hoped to be," Barber concluded, "but right here, right now, a Third Reconstruction is possible if we choose."

The day before Barber's sermon, at the swearing-in of Joe Biden as president and Kamala Harris as vice president, Amanda Gorman delivered an inauguration poem that spoke to the same hopes and frustrations as Rev. Barber's sermon. "Where can we find light in this never-ending shade?" she began. She was a "skinny Black girl descended from slaves," numbered among those who have "braved the belly of the beast," and are "weathered," "grieved," "hurt," and "tired." She rejected the call to "form a union that is perfect," replacing it with a charge to "forge a union with purpose." Gorman's proposed purpose for the union, like Barber's, embodied the Social Gospel: that "everyone will sit under their own vine and fig tree," where "love becomes our legacy" and "our people diverse and beautiful will emerge, battered and beautiful."

Amanda Gorman reciting her poem at the 2021 presidential inauguration. Office of the Chairman of the Joint Chiefs of Staff for Public Affairs. https://flickr.com/photos/42310076@N04/50861321057.

Like Barber and generations of African American speakers before her, Gorman saw in America's promise the possibility of the Social Gospel. But she simultaneously recognized the frustrating reality that the nation has turned its back on that promise so many times, most recently with the storming of the U.S. Capitol on January 6. Still, Gorman declared her faith that goodness and democracy would prevail.

At the second day of Senate confirmation hearings for Judge Ketanji Brown Jackson, Senator Cory Booker of New Jersey yet again summarized those feelings of hope and frustration in an impromptu statement. "There is a love of this country that is extraordinary," Booker said, exhibited time and again by the dispossessed and marginalized, from African Americans to women to Chinese immigrants to the LGBTQ community. Quoting Langston Hughes's famous poem, Booker recited from memory the attitude of these hopeful populations: "America was never America to me, but let America be America again." In Judge Jackson, said Booker, he saw another step forward in America's progress and promise. His hero, Harriet Tubman, had used a star to guide her way north and south. "The star was a harbinger of hope," he told Judge Jackson, and "today, you're my star. You're my harbinger of hope." In light of that hope, he declared, "I am not letting anybody in the Senate steal my joy. . . . Nobody's going to make me angry." He summed up his thoughts with a conclusion that in its fundamental message could be applied to so many across the course of American history, from Flora of Massachusetts to Ketanji Brown Jackson: "When you ascend onto the highest court in the land, I'm going to rejoice. And I'm going to tell you right now, the greatest country in the world, the United States of America, will be better because of you."

# A Note on Sources

## GENERAL SOURCES

General anthologies are helpful guides that can introduce the reader to the larger historical study of African American speech texts. Important anthologies include Carter G. Woodson, *Negro Orators and Their Orations* (New York: Russell and Russell, 1925); Marcus Boulware, *The Oratory of Negro Leaders, 1900–1968* (Westport, CT: Greenwood Press, 1969); Philip S. Foner, *The Voice of Black America: Major Speeches by Negroes in the United States 1797–1971* (New York: Simon and Schuster, 1972); Philip S. Foner and Robert Branham, *Lift Every Voice: African American Oratory, 1787–1900* (Tuscaloosa: University of Alabama Press, 1998); Molefi K. Asante and Steven Robb, *The Voice of Black Rhetoric: Selections* (Boston: Allyn and Bacon, 1971); Robbie Jean Walker, *The Rhetoric of Struggle: Public Address by African American Women* (New York: Garland, 1992); Catherine Ellis and Stephen Drury Smith, *Say It Plain: A Century of Great African American Speeches* (New York: The New Press, 2005); Martha Simmons and Frank A. Thomas, *Preaching with Sacred Fire: An Anthology of African American Sermons, 1750 to the Present* (New York: W. W. Norton, 2010); and Richard W. Leeman and Bernard K. Duffy, *The Will of a People: A Critical Anthology of Great African American Speeches* (Carbondale: Southern Illinois University Press, 2012). The general anthologies assembled by Woodson and Foner and the anthology of religious speeches by Simmons and Thomas were especially helpful for writing this book.

Important scholarly analyses of African American public speaking include Molefi K. Asante, *The Afrocentric Idea* (Philadelphia: Temple University Press, 1987); Celeste Michele Condit and John Louis Lucaites, *Crafting Equality: America's Anglo-African Word* (Chicago: University of Chicago Press, 1993); Teresa Zackodnik, *Press, Platform, Pulpit: Black Feminist Publics in the Era of Reform* (Knoxville: University of Tennessee

Press, 2011); Wilson Moses, *Black Messiahs and Uncle Toms: Social and Literary Manipulations of a Religious Myth* (University Park: Pennsylvania University Press, 1982); and David Howard-Pitney, *The Afro-American Jeremiad: Appeals for Justice in America* (Philadelphia: Temple University Press, 1990). Two useful scholarly anthologies include Elaine B. Richardson and Ronald L. Jackson II, *African American Rhetoric(s): Interdisciplinary Perspectives* (Carbondale: Southern Illinois University Press, 2007), and Richard W. Leeman, *African-American Orators: A BioCritical Sourcebook* (Westport, CT: Greenwood Press, 1996).

## CHAPTER 1: LIBERTY, EQUALITY, AND SALVATION: AFRICAN AMERICANS AT THE START OF THE NATION

*Preaching with Sacred Fire: An Anthology of African American Sermons, 1750 to the Present* (New York: W. W. Norton, 2010), written and edited by Martha Simmons and Frank A. Thomas, provided important texts and analyses of early religious speaking by African Americans. Christopher Cameron's *To Plead Our Own Cause: African Americans in Massachusetts and the Antislavery Movement* (Kent, OH: Kent State University Press, 2014) is an excellent analysis of Black abolitionist speaking during the colonial and early national periods. *Lift Every Voice: African American Oratory, 1787–1900* (Tuscaloosa: University of Alabama Press, 1998), edited by Philip S. Foner and Robert Branham, was a helpful source of speech texts. Jean McMahon Humez's *Gifts of Power: The Writings of Rebecca Jackson, Black Visionary, Shaker Eldress* (Amherst: University of Massachusetts Press, 1981) provides helpful insight into early folk preaching by women and men.

## CHAPTER 2: ALL MANNER OF REFORMS

Philip S. Foner and Robert Branham's *Lift Every Voice: African American Oratory, 1787–1900* (Tuscaloosa: University of Alabama Press, 1998) is again the best starting point, as it supplies a wide variety of speech texts for the period. Richard W. Leeman's *African-American Orators: A Bio-Critical Sourcebook* (Westport, CT: Greenwood Press, 1996) provides helpful introductions to the public speaking of Maria Miller Stewart, Charles Lenox Remond, William Whipper, Henry Highland Garnet, Frederick Douglass, William Wells Brown, Frances Watkins Harper, and Sojourner Truth. Richard W. Leeman and Bernard K. Duffy provide comprehensive analyses of several of the era's most notable speeches in *The Will of a People: A Critical Anthology of Great African American Speeches* (Carbondale: Southern Illinois University Press, 2012). Detine Bowers's article "A Place to Stand: African-Americans and the First of August Platform," *Southern Communication Journal* 60 (1995): 348–61, provides an excellent overview of the First of August ceremonial speeches.

Ministers and preachers continued to occupy a central role in Black public speaking during this era. Simmons and Thomas's *Preaching with Sacred Fire: An Anthology of African American Sermons, 1750 to the Present* was again helpful in tracing the evolution of Black preaching during the antebellum period. From the preaching tradition emerged the jeremiad as an important speech form. Wilson J. Moses's *Black Messiahs and Uncle Toms: Social and Literary Manipulations of a Religious Myth* (University Park: The Pennsylvania State University Press, 1982) and David Howard-Pitney's *The Afro-American Jeremiad: Appeals for Justice in America* (Philadelphia: Temple University Press, 1990) are fundamental to understanding the Black jeremiad in America.

Women speakers emerged to assume an especially central speaking role during the antebellum period. Teresa Zackodnik's *Press, Platform, Pulpit: Black Feminist Publics in the Era of Reform* (Knoxville: University of Tennessee Press, 2011) and Robbie Jean Walker's *The Rhetoric of Struggle: Public Address by African American Women* (New York: Garland, 1992) provide analyses and texts respectively that highlight the important contributions of African American women during the antebellum era of reform. Preeminent among these speakers was Sojourner Truth. Most readers turn first to her autobiography, the *Narrative of Sojourner Truth,* edited by Olive Gilbert (Battle Creek, MI: Review and Herald Office, 1884; reprint, New York: Arno Press, 1968), and Nell Painter's insightful analytical study *Sojourner Truth: A Life, A Symbol* (New York: W. W. Norton & Company, 1996).

The predominant speaker of the era was Frederick Douglass, and there are many excellent works available by and about Douglass, including his four autobiographies and the multivolume *Frederick Douglass Papers* from Yale University Press. Gregory Lampe's *Frederick Douglass: Freedom's Voice, 1818–1845* (East Lansing: Michigan State University Press, 1998) is an excellent analysis of Douglass's entry into public speaking and his early experiences as an antislavery platform speaker. *The Speeches of Frederick Douglass*, edited by John R. McKivigan, Julie Husband, and Heather L. Kaufman (New Haven, CT: Yale University Press, 2018), is an important compilation of important speeches, with helpful introductions provided. David Blight's

*Frederick Douglass: Prophet of Freedom* (New York: Simon and Schuster, 2018) provides an important look into the orator's contributions across the course of his speaking career.

CHAPTER 3: EMANCIPATION, SEGREGATION, AND MIGRATION

Speech texts for this era are more readily available, although Foner and Branham's *Lift Every Voice* remains an important mainstay for surveying the oratory of the period. Carter G. Woodson's *Negro Orators and Their Orations* (New York: Russell and Russell, 1925) is an important supplement to Foner and Branham's volume. Woodson made extensive use of the *Congressional Record* and the minutes from African American organizations to supply the speeches reprinted in his volume. Speakers analyzed in Leeman's *African-American Orators* are Anna Julia Cooper, Alexander Crummell, Frances Ellen Watkins Harper, Booker T. Washington, Fannie Barrier Williams, and Ida B. Wells-Barnett.

McKivigan, Husband, and Kaufman's *The Speeches of Frederick Douglass* is an important resource for understanding Douglass's speaking across this period. Kirt Wilson's *The Reconstruction Desegregation Debate: The Politics of Equality and the Rhetoric of Place, 1870–1875* (East Lansing: Michigan State University Press, 2002) examines the public speaking of "establishment" African Americans as they campaigned for equal rights and insightfully analyzes the difficult choices these speakers faced. Nell Painter's *Exodusters: Black Migration to Kansas after Reconstruction* (New York: W. W. Norton & Company, 1976) is an excellent survey that covers the speakers who agitated for westward migration and illustrates how these speakers served as a counterpoint to the mainstream Black speakers. Andre Johnson's *The Forgotten Prophet: Bishop Henry McNeal Turner and the African American Prophetic Tradition* (Lanham, MD: Lexington Books, 2012) explores the speaking of another leader who stood counter to the mainstream. Johnson examines how Turner's political speaking evolved over time, as he drew from different prophetic traditions to suit his changing views and purposes. Booker T. Washington's autobiography *Up from Slavery* (New York: Doubleday, Page and Company, 1901) provides useful descriptions of Washington's thinking regarding his public speaking. Richard W. Leeman's "Fighting for Freedom Again: African American Reform Rhetoric in the Late Nineteenth Century" in *The Rhetoric of Nineteenth-Century Reform*, edited by Martha M. Watson and Thomas Burkholder (East Lansing: Michigan State University Press, 2008), 1–35, surveys the speakers of this era in light

A NOTE ON SOURCES 225

of how they responded to Social Darwinism, a major line of thought developed by white Americans that supported de jure and de facto discrimination against African Americans.

Karlyn Kohrs Campbell's "Style and Content in the Rhetoric of Early Afro-American Feminists," *Quarterly Journal of Speech* 72 (1986): 434–45, ably draws connections between African American feminist speakers across the nineteenth century. Frances Smith Foster's *A Brighter Coming Day: A Frances Ellen Watkins Harper Reader* (New York: Feminist Press at the City University of New York, 1990) is a useful introduction to the work of this influential woman who worked in the fields of abolition, temperance, woman suffrage, and equal rights for Blacks. Like Washington's *Up from Slavery*, Ida B. Wells-Barnett's *Crusade for Justice: The Autobiography of Ida B. Wells* (Chicago: University of Chicago Press, 1970) supplies a fascinating look at how Wells-Barnett approached the art of platform speaking.

CHAPTER 4: LIFTING AS WE CLIMB: ADVANCING THE CAUSE

Because Foner and Branham's *Lift Every Voice* ends at 1900, readers must shift to the earlier volume by Philip Foner, *The Voice of Black America: Major Speeches by Negroes in the United States 1797–1971* (New York: Simon and Schuster, 1972). This volume, too, is encyclopedic, but more of the speech texts are abridged in this earlier work. Woodson's *Negro Orators and Their Orations* is useful for the first quarter century, and Marcus Boulware's *The Oratory of Negro Leaders, 1900–1968* (Westport, CT: Negro Universities Press, 1969) is also a useful resource. Simmons and Thomas's *Preaching with Sacred Fire: An Anthology of African American Sermons, 1750 to the Present* is very helpful for studying the rise of Black preachers during the early days of records and radio.

Single-speaker anthologies and biographies are particularly helpful to understanding this often overlooked period of African American oratory. Philip Foner's two-volume set of *W.E.B. Du Bois Speaks: Speeches and Addresses* (New York: Pathfinder Press, 1970) is invaluable to understanding this intellectual's public speaking, which is often overshadowed by the power of his written words. Similarly helpful is Amy Jacques Garvey's comprehensive two-volume compilation of her husband's speeches and essays in *Philosophy and Opinions of Marcus Garvey, vols. 1 and 2* (New York: Universal Publishing House, 1923, 1925). Cornelius Bynum's *A. Philip Randolph and the Struggle for Civil Rights* (Urbana: University of Illinois Press, 2010) does an admirable job of interpreting Randolph's role in the march for political and economic rights. Shorter essays on Mary McLeod Bethune, Father Divine, Francis Grimké, Vernon Johns, Thurgood Marshall, Mary Church Terrell, and Adam Clayton Powell Jr. may be found in Leeman's *African-American Orators: A BioCritical Sourcebook*.

CHAPTER 5: WAVES OF REFORM AND REVOLUTION: THE MODERN CIVIL RIGHTS MOVEMENT

Speech texts, biographies of speakers, and detailed accounts of speech events and audience reactions become far more plentiful with the advent of the modern civil rights movement. Encyclopedic anthologies like Foner's *The Voice of Black America: Major Speeches by Negroes in the United States 1797–1971* and Simmons and Thomas's *Preaching with Sacred Fire: An Anthology of African American Sermons, 1750 to the Present* continue to provide a helpful foundation, but readers have many other resources from which to choose. For the mainstream movement headed by Martin Luther King Jr., Taylor Branch's three-volume set includes many detailed discussions of speeches, contexts, and audiences: *Parting the Waters: America in the King Years 1954–63* (New York: Simon and Schuster, 1988); *Pillar of Fire: America in the King Years 1963–65* (New York: Simon and Schuster, 1998); *At Canaan's Edge: America in the King Years, 1965–68* (New York: Simon and Schuster, 2006). Helpful anthologies of King's work include Martin Luther King Jr., *Strength to Love* (New York: Harper and Row, 1963), and Martin Luther King Jr., *The Trumpet of Conscience* (New York: Harper and Row, 1967). Audio and video recordings of King speaking are now widely available on the Internet. Michael Eric Dyson's *I May Not Get There with You: The True Martin Luther King, Jr.* (New York: Simon and Schuster, 2000) is an outstanding analysis of King's speaking that reminds the reader how radical his voice was for contemporary audiences.

A similar treasure trove of sources is available for studying the speaking of Malcolm X. The most helpful anthologies for this chapter were Malcolm X, *Malcolm X Speaks: Selected Speeches and Statements*, ed. George Breitman (New York: Merit, 1965), and Malcolm X, *The Speeches of Malcolm X at Harvard*, ed. Archie Epps (New York: William Morrow, 1968). Louis Lomax's *When the Word Is Given* (New York: Signet, 1964) is particularly helpful for studying Malcolm's Nation of Islam speaking. Lomax includes detailed descriptions of Malcolm's speaking and his NOI audiences as well as extended speech excerpts. Malcolm X's *The Autobiography of Malcolm X (as told to Alex Haley)* (New York: Ballantine, 1964) provides a very helpful first-person perspective into his approach to public speaking. The most complete and reliable biography is Les Payne and Tamara Payne's *The Dead Are Arising: The Life of Malcolm X* (New York: W.W. Norton, 2020). The analysis in this chapter of Malcolm X and other Black Power speakers, and the impact of Malcolm X's speaking, owes much to Robert Terrill's idea of emancipatory rhetoric, as outlined in *Malcolm X: Inventing Radical Judgment* (Lansing: Michigan State University Press, 2004).

Important sources for understanding other important speakers during this era include Maegan Parker Brooks and Davis W. Houck's *The Speeches of Fannie Lou Hamer: To Tell It Like It Is* (Jackson: University Press of Mississippi, 2011); Stokely Carmichael (Kwame Toure), *Stokely Speaks*, ed. Ethel N. Minor (New York: Random House, 1971); and Philip S. Foner, *The Black Panthers Speak* (Philadelphia: Lippincott, 1970). Shorter essays on Eldridge Cleaver, Angela Davis, John Lewis, Louis Lomax, Robert Moses, and Andrew Young appear in Leeman's *African-American Orators: A BioCritical Sourcebook*. Audio and video recordings on the Internet of many speakers from this era, particularly Hamer, Carmichael (Toure), Cleaver, Davis, Huey Newton, and Bobby Seale, yield a fuller understanding of the range of compelling styles employed by speakers of this era. Molefi K. Asante's (Arthur L. Smith) *Rhetoric of Black Revolution* (Boston: Allyn and Bacon, 1970) is an important critical analysis of the Black radical speaking during the era.

## CHAPTER 6: "I AM SOMEBODY": PUBLIC SPEAKING IN THE AGE OF INTEGRATION

Following the close of the modern civil rights movement, the encyclopedic anthologies of Black public speaking are not as helpful. Foner's *The Voice of Black America* ends at 1971. Simmons and Thomas's *Preaching with Sacred Fire* continues to provide a helpful survey of Black preaching up until 2010. Anthologies, autobiographies, and biographies supplied much of the material needed for this chapter. Important such sources include Shirley Chisholm, *The Good Fight* (New York: Harper and Row, 1973); Barbara Jordan and Shelby Hearon, *Barbara Jordan: A Self-Portrait* (Garden City, NY: Doubleday, 1979); Barbara Jordan, *Barbara C. Jordan: Selected Speeches*, ed. Sandra Parham (Washington, DC: Howard University Press, 1999); Jesse L. Jackson, *Keep Hope Alive: Jesse Jackson's 1988 Presidential Campaign*, ed. Frank Clemente and Frank Watkins (Boston: South End Press, 1989); Jesse L. Jackson, *Straight from the Heart*, ed. Roger D. Hatch and Frank

E. Watkins (Philadelphia: Fortress Press, 1987); Louis Farrakhan, *Seven Speeches by Minister Louis Farrakhan* (Chicago: WKU and the Final Call, 1992); and Al Sharpton and Anthon Walton, *Go and Tell Pharaoh: The Autobiography of the Reverend Al Sharpton* (New York: Doubleday, 1996).

Mark MacPhail's trenchant analyses, "Louis Abdul Farrakhan," *African-American Orators: A BioCritical Sourcebook*, ed. Richard W. Leeman (Westport, CT: Greenwood, 1996), 120–33, and "Louis Abdul Farrakhan," *American Voices: An Encyclopedia of Contemporary Orators*, ed. Bernard K. Duffy and Richard W. Leeman (Westport, CT: Greenwood Press, 2005), 155–64, make the case that Farrakhan supplies an important prophetic critique of the United States. Additional useful chapters in Duffy and Leeman's *American Voices* include essays on Angela Davis, Marian Wright Edelman, Jocelyn Elders, Jesse Jackson, Audre Lorde, Colin Powell, Al Sharpton, and Faye Wattleton. Similar chapters surveying the speaker and their speeches in Leeman's *African-American Orators* examine the work of Shirley Chisholm, Lenora Fulani, Benjamin Hooks, Barbara Jordan, Eleanor Holmes Norton, Douglas Wilder, and Walter Williams. The Internet also provides many good audio and video recordings of speeches by major and minor figures of this era.

## CHAPTER 7: BARACK OBAMA AND THE "POST-RACIAL" SOCIETY

The nation's first African American president dominates the first decade of this period, from Obama's first presidential campaign through his farewell address. All of his presidential speeches are available online through the White House archives at https://obamawhitehouse.archives.gov. Barack Obama's *The Audacity of Hope* (New York: Crown Publishers, 2006) helps illuminate his approach to writing and giving speeches and the important role speaking plays in making tangible policy change. Richard W. Leeman's *The Teleological Discourse of Barack Obama* (Lanham, MD: Lexington Books, 2012) argues that Obama's public speaking, both prior to and during his presidency, is widely attractive to audiences because it centers around the teleological ethics of communication. In this chapter, the analysis of Obama's speaking rests solidly on this understanding. Many scholarly articles similarly seek to answer the question as to why Barack Obama appealed so eloquently to so many people. Some of the articles that provide especially fine analyses include James Darsey, "Barack Obama and America's Journey," *Southern Communication Journal* 74 (2009): 88–103; Robert E.

Terrill, "Unity and Duality in Barack Obama's 'A More Perfect Union,'" *Quarterly Journal of Speech* 95 (2009): 167–94; Robert C. Rowland and John M. Jones, "Recasting the American Dream and American Politics: Barack Obama's Keynote Address to the 2004 Democratic National Convention," *Quarterly Journal of Speech* 93 (2007): 425–48; Judy L. Isaksen, "Obama's Rhetorical Shift: Insights for Communication Studies," *Communication Studies* 62 (2011): 456–71; and David A Frank, "The Prophetic Voice and the Face of the Other in Barack Obama's 'A More Perfect Union' Address, March 18, 2008," *Rhetoric and Public Affairs* 12 (2009): 167–94.

Robert Terrill's *Double-Consciousness and the Rhetoric of Barack Obama: The Price and Promise of Leadership* (Columbia: University of South Carolina Press, 2015) explores the difficult line Obama walked between governing the U.S. as a popular president and also giving voice to the historic and contemporary problems experienced by the Black community. David A. Frank and Mark L. McPhail's "Barack Obama's Address to the 2004 Democratic National Convention: Trauma, Compromise, Consilience, and the (Im)possibility of Racial Reconciliation," *Rhetoric and Public Affairs* 8 (2005): 571–93, similarly addresses the difficulties Obama faced reconciling his two roles and the sense of frustration that many felt in the wake of his generally optimistic approach to American politics. An excellent entry to the scholarly discussions of Barack Obama's public speaking is provided in the anthology edited by Robert E. Terrill, *Reconsidering Obama: Reflections on Rhetoric* (New York: Peter Lang, 2017).

For other contemporary speakers, Internet sources such as audio and video recordings or organizational websites are the primary resources. Some of the current, important websites belong to Black Lives Matter (https://blacklivesmatter.com), the Equal Justice Initiative (http://www.eji.org), Repairers of the Breach (http://www.breachrepairers.com), and the Poor People's Campaign (http://www.poorpeoplescampaign.org). Popular press articles about figures were also helpful in writing this chapter. Jelani Cobb's "The Southern Strategist," *The New Yorker* (14 May 2018): 68–75, is a detailed discussion about how Rev. Barber continues the tradition of great Black preaching and commitment to the Social Gospel and the reactions of audiences when they hear his speaking. Helpful scholarly analyses of the Black Lives Matter movement include Alissa V. Richardson, "Dismantling Respectability: The Rise of New Womanist Communication Models in the Era of Black Lives Matter," *Journal of Communication*, 69 (2019): 193–213; Russell Rickford, "Black Lives Matter: Toward a Modern Practice of Mass Struggle," *New Labor Forum* 25 (2016): 34–42; Ashlee A. Lambert and Mark P. Orbe, "#BlackLivesMatter Political Discourse: A Burkean Analysis of Controversial Comments at Aretha Franklin's Funeral," *Journal of Contemporary Rhetoric* 9 (2019): 126–38; Andre E. Johnson, "Dislocations and Shutdowns: MLK, BLM and the Rhetoric of Confrontation," *Journal of Contemporary Rhetoric* 8 (2018): 137–45; Christopher A. House, "Crying for Justice: The #BLACKLIVESMATTER Religious Rhetoric of Bishop T.D. Jakes," *Southern Communication Journal* 83 (2017): 13–27; and Jennifer L. Borda and Bailey Marshall, "Creating a Space to #SayHerName: Rhetorical Stratification in the Networked Sphere," *Quarterly Journal of Speech* 106 (2020): 133–55.

# Index

AAMC. *See* Association of American Medical Colleges
Abernathy, Ralph, 124
abolition: during antebellum era, 2–3; motivation for, 46; petitions for, 26–27; in politics, 51–52; speaking for, 47–56; white abolitionists, 44
ACS. *See* American Colonization Society
activists: Black preaching and, 208–14; for change, 201–14; criminal justice system and, 203–8; exposure of, 175–76; in 1980s, 175–85; organizational leaders of, 175–77. *See also* community activism
*Adam by Adam* (Powell, A.), 118
Adams, Ennals J., 69–70
advocates, 31
affirmative action, 159, 167
AFL. *See* American Federation of Labor
Afric-American Female Intelligence Society, 46
African American community. *See specific topics*
African American rights. *See specific topics*
African Free School, 38
African Methodist Episcopal Church (A.M.E.), 19, 71
African religions, 16
*The Afrocentric Idea* (Asante), 182
*Afrocentricity* (Asante), 182
Afrocentrism, 5
Ali, Noble Drew, 116
Allen, Richard, 2, 19
A.M.E. *See* African Methodist Episcopal Church
American Anti-Slavery Society, 38, 42
American Civil Liberties Union, 183

American Colonization Society (ACS), 38, 62
American Communist Party, 6
American Dream, 190
American Federation of Labor (AFL), 101
American Revolution, 23, 24, 186
American Society of Muslims, 177
Anderson, Marian, 133
antebellum era: abolition during, 2–3; racial equality during, 2–3; religion during, 2–3; slavery during, 11; women in, 46
Anthony, Susan B., 56, 73
*Anti-Slavery Bugle*, 40
Anti-Slavery Convention of American Women, 46–47
antislavery societies, 37–38, 42, 44, 46–47, 49, 53
antiwar movement, 5
Arab Spring, 6
ASALH. *See* Association for the Study of Afro-American Life and History
Asante, Molefi K., 7, 182
Association for the Study of Afro-American Life and History (ASALH), 166
Association of American Medical Colleges (AAMC), 207
*The Autobiography of an Ex-Colored Man* (Johnson, J. W.), 97

Baker, Ella, 126–27, 145
Baldwin, Maria, 97–98
Ballou, Hosea, 20
Barber, William, II, *210*; fame of, 209–10; goals of, 212; leadership of, 218–19; religion of, 210–11; speaking style of, 209; support of, 211

## INDEX

Barry, Marion, 163–64
Beecher, Henry Ward, 76
Benezet, Anthony, 29
Bethune, Mary McLeod, 4, 12, 103
Bethune-Cookman Institute, 103
Bible, 68–69, 209; Book of Daniel, 79; Psalm 68, 18–19; Psalm 92, 32; relevance of, 17–18
Biden, Joe, 218–19
Black abolitionists, 11
Black Baptist preacher speaking style, 8–9
Black Codes, 38
Black Diamond Express sermon, 114–16
Black Lives Matter movement (BLM), 6, 178, 189–90, 199, 203–5, 214
*Black Messiahs and Uncle Toms* (Moses, W. J.), 114
Black millionaires, 41
Black National Baptist Convention, 124
Black nationalism, 4, 143, 148
Black Panther Party for Self Defense, 152–53
Black Power, 5, 10, 147–51; movement of, 153; refrain of, 152; speaking style of, 12
Black preaching: activism and, 208–14; fame of, 16–17
Black pride, 5
Black Star Line, 111
Black studies, 5
Black Talcott Congregational Church, 32
Blassingame, John, 16
BLM. *See* Black Lives Matter movement
Bloody Sunday march, 186
Booker, Cory, 201, 220
Borders, William, 159
Bowdoin College, 24
Bradley, Tom, 163–64
Branch, Taylor, 134
*Breaking Bread* (hooks and West), 181
British Empire, 63–64
Brockwell, Charles, 17
Brooklyn African Woolman Benevolent Society, 21
Brotherhood of Pullman Car Porters, 125
Brown, H. Rap, 12, 152, 157–58
Brown, John, 39
Brown, Michael, 199–200

Brown, William Wells, 3, 7, 44, 50–51
*Brown v. Board of Education*, 5, 12, 109, 121
Bruce, Blanche K., 79
Bruce, John E., 93
Bryant, M. Edward, 89, 93
Bunche, Ralph, 109–10, 148
Bush, George W., 183–84
Bustil, Cyril, 20

call-and-response technique, 8
Cameron, Christopher, 17, 27
Campbell, J. P., 68
Camus, Albert, 128
capitalism, 151–53
Carmichael, Stokely, 12, 132; on capitalism, 151–52; on condemnation, 150; exile of, 157–58; reach of, 5; speaking style of, 149–50; on violence, 151
Carver, George Washington, 166
Cary, Mary Ann Shadd, 73
Chaney, John, 145–46
Charles, C., 41–42
Chauncy, Charles, 17
Chavis, Benjamin, 6, 178–79
*Chicago Defender*, 106
Children's Defense Fund, 5, 13, 175
Chisholm, Shirley, 158, 168; tradition of, 183; on Vietnam War, 5–6; on violence, 160–61
CHR. *See* Council for Human Rights
Christianity, 90; commitment to, 126; ethics of, 122; hope in, 19–20; hypocrisy of, 15–16; sins of, 55; Social Gospel, 154–55. *See also* preaching
church: burning of, 32; discrimination in, 11; doctrine of, 20; integration of, 2–3. *See also specific topics*
cities, 4, 46–47
citizenship: full, 113; right to, 11, 55; school for, 145; second-class, 152–53
civil rights, 5; Black rights as, 46; challenges of, 33, 73–77; equal rights, 81; human rights as, 143–44; King, M. L., Jr., on, 137; legislation of, 1; loss of, 81–82; modern movement of, 121–58; opposition of, 30. *See also* modern civil rights movement; women's rights

# INDEX

Civil Rights Act (1875), 74, 88
Civil Rights Act (1964), 5, 148, 157–58, 186
Civil War: defining the, 66–67; discrimination during, 68; Douglass, F., on, 67; emancipation and, 80–81; fighting in, 65–68; influence of, 11; participation in, 75; reconstruction during, 68–81; slavery and, 65–66; soldier rights during, 67–68; support of, 3
Clay, Henry, 44, 62
Cleage, Albert B., Jr., 139
Cleaver, Eldridge, 12, 152
clergy. *See specific clergy*
Clinton, Bill, 185
Clinton, Hillary, 165, 183
Cobb, Jelani, 212
COFO. *See* Council of Federated Organizations
colonial period, 11
colonization, 62–63, 102
colonization movement, 34–35
Colored Reading Society, 41
Coloured American Conventional Temperance Society, 56
community: benefits of, 26; building, 21–26; challenges of, 22–23; Johnstone on, 25; King, M. L., Jr., on, 123–24; Obama, B., on, 187; programs for, 176; speaking within, 110–17; unity of, 166–67
community activism, 164–67, 175–82
*Confession* (Flora), 17–18
Congress, U. S., 74, 159–60
Congress on Racial Equality (CORE), 125, 132
Constitution, U. S., 33, 51, 55, 161–63
Cooper, Anna Julia, 83
Cooper, Ann Nixon, 195–96
CORE. *See* Congress on Racial Equality
Cotton States Exposition, 85
Council for Human Rights (CHR), 139
Council of Federated Organizations (COFO), 128, 145
crime, 24–25, 49
*The Crisis*, 7, 99
Cronon, Edmund David, 113–14
Crummell, Alexander, 77, 125
Crump, Benjamin, 214–15

Cullors, Patrisse, 178, 203–5
Cummings, Elijah, 217

Davidson, Olivia, 82
Davis, Angela, 5–6, 12, 153, 179
Davis, Samuel, 61–62
Dawson, William, 117
death: of Kennedy, 142; of King, M. L., Jr., 157–58; of Malcolm X, 149; of Martin, 6; in riots, 39
Declaration of Independence, 49, 135–36
Declaration of Sentiments, 58–59
Delaney, Martin R., 77
democracy: education and, 34; foundation of, 34; justification of, 122; MFDP for, 145–46; war for, 102
Democratic National Convention (DNC), 146, 168, 170, 186, 201, 209–10
Democratic Party, 71, 75, 106, 107, 143, 160, 163, 168, 186
De Priest, Oscar Stanton, 106–7
Deval, Patrick, 201
Dexter Avenue Church, 121
discrimination, 8; in church, 11; during Civil War, 68; de facto, 3; economic, 6, 156; in freedom, 60–62; in laws, 105; perception and, 199–200; racial, 1, 3–4; systemic economic injustice, 156
DNC. *See* Democratic National Convention
Douglass, Frederick: anger of, 55–56; background of, 44–45; on Civil War, 67; on Constitution, US, 55; criticism of, 88; "Fourth of July" Oration by, 53–56; on Lincoln, 80–81; livelihood of, 7; on migration, 79; on religion, 53–55; in slavery, 3; on slave trade, 55; speaking style of, 9; support of, 58–59; teachings of, 16
Douglass, Sarah, 46–47
*Dreams from My Father* (Obama, B.), 193
Drew, Charles, 166
Du Bois, W. E. B., 1, 4, 87, 175; education of, 96–97; on equality, 105; organization of, 97; Pan-Africanist, 117; in politics, 96–97; on Social Darwinism, 105–6; support for, 97
Dyer Anti-Lynching Bill, 103

early national period, 11
East Baltimore Mental Improvement Society, 44
Easton, Hosea: background of, 31–35; on liberty, 32; on moral improvement, 35; passion of, 35; on religion, 34; speaking style of, 32
Ebedmelech the Ethiopian, 23
economic discrimination, 6, 156
economic self-sufficiency, 10
Edelman, Marian Wright, 5, 128–29; criticism of, 184; fame of, 183; lobbying of, 165–66; speaking style of, 165, 175–76; on taxes, 175–76
Edgefield Real Estate and Homestead Association, 77–78
education, 5, 12, 109, 121, 199; of children, 98–99; democracy and, 34; of Du Bois, 96–97; fight for, 82–87; of Hooks, Benjamin, 165–66; "industrial education," 85, 88; literacy tests, 76; literary societies, 37–38; NEA and, 85, 165, 175; "No Child Left Behind," 183–84; of preachers, 33–34; progress of, 166; public speaking and, 98; value of, 103; of women, 71; women's rights to, 58
Edwards, Jonathan, 2
Egyptians, 23, 29, 54
Eisenhower, Dwight D., 125
EJI. *See* Equal Justice Initiative
emancipation, 131; Civil War and, 80–81; migration and, 65–93; segregation and, 65–93; universal suffrage and, 69–72
Emancipation Proclamation, 66, 135
emigration, colonization compared to, 62–63
employment: FEPC for, 108; sanitation workers' strike and, 157; in trade careers, 98; during World War I, 95–96
equality, 2–3, 6; agitating for, 96–110; CORE for, 125, 132; Du Bois on, 105; fight for, 95–119; legal, 3–4; liberty and, 15–36; organizing for, 96–110; principle of, 109; progress of, 63; through public speaking, 3; social, 70; Truth on, 59–60; of women, 59–60
Equal Justice Initiative (EJI), 7, 178, 206, 211

Equal Rights Amendment, 160–61
Evers, Medgar, 145
Exodusters, 77, *78*

Fair Employment Practices Commission (FEPC), 108
Farrakhan, Louis, 6, 177, 184, 208–9
Fauntroy, Walter, 183
Federal Communications Commission (FCC), 166
Federal Court of Appeals, U. S., 178–79
Female Literary Society of Philadelphia, 46–47
FEPC. *See* Fair Employment Practices Commission
Ferguson Commission, 212
First African Baptist Church, 38
First Congregational Church, 17
First Gulf War, 182
First National Conference of Colored Women, 83
First National People of Color Environmental Summit, 6
Flora (slave), 17–19, 23
Floyd, George, 13, 214
folk preaching: call-and-response pattern, 16; Great Awakening and, 16–19; style of, 16; tradition of, 114; whooping, 16
Forman, James, 147–48
Forten, James, Jr., 41
*Fortune*, 208
Fortune, T. Thomas, 89–90
Founding Fathers, 53
Fourth Convention of Colored Citizens, 62–63
Franklin, C. L., 139
Franklin, John Hope, 95
freedom: achieving, 26; discrimination in, 60–62; legal, 65; MFDP for, 145–46; of politics, 15; of religion, 15–16
Freedom Riders, 128, 149, 212
Freedom Rides, 125–27, 144
*Freedom's Journal*, 24
Freedom Summer, 149, 183
Freedom Voters, 129
*Free Speech*, 91
French Revolution, 24

## INDEX

Fugitive Slave Law, 39, 45, 47, 53, 55, 63–64
Fulani, Lenora, 6
fund-raising, 5, 13, 38, 103–4, 175

Gage, Frances, 59
Gandhi, Mahatma, 126–27
Garnet, Henry Highland, 2–3, 39, 50–53, 61–63, 68–69, 77, 97
Garrison, William Lloyd, 31–32, 41–42, 44
Garvey, Marcus, *112*, 143; background of, 110–11; criticism of, 113–14; deportation of, 4; fame of, 12; Malcolm X compared to, 10; passion of, 7–8; speaking style of, 9, 111–13
Garveyites, 4, 10
Garza, Alicia, 178, 203–5
Gates, Henry Louis, 5, 181–82
Gates, J. M., 114
Giffords, Gabrielle, 198–99
God, 21
Goetz, Bernard, 178
Goldwater, Barry, 147
Goodman, Andrew, 145–46
Good Samaritan, 23
Gorman, Amanda, 218–19, *219*
da Graca, Marcelino Manoel "Sweet Daddy Grace," 116
Grace, Charles "Big Daddy," 4
Grady, Henry, 85
grassroots mobilization, 214
grassroots public speaking, 5
Great Awakening, 16–19, 40
Great Migration, 4, 12, 95
Green, John P., 88
Grimké, Archibald, 4, 97
Grimké, Francis, 4, 97, 125

Haiti: crime in, 24–25; government of, 24; representatives of, 42; Russwurm on, 24–25
Haitian slave revolt (1791), 24
Hall, Prince, 2, 22, 23, 27
Hamer, Fannie Lou, 5, 12, 128–29, 144–45, 146–47, 186
Hamilton, William, 26–28, 31, 62–63
Harper, Frances Ellen Watkins, 3–4, 7, 9, *45*, 70–73, 90

Harris, Kamala, 201–3, 218–19
Hart, Gary, 168
Harvey, Burwell T., 87
Hayes, Rutherford B., 79–80, 211
Haynes, Lemuel, 20, 22
Henery, Mary, 19
Henry, Patrick, 52
Hiram, Revels, 70
*The History of Woman Suffrage* (Gage), 59
Holder, Eric, 201
Holmes, Eleanor, 128–29
Holt Street Baptist Church, 122
*The Holy Koran of the Moorish Science Temple* (Ali), 116
hooks, bell, 5, 180–82
Hooks, Benjamin, 165–67
Hope, John, 87
House of Representatives, US, 5, 39, 79–80, 161
Hughes, Langston, 136, 220
humanity, 50–51
human rights reforms, 5
Humez, Jean, 40
Hurricane Katrina, 204

Independence Day, 53–54
integration: agitating for, 96–110; of church, 2–3; organizing for, 96–110; promotion of, 116; public speaking and, 159–88; of religious movements, 11
intellectual voices, 179–82
International Society of Christian Endeavor, 82–83

Jackson, Andrew, 49
Jackson, Jesse, 4, *172*, 177–78, 208–9; campaign of, 5–6; childhood of, 171–72; in politics, 168–70, 183; retirement of, 164–65; speaking style of, 165
Jackson, Joseph H., 124–25
Jackson, Ketanji Brown (Ketanji Onyika), 1–2, 220
Jackson, Mahalia, 133, 136, 178
Jackson, Rebecca Cox, 40
Jackson, Thomas, 127
Jefferson, Thomas, 31
Jemison, T. J., 124

235

Jennings, Elizabeth, 57–58
Jim Crow culture, 34, 42, 61, 89–90
Johnson, James Weldon, 97, 102–3, 112
Johnson, Lyndon, 143, 146, 158
Johnson, Mordecai, 4, 97, 103, 125
Johnstone, Abraham, 25–26
Joint Chiefs of Staff, 182–83
Jones, Absalom, 2, 19, 27, 30–31
Jordan, Barbara, 5, 161–64, *162*, 168
Julian, Percy, 166
justice, 131
*Just Mercy* (Stevenson), 206

Kennedy, John F., 138, 142, 190
Kerner Commissions Report, 158
King, Don, 178
King, Martin Luther, Jr.: anger of, 138–39; assassination of, 12–13; on civil rights, 137; on community, 123–24; death of, 157–58; Gallup poll on, 155–56; "I Have a Dream," 134–37; impact of, 134–35; legacy of, 185; on Malcolm X, 137–38; Nobel Peace Prize for, 148; nonviolent protests led by, 12; Obama, B., compared to, 9–10, 190, 195; reach of, 5; religion of, 123, 156–57; skill of, 8; speaking style of, 8, 135–36; on Vietnam War, 5, 8, 154–56; on violence, 137–38; warnings from, 137–38
Ku Klux Klan, 75, 123

labor organizers, 4
Ladies' Anti-Slavery Society, 53
Ladies' Literary Society of New York, 46–47, 57
Langston, John Mercer, 60
Lawson, James, 126–27
lay speakers, 40–42
LDF. *See* Legal Defense Fund
lecturing, 42–45
Legacy Museum: From Enslavement to Mass Incarceration, 206
Legal Defense Fund (LDF), 103–4
Lewis, John, 12, 127–28, 147–48, 217
LGBTQ movement, 182–83
*Liberator*, 46
liberty, 15–36, 55

Liberty Party, 51–52
Lincoln, Abraham, 65–66, 80–81, 190–91
Little, Earl, 4, 129
Loguen, Jermain Wesley, 39
Lomax, Louis, 131, 159
Lorde, Audre, 5, 179–80
*Lord of the Rings* (Tolkien), 128
Lynch, Loretta, 201
Lyon, Danny, 128

MacPhail, Mark, 188
Madison, James, 44
Malcolm X, 4, *141*; background of, 129–30; criticism of, 132, 140–41; death of, 149; emancipatory rhetoric of, 131; evolution of, 148; Garvey compared to, 10; influence of, 10; inspiration of, 152–53; King, M. L., Jr., on, 137–38; legacy of, 6; on politics, 142–43; reach of, 5; revolution of, 141–42; speaking style of, 12, 130, 152–53; theme of, 139–40; on Vietnam War, 143–44; on violence, 144
Mann, Kenneth, 106
manumission, 38–39
Marrant, John, 23
Marshall, Thurgood, 103–4, 109
Martin, Trayvon, 6, 199
Masonic African Lodge No. 1, 21, 23
Masons (fraternal order), 2
Massachusetts Anti-Slavery Society, 49
mass movements evolution, 4
Matthews, Victoria Earle, 82–83
McCain, John, 189, 194
McKissick, Floyd, 132
McNeal Turner, Henry, 78
McPhail, Mark, 184
media, 2
men, 46, 52, 97, 184
Mercer, John, 41–42
MFDP. *See* Mississippi Democratic Freedom Party
MIA. *See* Montgomery Improvement Association
migration: benefits of, 77–79; challenges of, 78–79; Douglass, F., on, 79; emancipation and, 65–93; Great Migration, 4, 12, 95; motivation for,

INDEX 237

93; risks of, 79; segregation and, 65–93; Washington, B. T., on, 107
militancy: mainstream influence of, 154–58; moving to, 51–53; rise of, 129–32
millennium, 182–86
Millerites, 40
Million Man March, 184
ministerial voices, 177–79
ministers, 17, 19–21. *See also specific ministers*
Mississippi Democratic Freedom Party (MFDP), 145–46
Mississippi Freedom Summer, 183
Mitchell, Arthur, 107
modern civil rights movement, 12
Mondale, Walter, 168
Montgomery bus boycott, 5, 8, 124–26
Montgomery Improvement Association (MIA), 121
Moral Reform, 47
Moses, Bob, 144
Moses, Robert Parris, 128
Moses, Wilson Jeremiah, 114
Mother Emmanuel Church, 9
Mother Pollard, 133
Motley, Constance Baker, 1–2
Mount Zion Baptist Church, 124
Muhammad, Elijah, 116, 130–32, 142, 177
Muhammad, W. Deen, 177

NAACP. *See* National Association for the Advancement of Colored People
NACW. *See* National Association of Colored Women
NAM. *See* Non-Aligned Movement
NAN. *See* National Action Network
*Narrative* (Brown, W.), 44
*Narrative of the Life of Frederick Douglass, an American Slave* (Douglass, F.), 45
National Action Network (NAN), 185
National Afro-American League, 89
National Association for the Advancement of Colored People (NAACP), 4, 12, 93, 96–99, 108
National Association of Colored Women (NACW), 84, 103
National Cathedral, 156

National Convention of Colored Citizens, 52, 61
National Council of Colored Men, 90–91
National Education Association (NEA), 85, 165, 175
National Guard, U. S., 125
National Mall, 132–33
National Memorial for Peace and Justice, 206
National Negro Conference, 95, 101
*National Reformer*, 41
National Security Council, 5–6
National Woman Suffrage Association, 73
Nation of Islam (NOI), 6, 116, 129, 130, 177
NEA. *See* National Education Association
*Negro World*, 111
Nell, William, 57
New Alliance Party, 6
New England Anti-Slavery Society, 42
Newton, Huey, 5, 152, 157–58
New York African Mutual Relief Association, 26
New York African Society for Mutual Relief, 21
*New York Age*, 89
New York City Third Avenue Railroad Company, 46–47
*New Yorker*, 212
*New York Times*, 87, 112–13, 155, 197–98
Night Riders, 147
Nix, A. W., 114–16
Nixon, Richard, 5, 160–63
Nobel Peace Prize, 148
NOI. *See* Nation of Islam
*nommo* (word), 182, 203–4
Non-Aligned Movement (NAM), 140
nonviolent protests, 12
North Carolina State Human Relations Commission, 209
*The North Star*, 53
Norton, Eleanor Holmes, 183
*Notes on the State of Virginia* (Jefferson), 31
"No Union with Slaveholders," 51

Obama, Barack, 170; acceptance speech from, 194–95; background of, 187; campaign of, 192–96; on community,

187; criticism of, 188, 193; election night victory speech from, 195–96; first term of, 196–98; on foreign policy, 196–97; goals of, 194; impact of, 200; influence of, 6; King, M. L., Jr., compared to, 9–10, 190, 195; legacy of, 191–92; legitimacy of, 6; on Lincoln, 190–91; Nobel Peace Prize for, 197; on police, 200; post-racism and, 189–216; presidency of, 13, 189–90; second term of, 198–200; on September 11, 2001, 198; Sharpton and, 186–88; skill of, 192; speaking style of, 9, 190–92; support for, 194; on Trump, 200; on war, 197–98
Obama, Michelle: as mother, 201; speaking style of, 201; on Trump, 202
Oberlin College, 47
Onyika, Ketanji. *See* Jackson, Ketanji Brown
Open Housing Act (1965), 5
Operation PUSH, 13
Organization of African American Unity, 142
Osborne, Peter, 49

Painter, Nell, 77, 79
Parker, Kathleen, 198
Parks, Rosa, 121, 122–23
*Parting the Waters* (Branch), 134
Paul, Nathaniel, 38, 62
Paul, Thomas, 49–50
Payne, Daniel, 38, 50
Peace Missions, 116
Pennington, James W. C., 39, 67
Pennington, J. C., 66
People United for Saving (later Serving) Humanity (PUSH), 164–65
Pfeffer, Paula, 101
Phyllis Wheatley Club, *104*
Pickens, William, 97
*The Plague* (Camus), 128
Planned Parenthood, 5, 13, 183
politics: abolition in, 51–52; African Americans in, 5–6; Du Bois in, 96–97; freedom of, 15; influence in, 168–75; Jackson, Jesse, in, 168–70, 183; Malcolm X on, 142–43; power of, 215–16; public

speaking and, 159–64; racial, 211; Sharpton in, 185; Wilson, S. on, 213–14
Poor People's Campaign, 156
post-racism, 189–216
post-reconstruction, 81–93
post-Reconstruction period, 4, 11–12, 90–91
poverty, 6, 8, 26, 156
Powell, Adam Clayton, Jr., 4, 12, 121–22; leadership of, 119; protests of, 118; speaking style of, 117; strategy of, 118
Powell, Colin, 5–6, 173–75
power, 21, 29–31. *See also* Black Power
preachers, 8–9, 15–19, 21, 33–34. *See also* Black preaching; folk preaching
*Preaching with Sacred Fire* (Simmons and Thomas), 21, 124
prejudice, 24–25, 109–10
*Press, Platform, Pulpit* (Zackdonik), 84
Price, Joseph E., 85, 88
pride, 5, 22–23
principles, 1, 109
protests: of change, 88–90; elections and, 214–16; Freedom Rides, 125–26; of Powell, A., 118; preaching for, 122–25; sit-ins, 125–26; State House Building, 209; on Vietnam War, 151; youth in, 125–29
*Provincial Freeman*, 47
Pseudo-Longinus, 192
public speaking: access to, 5–13; all manner of, 37–47; challenges for, 3; education and, 98; equality through, 3; fighting prejudice with, 24; focus of, 110; history of, 216–17; importance of, 2; influence of, 1–13; integration and, 159–88; international affairs in, 108–9; legacy of, 217–18; media and, 2; outcomes of, 2, 104–5; politics and, 159–64; preservation of, 15–16; risk of, 26; style of, 9–13; themes of, 15–16; unity from, 84; value of, 24, 216–17. *See also specific speakers*
Purvis, Robert, 66
PUSH. *See* People United for Saving (later Serving) Humanity

Quarles, Benjamin, 56

INDEX

race riots, 4
racial integration. *See* integration
racial prejudice. *See specific topics*
racism: capitalism and, 153; environmental, 6; systemic, 5
Rainbow Coalition, 169–71
Randolph, A. Philip, 4, 12, 100, 107–8, 117
rape, 91
Rapier, James, 74–75
Reagan, Ronald, 169–70
reconstruction, 79–81. *See also* post-reconstruction
Reconstruction period: amendments in, 11; challenges during, 11–12; after Civil War, 68–81; end of, 3–4. *See also* post-Reconstruction period
reform movements: contemporary, 3; manner of, 37—64; moral reform, 57–58; preaching for, 122–25; revolution and, 121–58; temperance of, 56–57; wide circle of, 56–63; youth in, 125–29
*Regents of the University of California v. Bakke*, 167
religion: of Africa, 16; during antebellum era, 2–3; of Barber, 210–11; Douglass, F., on, 53–55; Easton on, 34; of Flora, 17–19; freedom of, 15–16; of King, M. L., Jr., 123, 156–57; secrecy of, 16; of White, 19–20; of Wilson, S., 212–13
religious improvement, 33–34
religious movements, 11
Remond, Charles Lenox, 3, 42, 47, 49–51, 58–59, 61
Remond, Sarah Parker, 47, 66
reproductive rights, 177
Republican Party, 81
reverse stereotyping, 187
revolution: American, 23, 24, 186; Black, 140; French, 24; of Malcolm X, 141–42; reform movement and, 121–58
Richardson, Lewis, 43–44
riots: Chicago, 1919, 95–96; death in, 39; Wilmington Riot of 1898, 90
*The Rising Tide of Color* (Stoddard), 105
Rock, John S., 66
*Roe v. Wade*, 160–61
Rogers, Daniel, 17–18, 21

Roosevelt, Franklin, 107–8, 196
Ruffin, Josephine St. Pierre, 83, 98
Russwurm, John Brown, 24–25
Rustin, Bayard, 124

salvation, 15–36
Sampson, B. K., 71
Sandy Hook Elementary School, 199
sanitation workers' strike, 157
SCHR. *See* Southern Center for Human Rights
Schwerner, Michael, 145–46
SCLC. *See* Southern Christian Leadership Conference
Scott, Tim, 201
Seale, Bobby, 152, 157–58
Second Great Awakening, 16–17
second postwar period, 107–10
segregation: economic legacy of, 8; emancipation and, 65–93; in institutions, 60; migration and, 65–93. *See also Brown v. Board of Education*
Senate Judiciary Committee, US, 1
separatism, 4, 130
Sermon of Thanksgiving (1808), 26
Shadd, Mary Ann, 47
Sharpton, Al, 4, 178, 185–88, 208–9
*The Signifying Monkey* (Gates, H. L.), 181–82
Simmons, Martha, 16–19, 21, 124–25
Simpson, Ivesta, 146–47
Singleton, Benjamin "Pap," 77–79
Sixteenth Street Baptist Church, 138
*The Slave Community* (Blassingame), 16
slave importation ban, 31
slavery: abolition of, 26–27; American Anti-Slavery Society, 38, 42; during antebellum era, 11; antislavery petitions, 27; blackbirding, 204; British Empire on, 63–64; Civil War and, 65–66; coping with, 16, 50; cost of, 50; cruelty of, 27–28, 32–33; denouncing of, 25; Douglass, F., on, 3; economic legacy of, 8; in Egypt, 29, 54; escape from, 39; evil of, 50–51; fugitives of, 11, 44; hypocrisy of, 28–29, 49–51; immorality of, 48–49; impact of, 57; Johnstone on, 25–26; Massachusetts

Anti-Slavery Society, 49; New England Anti-Slavery Society, 42; opposition to, 26–31; racial prejudice and, 26–27; rape in, 91; reparations for, 184–85; revolts of, 52; traders of, 44; war compared to, 47; Western New York Anti-Slavery Society, 44
slave trade, 55
Smith, James McCune, 39
SNCC. *See* Student Nonviolent Coordinating Committee
Social Darwinism, 105–6
Social Gospel, 219
social injustice, 5, 13
*The Souls of Black Folk* (Du Bois), 96
Southern Center for Human Rights (SCHR), 206
Southern Christian Leadership Conference (SCLC), 8, 124–26, 137, 217
Southern Youth Legislature, 109
Stanley, J., 67
Stanton, Elizabeth Cady, 56, 73
Stanton, Lucy, 47, 50, 61
Stevenson, Bryan, 7, 178, 206–8
Steward, Austin, 27–28
Stewart, Maria Miller, 46, 58, 60–61, 99
Still, William, 7, 43
Stoddard, Lothrop, 105
*Stranger at the Gates* (Sugarman), 145
St. Thomas African Episcopal Church, 19
Student Nonviolent Coordinating Committee (SNCC), 126, 132
suffrage, 69–72
Sugarman, Tracy, 145
Supreme Court, US, 104–5

Talented Tenth, 175
television, 5–7
Terrell, Mary Church, 3–4, 84, 97–100
Terrell, Robert, 131
Third Avenue Streetcar Company, 57
Thomas, Frank, 16, 21, 124–25
Till, Emmett, 5, 121
Tillman, Juliann Jane, *18*
de Tocqueville, Alexis, 2
Tolkien, J. R. R., 128
Tometi, Opal, 178, 203–5

traditions, speaking, 13
Trinity United Church of Christ (UCC), 192–93
Trotter, William Monroe, 97
Truman, Harry, 117
Trump, Donald, 200, 202
Truth, Sojourner, 7; "Ar'n't I a Woman?," 40, 59; children of, 40; on equality, 59–60; fame of, 40, 46; speaking style of, 9
Tubman, Harriet, 220
Turner, Henry McNeal, 71–72, 87, 90–91
Tuskegee Institute, 7

UCC. *See* Trinity United Church of Christ
Underground Railroad, 7, 41
UNIA. *See* Universal Negro Improvement Association
Union, 51, 65–66
United House of Prayer, 116
United Nations General Assembly, 203–4
Universal Negro Improvement Association (UNIA), 111, 129
universal suffrage, 69–72
Urban League, 108

Versailles peace talks, 102
Vietnam War: Chisholm on, 5–6; economic impact of, 12; King, M. L., Jr., on, 5, 8, 154–56; Malcolm X on, 143–44; opposition to, 12; protests of, 151
violence: answering to, 90–93; Carmichael on, 151; against children, 138–39, 178; Chisholm on, 160–61; evidence of, 92–93; King, M. L., Jr., on, 137–38; lynching, 90–93, 102–3, 211; Malcolm X on, 144; police, 214–15; during post-Reconstruction, 90–91; rape, 91; torture, 102–3; of Whites, 81–82; Wilson, S. on, 213–14. *See also* death; riots
voter rights, 144–45
Voting Rights Act of 1965, 5, 157–58, 186

Walker, David, 51–52, 60–61
Walker, Wyatt Tee, 124–25
War Production Board, 108

Washington, Booker T., 7, 86, 93; criticism of, 96–97; on migration, 107; speaking style of, 85–87; tradition of, 107
Washington, D. C. march, 132–39
Washington, George, 29
Washington, Harold, 173
*Washington Post*, 211
Watkins, Frances Ellen, 43, 46, 56
Watkins, Gloria. *See* hooks, bell
Watkins, William, 43, 44
Wattleton, Faye, 5, 176–77, 183
wealth, 41
Wears, Isaiah C., 67
Wells-Barnett, Ida B., 9, 91–93, 95, 98
West, Cornel, 5, 181–82
Western New York Anti-Slavery Society, 44
Wheatley, Phyllis, 49
Whipper, William, 40–41, 50
White, George, 19–21
white abolitionists, 44
White Citizens Council, 123
white criticism, 57
Whitefield, George, 16–17
Whites, 29–31, 81–82
Whitten, James, 145
whooping, 16
Wilberforce, William, 29
Wilberforce Philanthropic Association, 21
Wilder, Douglas L., 5–6, 173, 177
Willard, Frances, 92–93
Williams, Eugene, 95–96
Williams, Fannie Barrier, 83, 90, 98
Williams, Joe, 75
Williams, Peter, Jr., 29–30, 49–50, 61
William Watkins Academy for Negro Youth, 43
Wilson, Starsky, 212–14

Wilson, Woodrow, 101–2
Winfrey, Oprah, 201
Woman's Christian Temperance Union (WCTU), 56, 92–93
Woman's Congress, 70–71
Woman's Medical College of Pennsylvania, 71
Woman's Rights Convention, 40
women: African American, 1; in antebellum era, 46; education of, 71; equality of, 59–60; First National Conference of Colored Women, 83; NACW, 84, 103; Terrell, M. C., support of, 97–100; white, 83–84, 100; World's Congress of Representative Women, 83, 90. *See also specific women*
women's club movement, 3–4, 82, 83
women's health, 176
women's liberation movement, 5
Women's Political Council, 121
women's rights, 46–47, 58–60. *See also* reproductive rights
Women's Rights Convention, 59
women's suffrage, 3, 72–73
Woolman, John, 29
word *(nommo)*, 182, 203–4
World's Congress of Representative Women, 83, 90
World War I, 12, 93, 95–96, 100–107
World War II, 107–10
Wright, Jeremiah, 192–94
Wright, Theodore, 38–39, 49
Wright, Thomas, 2–3
WTCU. *See* Woman's Christian Temperance Union

Young, Andrew, 159, 173
Young, Coleman, 163–64, 173

Zackdonik, Teresa, 84

# About the Author

**Richard W. Leeman** is professor of communication studies at the University of North Carolina at Charlotte. He is the author of several books, including *The Teleological Discourse of Barack Obama* (Lexington), and the editor/author of several more, including *African-American Orators: A BioCritical Sourcebook* and *The Will of a People: A Critical Anthology of Great African American Speeches*.

Lightning Source UK Ltd.
Milton Keynes UK
UKHW020117191022
410696UK00002B/56